THE
LOST
APOSTLE

THE LOST APOSTLE

❋

Searching for the Truth About Junia

Rena Pederson

JOSSEY-BASS
A Wiley Imprint
www.josseybass.com

Published by Jossey-Bass
A Wiley Imprint
989 Market Street, San Francisco, CA 94103–1741   www.josseybass.com

Jossey-Bass books and products are available through most bookstores. To contact Jossey-Bass directly call
our Customer Care Department within the U.S. at 800-956-7739, outside the U.S. at 317-572-3986, or
fax 317-572-4002.

Jossey-Bass also publishes its books in a variety of electronic formats. Some content that appears in
print may not be available in electronic books.

Credits are on page 280.

Library of Congress Cataloging-in-Publication Data
Pederson, Rena.
  The lost apostle : searching for the truth about Junia / Rena Pederson.
     p. cm.
  Includes bibliographical references and index.
  ISBN-13: 978-0-7879-8443-4 (cloth)
  ISBN-10: 0-7879-8443-4 (cloth)
  1. Junia (Biblical figure) 2. Apostles. 3. Christian saints. I. Title.
  BS2460.J88P43 2006
  227'.1092—dc22   2006017998

Printed in the United States of America
FIRST EDITION
HB Printing 10 9 8 7 6 5 4 3 2 1

CONTENTS

TO MY PARENTS, RUDY AND DORIS PEDERSON,
WHO SHARED THEIR FAITH WITH SEVEN CHILDREN.

ACKNOWLEDGMENTS

Special thanks go to the scholars who so generously shared their time and expertise with me:

Jean-Noel Alletti, dean of faculty, professor of New Testament exegesis, Pontifico Instituto Biblico, Rome, Italy

John Barnett, associate professor of New Testament, St. Vladimir Orthodox Theological Seminary, Crestwood, New York

Jouette Bassler, professor of New Testament, Southern Methodist University, Dallas, Texas

Darrell Bock, research professor of New Testament studies, Dallas Theological Seminary, Dallas, Texas

Bernadette Brooten, professor of Christian studies, Brandeis University, Boston, Massachusetts

Thomas H. Carpenter, Charles J. Ping Professor of Humanities and professor of classics, Ohio University, Athens, Ohio

Mary Rose D'Angelo, associate professor of theology, University of Notre Dame, Notre Dame, Indiana

Bart Ehrman, chair of the Department of Religious Studies at the University of North Carolina at Chapel Hill, North Carolina

Eldon J. Epp, Harkness Professor of Biblical Literature, emeritus, and
  dean of humanities and social science, emeritus, Case Western
  Reserve University, Cleveland, Ohio

Dr. Kyriaki Karodoyanes Fitzgerald, Orthodox scholar and author,
  Sandwich, Massachusetts

William Frank, director of the University of Dallas program in Rome,
  Italy

Karen King, professor of ecclesiastical history, Harvard University,
  Cambridge, Massachusetts

Cynthia Briggs Kittredge, assistant professor of New Testament,
  Episcopal Theology School of the Southwest, Austin, Texas

Peter Lampe, professor of New Testament, University of Heidelberg,
  Germany

Amy-Jill Levine, professor of New Testament studies, Vanderbilt
  University, Nashville, Tennessee

John Anthony McGuckin, professor of early church history, Union
  Theological Seminary, New York, New York

Wayne Meeks, Woolsey Professor of Biblical Studies, emeritus,
  Department of Religious Studies at Yale University, New Haven,
  Connecticut

Carolyn Osiek, professor of New Testament at Brite Divinity School,
  Texas Christian University, Fort Worth, Texas

Elaine Pagels, Harrington Spear Paine Professor of Religion at
  Princeton University, Princeton, New Jersey

Paige Patterson, president, Southwestern Theological Seminary,
  Fort Worth, Texas

Barbara Reid, professor of New Testament at Catholic Theological Union,
  Chicago, Illinois

Gail Thomas, founder, Dallas Institute of Humanities, Dallas, Texas

Karen Jo Torjeson, dean of Claremont Graduate University's School of
  Religion, Claremont, California

David Dawson Vasquez, director of Rome programs for Catholic
  University of America and DePaul University

L. Michael White, professor of classics and Christian origins, University of Texas at Austin

N. T. Wright, Bishop of Durham, England

A very special thanks to my brother, Michael Weldon White, professor of English at Odessa College, who helped with every chapter while carrying a full teaching load. And much thanks to George McLaughlin, former chancellor of Lamar University, the Rev. Susan Barnes, the Rev. Katherine Lyle, and the Rev. Pam Theodore, who generously read many chapters and made many thoughtful suggestions.

I am also grateful to

Debi Moses and the women of Lovers Lane Methodist Church, and to Dana Harkey and the women of Highland Park United Methodist Church, who helped me "road test" my first drafts

Deedie Leahy and Chuck Cox, for making connections

Nathan Wood for thoughtful research help.

Other faithful friends who helped read chapters:

J. D. Mason, Ann Simmons, Len Bourland, Libby Norwood, and Ann Carruth

Terry C. Peet, a former librarian at the Library of Congress, for finding Orthodox Church sources

Darren Moore, for the special map of Junia's world

Laura Flusche, director of the Institute of Design and Culture in Rome, and Renaissance scholar Carolyn Vallone in Rome, for all manner of assistance and good cheer

William and Therese Frank, for warm hospitality in Rome

My bosses, Randy Best and Mike Moses, for their faithful support

My sons, Grant and Greg, for sharing our home with Junia.

The Search Begins

There is meaning in every journey that is unknown to the traveler.
DIETRICH BONHOEFFER

Her name came as a surprise. Out of the blue. Or, more accurately, out of the past. I was speaking to a book club about women in the Bible when someone in the audience raised her hand and suggested that a woman named "Junia" was a little-known apostle who ought to be included.

Junia?

I had never heard of her before. No one else in the room had either.

"It's in *Romans*," the woman in the audience insisted. "Paul praises her as one of the *greatest* apostles, but the translators didn't think that a *woman* could be an apostle, so they changed it to a *man's* name. But it was a *woman*."

I was stunned. And perplexed. I had studied women of the Bible for a book about women and faith that I had written called *What's Missing*? I didn't remember running across Junia's name. Perhaps the apostle Junia was "what's missing" in my book. What irony! But how could that be? I had spent a lifetime of Sundays in church, paying attention most of the time, yet I had never heard a word about someone named Junia.

After the meeting, the thought stayed with me: "Who was this Junia? Was she *really* an apostle?"

1

It was the beginning of a search—a kind of missing-person search, if you will. It would take me through dozens of Bible translations, to theology schools around the country, and around the world to the catacombs in Rome.

The minute I got home from the meeting, I rushed to my bookshelves and looked up Junia in the Bibles I had on hand. First, I opened the *NIV Study Bible* and flipped hurriedly through Romans to find the verse that the woman had claimed was about Junia. There it was, in Romans 16:7: "Greet Andronicus and Junias, my relatives, who have been in prison with me. They are outstanding among the apostles and they were in Christ before I was."

But the scripture referred to a man—Junias. How disappointing. Then a footnote caught my eye. There was a tiny notation in agate type at the bottom of the page: "The preferred reading in the Greek text is Junia, a feminine name."

So it probably *was* a woman apostle. Why didn't they just say so? A good question.

I went to the new *Oxford Annotated Bible*—another reputable study Bible. It said, "Greet Andronicus and Junia, my relatives, who were in prison with me; they are prominent among the apostles, and they were in Christ before I was."

Aha! This time, Junia was a woman. There was a footnote there, too, but it simply explained that Junia was a woman's name.

So far, it was a tie: one male reference, one female reference.

Next, I turned to a new edition of the *Eerdmans Dictionary of the Bible*. There she was. "Junia: Probably the wife of Andronicus, member of a husband-wife team, who, like Paul, were Jews, Christians before him, imprisoned with him, and 'prominent among the apostles.'" The entry went on to say that Junia is the only woman called "Apostle" in the New Testament; she may have had a charge of some sort and may have been among the restricted leadership of the church. It concluded, "Paul approved of her role, calling her 'outstanding among apostles.'"

Bingo.

Wanting to confirm more, I pulled down a dusty 1960s edition of *Halley's Bible Handbook* from the shelf. It described Andronicus and Junius (a misspelling) as "two of Paul's kinsmen, now old men, for they had been Christians longer than Paul, and in prison with him." Not even a mention of the feminine possibility in the older reference book. Once again, it was a tie: one reference to a female apostle, one to a male apostle.

It was getting late. Jay Leno was starting his monologue on late-night TV. But I felt compelled to keep looking for the elusive Junia. And there she was in the 1998 *Women's Bible Commentary* and the 2002 *Intervarsity Press Women's Bible Commentary*. The newer reference books confirmed that Junia had been praised as an apostle in the early church but said that later church leaders, "uncomfortable with a woman apostle who had leadership within the church, changed her name. . . ."

So the lady in the audience was right. Junia's name had been changed for "political correctness." But her story, apparently, was beginning to resurface. Her role was being rediscovered by scholars who were going back to the early Greek translations. They were excavating through layers of false translations and assumptions, just like an archeological dig. It was as if Junia had been waiting all those years to be found in the original scriptures—hiding in plain sight, as it were—if only people would look.

❋

Junia's story intrigued me. The problem of "the invisible woman" in American culture had been on my mind for some time. It seemed as if every time I spoke to a women's group, a woman from the audience would come up afterward and shyly say, by way of introduction, "You don't know me. I'm nobody." The truth is that, despite having more freedom in today's more liberated world, many women still feel insignificant in our culture, unworthy of regard. They need reassurance that the stories of women count.

I felt compelled to sift through the layers of history and piece together a mosaic that would flesh out Junia's story. It would be a reminder that God works through women as well as men in the world—evidence that women of faith have *mattered*. Researchers had done something like that when they reconstructed the past of the mummified "iceman," who was found frozen in the Alps in the 1990s. Even though he had died more than five thousand years before, the scientists could pinpoint his likely birthplace. They determined that he was twenty-five to thirty-five years old and that he was 5 feet 2 inches tall and weighed 110 pounds. They deduced that he had died in autumn because he had sloeberries in his pouch, and those berries ripened in the fall. They initially theorized that he had died of hypothermia in the cold. Later, using a CAT scan, they discovered an arrowhead in his torso, which altered their conclusion. They realized he must have struggled some distance with a wound before he died. It was an amazing reconstruction.

Junia's case would be trickier because there was no physical evidence, just references in the writings of Christians from long, long ago. As Sherlock Holmes would say, this definitely was a "three-pipe problem." But it would be worth the effort to follow the clues as far as possible. If Junia had indeed been a brave and faithful apostle, more women of today should know about her. And men.

Since her story was a theological mystery of sorts, I decided to start asking questions like a detective: to inquire where she might have been last seen, who might have had a motive to do her in, what kind of life she led. Someone needed to bring Junia's story back to light. So I started searching for her.

Like any pilgrim, I encountered many interesting travelers on my way—scholars, saints, and scoundrels. I was drawn down paths to the stories of the other women of the early church and discovered that their heroic lives provided helpful parallels to what Junia's experience must have been like. Because the history of the church has largely been told by men, I also had to look at the stories of the fathers of the church to find out how attitudes toward women evolved. Why did the organized church disregard the roles of women like Junia?

Since there was no convenient cache of information, I had to look for Junia in shadows on walls, in fragments of scripture, and in the writings of other believers through the years. As it turned out, there was a surprising web of connections over the centuries from Junia's time to ours. The cast of characters who colored church views of women included Aristotle, Augustine, and Thomas Aquinas. I could not have imagined when I started out that the clues would take me from Nero's Rome in the first century to a church showdown with the Knights Templar in the Middle Ages to Martin Luther's rebellious reforms to the arcane world of Bible translation in the twentieth century. But by the end, the twists and turns would teach me much. As I would discover, the search for holiness is not a small matter.

CHAPTER ONE

Cherchez la Femme

All stories are true. Some of them actually happened.
RON WETHERINGTON, ARCHAEOLOGIST,
SOUTHERN METHODIST UNIVERSITY

he questions kept nagging me after I learned her name: *Who was Junia?* Why did her name disappear from the Bible? Might she *really* have been one of the apostles? I wanted to find out more about Junia but wasn't sure where to begin. How do you find someone who's been missing for hundreds of years?

There wasn't much to go on. The basic facts are these: The name "Junia" appears in the last chapter of Paul's theological masterpiece—his letter to the young Christian church in Rome. Specifically, in Romans 16:7, Paul sends greetings to Andronicus and Junia. He then provides a sprinkling of clues about them:

- He says they are his "kinsmen," or relatives. This has led analysts to believe they were Jews, like Paul.
- They became Christians even before Paul did, which means they were among the very earliest of believers.
- They were in prison with Paul, which means they were in the forefront of the Jesus movement, and authorities knew about their activism.

7

- They helped start the Christian church in Rome, which means they kept venturing out bravely after their imprisonment to spread the good news.
- They were considered outstanding, or "of note," among the apostles.

The clues offer just a brief glimpse, albeit a tantalizing glimpse. I could already see that finding out who Junia was, once and for all, could be important for biblical scholarship. But was it feasible for me to pursue the answers? Would it make a difference to anyone else?

❦ *Why is finding Junia important?* I decided that the search was worthwhile because "finding" Junia would establish an important precedent for women preaching and teaching. And since Paul often has been viewed as someone who wanted to keep women quiet, his praise for Junia seems to show that he was much more broadminded in practice.

If nothing else, establishing that Junia existed should provide a psychological boost for women of many Christian denominations. After all, women come to faith differently from the way men do. They have to reconcile a religion that says, on the one hand, that we should love everyone equally and generously—and, on the other, that women aren't exactly full members of the church. It seems counterintuitive. How can women be "less than" men in church standing—less worthy, less qualified to spread God's word—when Paul says, "There is no longer Jew or Greek, there is no longer slave or free, there is no longer male and female; for all of you are one in Christ Jesus" (Gal. 3:28 NRSV)?

It is to women's credit that they have kept the faith for centuries and have done much of the hard, hands-on work in caring for the sick and needy, in spite of restrictions in many denominations that they cannot be full participants in the front office and in the pulpit. It is not surprising that women today still yearn deeply for indications that their faith counts fully, that they are not secondary in God's eyes and in his house. Reclaiming the stories of early women of faith, such as Junia and the other

Icon courtesy of The Orthodox Church in America, www.oca.org. For more information about the three saints (L to R: St. Andronikos the Apostle; Saint Athanasius, Bishop of Christianopoulos; and Saint Junia), and to see a color image of the icon, please refer to the OCA web site at the following page: http://ocafs.oca.org/Caption.asp?FSID=101406

women in Romans 16, could be a great comfort to today's women. It would be more affirmation that God wants women to do his work in the world, hand-in-hand with men.

❧ *But how do we find out more about Junia?* I didn't feel qualified to conduct the search myself because I'm not a religious scholar. I'm just an ordinary believer—a moderate Methodist with Presbyterian roots. But I was always the kind of kid who would peek behind doors or pick up something in the road to look at it more closely and wonder, How did it get there? What did it mean to someone else?

Perhaps it would be helpful to have someone look with fresh eyes. Having been a journalist for three decades, I knew how to poke around and take notes. In newsroom circles, the adage is, "If your mother tells you she loves you, check it out." In theological circles, this is called the "hermeneutics of suspicion." You challenge information. The asking of pesky questions helps you get to the core of the matter.

To find traces of Junia, an obvious first step was to check what information was available about her on the Internet. Surprise! There were dozens of articles about Junia. There apparently has been a lively dispute going on about her in theological circles for some time. Yet that debate has gone on largely outside the notice of the general public. Most church-women still have not heard of Junia. It seemed time they did.

My next stop was to check out more Bible translations to see if they identified Junia as a woman. I gathered the motley assortment of Bibles in my house to check their rendition of Romans and then went browsing at the closest religious bookstore, taking notes Bible-by-Bible, smiling gamely when a clerk walked by to see what I was doing. It turned out that some Bibles had the female name and some didn't.

Those that used "Junias" to refer to a male apostle in Romans included:

Revised Standard Version (1946)
Amplified Bible (1958)
New English Bible (1961)
New American Standard Bible (1963)
Living Bible (1971)
New International Version (1973)
Harper Study Bible (RSV with notes, 1976)
New Jerusalem Bible (1985)

Those that referred to "Junia" as a woman apostle included:

King James Version (1611)
Good News Bible (1966)
New King James Version (1979)
New Century Version (1987)

10

New Revised Standard Version (1989)

HarperCollins Study Bible (NRSV with notes, 1993)

Oxford Study Bible (NRSV with notes, 1994)

New Living Translation (1996)

New Interpreter's Study Bible (2002)

Holman Christian Bible (2004)

Today's New International Version (2004)

It was almost evenly split, with newer translations tilting toward "Junia." The *Catholic Study Bible* acknowledged, "The name Junia is a woman's name. One ancient Greek manuscript and a number of versions read the name Julia." But the study Bible added, "Most editors have interpreted it as a man's name, *Junias.*" In other words, "The name is a woman's name, but most editors have said it's a man anyway." It was as if those editors were saying it was a man with a woman's name, like a boy named Sue. But that was a stretch. To its credit, the *Catholic Study Bible,* unlike the editors it cited, resisted the boy-named-Sue contortion and used the feminine name Junia in its text.[1]

To get a feel for other scholarly views, I went back to the bookstore and brought home an armload of commentaries on the book of Romans. All were written by men. Three out of the four said it is *probable* that Paul was referring to a woman, although it's difficult to be certain. Whether she was really a bona fide *Apostle,* they said, was another matter. Still, this was encouraging. Three of the authors agreed that Junia, most likely, was a "she." Theirs was not a warm embrace of Junia, mind you, more like having to kiss your sister on the cheek on her birthday, but it was recognition, nevertheless.

The next step was to see what *female* theologians were saying in *The Women's Bible Commentary, Women in Scripture,* and *Women in Bible Lands.* They all said Junia was a female apostle. No wavering or quibbling.

My book bills were piling up, but a pattern was emerging. Both male and female theologians increasingly were agreeing that Paul had praised a woman as an apostle.

11

I was beginning to realize that making sense of what Paul's praise meant would require more knowledge of the time and place than I had gotten in church over the years. How could I understand what I was finding without knowing the context? To put it into perspective, I would have to find out why Paul was writing the believers in Rome and why he singled out people like Junia. This search of mine was driving me back for more Bible study.

Enough detail can be found here and there to piece together a background sketch. Paul sent the letter to the new church in Rome about 57 C.E., probably while he was preaching in Corinth. It was a time of great ferment. The Mediterranean became even more of a bustling bazaar of competing religious views after Christianity had elbowed its way in. "The Way" offered by Jesus of Nazareth was the newcomer in a very superstitious world. People there already worshiped a variety of Roman and Greek gods, as well as Egyptian deities like Isis, Persian heroes like Mithras, and the "one God" of Abraham.

In the two decades after Jesus' resurrection, Paul had made many arduous missionary journeys into this fractious environment, establishing churches and collecting relief funds to shore up the needy Jerusalem church. His intention was to take the funds to Jerusalem and then fulfill a longtime dream to visit Spain, stopping by the church community in Rome on the way. His letter to the Romans was a self-introduction of sorts, an overview of his thoughts as a seasoned Christian. Paul could not have known that it would be three long years before he would make it to Rome. He was arrested when he returned to Jerusalem and imprisoned in Caesarea on trumped-up charges. When he finally arrived in Rome, it was as a prisoner, exercising his right as a Roman citizen to appeal his charges in person to the emperor. As Luke fatalistically put it in Acts 28, "and so we came to Rome."

Rome at the time was the center of the known world—a sprawling city of around one million, according to historian Edward Gibbon. The Roman Empire stretched from Britain to Africa, Arabia, and Asia Minor— where Turkey is today. Thanks to the enforcement of Pax Romana, travel

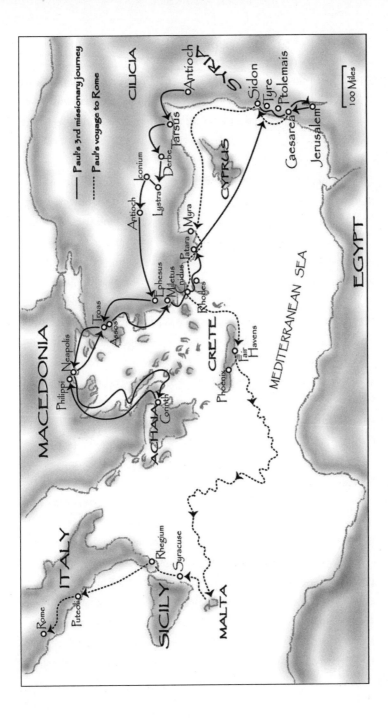

Source: Darren Moore.

was relatively safe. All roads really did lead to Rome. The city was a cosmopolitan crossroads of peoples.

At the time Paul wrote his letter to them, the Christian community in Rome is believed to have been small but growing (perhaps 1,000 to 1,400 members) and gaining converts all the time. The new Christians were an assortment of Jews and Gentiles (all those who were not Jewish by origin). There were freed slaves, as well as slave owners—men and women. They generally met in house churches; significantly, some of those houses were owned by women.

Women, according to scholars like Rodney Stark, Peter Lampe, and Gillian Clark, formed a very crucial part of the early church in Rome. Although Roman society was highly patriarchal, like most of the world, and men ruled the scene, it is significant that Roman women could inherit and own property. Women were expected to stay within the private parameters of the home, as opposed to the wider world of politics and public debate, but that confinement played to their advantage in the new Christian sect, because the first services were held in homes where women ruled the domain. Women helped spread the word to neighbors and local tradespeople, sometimes bringing their children with them as they visited other houses, telling the story of Jesus of Nazareth.

❀

What's in a name? Initially, I formed an image of Junia as a perpetually youthful, energetic person because some dictionaries list "youthful" as the translation for the Latin name "Junia." It was natural to see her as an ancient Roman version of the perky girl next door.

But most scholars say the name Junia actually indicates that she would have been a freed person or child of freed slaves of the prominent Junian family, which also included Brutus. British scholar John Thorley says in *Novum Testamentum*[2] that the bearer of the name most probably acquired it through manumission from slavery in the household of the Junian family resident in the Roman province, of which

Tarsus was part at that time. So Junia could have had connections to a worldly Roman family and to the same town where Paul was from.[3]

❧

To see how Junia fits into the picture in Rome, we must start at the source—the last chapter in Paul's letter, Romans 16. Once you break it apart, you can connect real people to the names. The chapter is, essentially, a list of personal greetings to people Paul knew in Rome. In effect, Paul is schmoozing. He is trying to establish a positive connection with the believers who will help pay for his upcoming trip to Rome and support his teaching. He begins with a glowing recommendation for Phoebe.

Paul's high praise for Phoebe immediately raises interesting questions. It's not the kind of thing we expect from Paul. Why would he do that, and how might this woman be important to Junia's story?

❧ *Who is Phoebe?* Apparently, she is carrying Paul's letter to the new church in Rome. Since there were fraudulent preachers traveling about, Paul emphasizes Phoebe's qualifications. He apparently wants the Romans to know she is trustworthy.

Paul goes on to say that Phoebe is a deacon of the church in Cenchreae, a seaport nine miles from Corinth. The Greek *diakonos* can mean "minister," or it can mean "servant" or "helper." Since the letter was written before church hierarchies such as bishop or deacon were officially established, the term is not a formal rank, but it is recognition of significant leadership, nevertheless. As centuries went by, patriarchal church leaders began referring to Phoebe with the least generous interpretation of *diakonos*. They identified her as merely a "servant," while maintaining the most flattering interpretation of *diakonos* as "deacon" or "minister" when men were described. Unlike Junia, Phoebe's name was not changed in later translations. But her role was subtly diminished, over time, in many translations.

So Paul is asking that Phoebe be given whatever assistance she needs. She appears to have traveled to Rome independently, rather than with a husband or brother, as was the custom of the time. She probably had servants or attendants of some sort to accompany her and must have been a woman of some means, because Paul also describes her as a "benefactor" (*prostates*) to him and others. As Leon Morris, the highly respected Romans scholar, observes, "There were not many wealthy people in the church of the day, but it seems that Phoebe was one of them."[4] We might presume that she was a patron who provided financial support for the new Jesus movement, but her role probably was even larger than that. The literal meaning of the Greek word *prostates* is "one who presides" or "a woman who is set over others."

Paul shows then, by his words of acceptance and admiration, that Phoebe is somebody *special.* He does not identify her by her husband, as was the custom, or by her *occupation,* which also was customary, but by her own history of leadership. This description of Phoebe is a crucial prelude to the praise for Junia a few verses later, because it establishes that women were serving as leaders in the early church. And it shows that Paul approved. Although other writings attributed to Paul were later used to diminish the role of women in specific church situations, he makes it clear with his praise for Phoebe at the outset of Romans 16 that he respects the efforts of women who were helping spread the gospel. Clearly, Paul embraces women as active participants in the Jesus movement.

❦ *And who are these other women?* After that auspicious beginning, Paul then praises the contributions of Prisca and Aquila, a husband-and-wife team. In some very dangerous situations, he says, they "risked their necks" for his sake. In Corinth, they had shared their home and their tent-making business with him. But notice who gets top billing in the greeting? Prisca, who is sometimes called by the longer nickname of Priscilla. She is mentioned before Aquila (Latin for "eagle") in four out of six references to the couple in the New Testament. In the ancient world, the first person named in a pair carried the greater distinction and honor. It is very likely that Prisca was the more gifted teacher and speaker, although she and her husband shared equally in their ministry. The two had helped plant the seeds of Christianity in Corinth and Ephesus and had come back to Rome to lead a house church. They apparently had enough resources to travel and to have a house large enough for small groups to gather.

Some scholars connect Prisca to a noble Roman family, which means she would have been trained in rhetoric, philosophy, and oratory. Prisca also is believed to have taken the lead in tutoring the gifted missionary Apollos about Jesus' teachings. She must have been dedicated and daring to keep leading the missionary movement, which was under suspicion from many sides. Christianity was not illegal, but there was angry resistance from some segments of the Jewish community. There was friction and there was great risk. Paul is openly appreciative of Prisca's brave efforts in Romans 16.

Paul goes on to greet Epaeneutus, who was the first convert in Asia, and Mary, "who has worked very hard among you." Then he salutes Andronicus and Junia, followed by a list of others, including six more women: Tryphaena and Tryphosa, Persis ("who has worked hard in the Lord"), Rufus's mother ("who was a mother to me also"), Julia, and Nereus's sister.

That is a lot of names to sort out, but we can learn from the list that Paul places Junia firmly in the company of women who were stalwarts of the early church. Ten women are named in the Romans list and nineteen men. Too often, believers skip over the list of names as if they were the titles at the end of the movie. But if you stay in your seat and read on, you will see that women had major roles in the movie.

I felt compelled to find out what those roles might have been. I was committed fully now to finding out everything I could that would lead to discoveries about Junia. At this point, I knew what Paul thought about Junia. But what about other people? What might they have said about her?

🌺 *What did people besides Paul have to say about Junia?* Quite a lot, as it turned out. Every leading scholar during the first thousand years of the

Christian church confirmed that Paul referred to a female apostle in
Romans 16, including Origen of Alexandria, one of the most prolific
scholars of the age; Jerome, the father of the Latin Vulgate Bible; Hatto, the
Bishop of Vercelli; Theophylact, a deacon at Constantinople; Bishop John
Chrysostom, who was later revered as a saint; and renowned scholar and
educator Peter Abelard.[5]

That's a formidable group of intellectuals. Of the group, John
Chrysostom is most often cited for his generous praise of Junia. Although
Chrysostom sometimes expressed misogyny in his writings, he had nothing but good things to say about Junia. He wrote that both Junia and
Andronicus were known for their good works and upright conduct. Then
he adds, with reference to Junia, "To be an apostle is something great. But
to be outstanding among the apostles—just think what a wonderful song
of praise that is! They were outstanding on the basis of their works and virtuous actions. Indeed, how great the wisdom of this woman must have
been that she was even deemed worthy of the title of apostle."[6]

As British commentator John Thorley points out, scripture does not
mention Junia's "works" or "virtuous" actions. Chrysostom may have had
some independent information at the time that is no longer available, or
he may have been being expansive and enthusiastic.[7] Even so, it is noteworthy that one of the most respected church leaders of the age, who had
a deep knowledge of Greek and church history, saw no problem in praising a woman's virtues as an apostle. Chrysostom underscores his admiration for the early church women by saluting Paul's greeting to Mary in
Romans 16:6:

> How is this? A woman again is honored and proclaimed victorious!
> Again we are men put to shame. Or rather, we are not put to
> shame only, but have even an honor conferred upon us. For an
> honor we have, in that there are such women among us, but we
> are put to shame, that we men are left so far behind by them.
> For the women of those days were more spirited than lions.[8]

His words were welcome affirmation. I felt as if I had been holding my breath while I pored over books, and now I could exhale. The search absolutely must go on.

No doubt about it, the consensus among the early Christian fathers was that Junia was a woman—and an impressive one at that. That should counter criticism that calling Junia an apostle is some kind of liberal, feminist revision of scripture. To the contrary, the more conservative way to interpret Paul's references to an apostle is actually the *older* way, the way that the early church fathers saw it, as a female apostle.

If we were in a court, we could throw several more exhibits on the judge's desk corroborating that Junia was a woman. One of the most persuasive is that Junias was not known as a man's name in those days. Several philological studies have shown that the name Junias was never in usage in antiquity, whereas the name Junia was a well-known woman's name. According to Daniel B. Wallace of the Biblical Studies Foundation, no instances of the male name Junias have surfaced in Greek literature.[9] The name Junia is found on ancient grave inscriptions numerous times and always in the feminine form.

Hans Lietzman, who was considered a superb philologian in the early 1900s, made an investigation into all surviving names in antiquity and came to the conclusion that the name Junias did not exist. The name Junianus existed, yes, and it is possible that Junias was a short form for that name, Lietzman said, but he could find no trace that the short form was ever used. That research certainly increased the odds that the male name Junias was a fabricated name, contrived by simply adding an *s* to transform Junia into a man.

But wouldn't you know it? Despite his own evidence, Lietzman still balked at conceding that Junia was a female apostle. Lietzman acknowledged that there is no philological evidence that there was a man named Junias, but still he insisted it was unthinkable that a woman was an apostle and therefore he would continue to read the male name anyway.[10] Perhaps we can accept his scholarship today with a more open mind than Professor Lietzman was able to do himself.

❧

Junia was not the only woman of faith to have her identity tampered with.

- If you look up above the high arch over the door in St. Zeno's Chapel in the Basilica of Santa Prassede in Rome, you will find a mosaic portraying four figures: two female saints, Prassede and Pudentiana, along with Mary the mother of Jesus, and a woman whose head is surrounded by a square halo. The square halo indicates the person was still living when the portrait was made, and the ninth-century portrait is believed to be the mother of Pope Pascal I. If you peer closely at the inscription, you can read "Theoda Episcopa," which means "Bishop Theodora." The picture clearly is that of a woman. But look again at the inscription. The *a* on the name Theodora is defaced to make it look like an *o*. Attempts apparently were made to deface it after the mosaic was installed. Scholars like Karen Jo Torjesen of Claremont Graduate School in California and others have concluded that those efforts were made centuries ago to hide the fact that a female bishop was revered.[11]
- In the "Greek Chapel" of the Priscilla Catacombs in Rome, there is a fresco showing numerous female figures gathered at table, perhaps celebrating a funeral banquet or Eucharist. Centuries after the fresco was painted, someone added beards to a replica of the figures, possibly in the belief that the scene was a communion service and that women should not be seen leading the Eucharist.[12]
- Several ancient versions of the New Testament transformed Nympha's name in Colossians 4:15 into a masculine form, ap-

parently as a reaction against a woman leading a house church. The name means "bride" in Greek, or "young wife." Confusion may have occurred because when used as a direct object, both the masculine name Nymphas and the feminine name Nympha are written as Nymphan. Faced with a choice, older translations leaned to the male translation. Yet modern scholars have discovered the masculine name is nowhere to be found in inscriptions of the period, whereas the feminine name is attested more than sixty times. The feminine name is now preferred in many new translations.[13]

- In the Domitilla catacombs, one of the showplace crypts is the so-called "arcosolium of the little apostles." Underneath the arch of the crypt, there is a painting of the twelve apostles sitting around Christ. In the center there once was a fresco of a woman praying. Her image was later blacked out. To the right and left side of the woman's portrait are paintings of the saints Peter and Paul. The woman in the portrait was obviously a very prominent person, perhaps the Christian for whom the crypt was made. But who was she? We cannot say, because her image has been totally obscured.[14]

- In the Codex D, an early flat-bound version of scripture, the reference to a woman convert in Athens named Damaris in Acts 17:34 is eliminated. Other references cite her as "high standing," but even that recognition was dropped. The Codex D also rewrote the Acts 17:4 reference to the role of some "noble women," so that the women become the wives of the noble men instead of the participants.[15]

❧

Most of the scholarly world knows about such changes, but people in the pews do not. Likewise, most scholars also know about Junia the apostle, but most church women do not.

The first scholar I checked with was Carolyn Osiek, who is a New Testament expert at Brite Divinity School in Fort Worth. Professor Osiek, who received her divinity degree from Harvard, has written several highly regarded books on the early Christian communities.

"Oh, yes, *Junia,*" she said when I called, as if it were somebody she had spent time with.

Was she an apostle? "Yes."

A woman? "Yes."

How would you describe her? "As a dedicated first-generation follower of the Jesus movement, someone engaged in full-time apostolic ministry, probably with her husband."

Osiek said she found John Chrysostom's praise in the fourth century for Junia particularly compelling. "By the twelfth century, when Junia's name was probably changed to a man's name, it was *unimaginable* for them that a woman could have been an apostle. But it was not unimaginable for Chrysostom, who was a native Greek speaker and knew the early Greek translations very well. Although there was rhetoric of the time that women were weak or untrustworthy, one of his closest friends and supporters was Olympias—a very powerful woman. She was the superintendent of a monastery in Constantinople, a deaconess, and a major supporter of his. He regularly went to her for advice during his brief time as bishop there. He knew that God could work through women."

We talked for quite a while about where Junia might have lived and how she might have died. "You really should talk to Bernadette Brooten," Osiek recommended. "She has written extensively about Junia."

So I did. I tracked Brooten down at Brandeis University, where she is a professor of Christian studies. She, too, holds a doctorate in theology from Harvard and has written several noteworthy books about early Christians. More to the point, she wrote a series of scholarly papers on Junia that helped launch new interest in her story.[16]

Was the person mentioned along with Andronicus in Romans 16 a woman?

"Absolutely."

And an apostle?

"Oh, yes."

"What makes you so sure?"

"There are three strikes against this being a masculine name," she said. "One: the early church interpreted it as feminine. Two: it is a Latin name and would not normally have been changed into Junias in Greek. Three: Junia is found only as a *female* name in antiquity."

Later I would come to admire how Brooten had distilled the complicated debate into a one-two-three case. She was positive that Junia was an apostle and got right to the point. How would she compare Junia to other women mentioned briefly in the New Testament, such as Lydia and Prisca?

"Lydia was a slaveholding woman whose household converts to Christianity, but we don't have direct evidence of her either preaching or teaching beyond her household. Prisca, according to Acts, teaches. Junia, as an apostle, would have taught or preached," she said, "because those are the standards Paul sets in describing himself as an apostle."

We talked for so long about Junia and the ins and outs of gender controversy that I felt guilty taking so much of Brooten's time on a Saturday afternoon. She not only was patient with my questions; she offered to resume the conversation after an appointment with a graduate student. I was to find a similar response from other New Testament scholars, male and female. They seemed to find the Junia case fascinating and were eager to help set the record straight.

Elaine Pagels, the author of *Beyond Belief* and *The Gnostic Gospels,* was gracious, even though I caught her after a long day of teaching at Princeton. She said that the Junia story was typical of church tradition that was lost over time—or ignored. "It just wasn't in the interest of those preserving the tradition to include it," she said. That seemed a tactful way of saying that winners get to write the history, and sharing power with women was not on their minds.

Pagels pointed out that as Christianity became more popular in Rome, it included more wealthy members, not just the odd lot of poor people, slaves, and tradespeople it attracted at the outset. Over time, the church became more accommodating to the values of those affluent house-holds, whose belief codes came from traditional sources like the Greek philosopher Aristotle, who believed that a man must be master of the house and be in charge of the slaves, women, and children. Patterns of domination and submission were considered essential to running a well-ordered house in the Greco-Roman world, she told me.

> Those changes were subtle but very effective. I don't like conspir-acy theories, so I don't think it was out of malice. Most men didn't feel ill will toward women; they just didn't see them as part of the ruling structure of the world. You know that prejudice of any kind, racial or ethnic, is often quite unconscious. Most people don't know they have it and would be distressed to know that they do. It's not on their radar screen to question.

Though the evidence pointing to Junia is limited, she said, it's some-thing of a miracle that it still exists at all. "The fact that we even have these traces about Junia is very interesting—some made it in anyway! All of this really is like a detective story. We are rewriting the story of Christianity, but not just from a woman's point of view—from the *original* view," she said.

Perhaps then, Junia could take us "back to the future," where women could be praised once again as leaders in the church.

❦

When I told friends what I was working on, they not only wanted to hear more; they wanted me to hurry. "Now tell me more about Junia," they would say the next time I saw them. The idea of Junia taps into a sublimi-nal frustration of women believers who have read scriptures all their lives in which women were nameless or not valued. I understood that quiet frustration. As a young girl, I had wondered why Noah's sons were all named in Genesis, but not his wife. Her name is not given in scripture, although in Jewish tradition she is called Na'amah.

Likewise, it says in the Gospel of Mark that Jesus had four brothers and "*sisters.*" Mark identifies the brothers as James and Joses and Judas and Simon. The sisters are not named.

And then there's the story in Matthew 14 about how five thousand were fed with the loaves and fishes, "not counting women and children." The not-so-subtle message is that women and children did not count.

Perhaps that seems a petty concern, like carping about who cooked the Last Supper and had to do the dishes while the men talked theology. Yet it is possible to intellectually accept that such was the patriarchal culture of those times and still chafe at the thought of all those undervalued women. Passing along such traditions unthinkingly has done a disservice to the successive generations of young women.

This was brought home to me in an embarrassing way when I was teaching a fourth-grade Sunday school class. We were studying the story of Moses and how his mother and sister hid him in a basket in the bulrushes so the Pharaoh of Egypt would not kill him along with other newborn male babies who might someday pose a threat. As we put the felt cutout of a baby boy in the brown basket on the story board, one of the fourth-grade girls asked, "What was Moses' mother's name?"

Hmmm. I was stumped. Well, his sister's name was Miriam, I offered.

The little girl persisted, "But what about the *mother?*"

I desperately looked in the Sunday school teacher's guide. No mother's name. The little girl would not relent. "Where is this story from?" she asked.

I grabbed a Bible so we could look up the story in Exodus. No mother's name.

"Who wrote this book?" the girl asked.

I told her that I had learned in Sunday school that it was Moses, but there may have been other contributors.

She was not deterred. "But he should have put his mother's name in! She's the most important person. If she hadn't thought of putting him in the basket, he would have died," the girl protested. She had a good point.

For months after that, I kept looking for the name of Moses' mother. I later found out it was Jochebed. You can find her name through other Biblical sources but not the names of many other women alluded to in scripture—like the Samaritan woman at the well, who was the first person to learn Jesus was the Messiah—or the anonymous woman "with issues of blood," who touched the hem of Jesus' garment as he passed in the midst of a throng and was healed through her own powerful faith. Jesus "felt the spirit go out of him" and suddenly asked, "Who touched me?" But we do not learn the woman's name; we just learn about her faith.

In later centuries, the name Photina was attached to the story of the Samaritan woman at the well. That became a popular tradition in the Eastern Church. But in scripture she was nameless. In a similar manner, the name Veronica was attached in the second century to the woman with "the issues of blood." The story that she wiped Jesus' face with her veil, which was left with a likeness of his face, also became a revered tradition. But again, in scripture, the woman was nameless.

It was for those "invisible" women who have been unnamed in history, as well as the women today who still bake the church suppers, who rock the wailing babies in the church day care, who take out loans to go to a seminary and then are offered lesser jobs as assistant ministers or at the smallest churches—it was for those women that I wanted to tell Junia's story. Those women—and their daughters and sons—might have their faith deepened by knowing more about the intrepid women of the early church.

But there were more questions that needed to be answered. Once we can establish that Junia was a woman, what does it mean to say Junia was an *apostle*? That's the controversial designation.

Were there *other* apostles in addition to the twelve disciples?

And could one of them have been a woman?

CHAPTER TWO

Who Was in the Apostle Club?

And afterward, I will pour out my Spirit on all flesh;
your sons and daughters shall prophesy, your old men shall
dream dreams, and your young men will see visions. Even on the
male and female slaves, in those days, I will pour out my spirit.
JOEL 2:28–30 NRVS

f you accept that the "Junia" who was praised by Paul is a woman, then there's an even more tantalizing question to answer: Was she really an apostle?

It's one thing to say Junia was a leader in the early church; it's quite another thing to say she was an *apostle*. One of my most conservative friends—a strait-laced Episcopalian—would bristle at the very mention of a *woman* apostle. He'd huff, "No good can come of this." At which point, his wife would caution him with a knowing look: "Settle down." In that same wise spirit, we should carefully and dispassionately track the provenance of the term *apostle* and its application to women like Junia.

❧ *Tracing back to roots.* The word in Greek (*apostolos*) derives from the verb *apostello,* which means "to send," so the noun came to mean "messenger" and "one sent on a mission."

Many Christians make the mistake of thinking that the only "apostles" in the early church were the twelve disciples chosen by Jesus of Nazareth to lead his ministry. That's understandable. The image of twelve men gathered around a table, discussing business over dinner, is firmly cemented in Western imagination.[1]

But there were others mentioned as "apostles" during the early years of the church. They included

> *Matthias,* who replaced Judas Iscariot (Acts 1:21, 22, 24, 26)
>
> *Paul,* the apostle to the Gentiles (Rom. 11:13)
>
> *Barnabas,* who disposed of his land to help the apostles and who assisted Paul (Acts 14:4, 14)
>
> *Andronicus and Junia,* Paul's kinsmen and missionary colleagues (Rom. 16:7)
>
> *James,* brother of Jesus (Gal. 1:19, Luke 10:1–20)
>
> *Silvanus,* also known as Silas, who accompanied Paul and conveyed Peter's first Epistle (1 Thess. 2:6)
>
> *Timothy,* Paul's steadfast companion (1 Thess. 2:6)

Some scholars also include the eloquent preacher *Apollos,* who is included in Paul's comments in 1 Corinthians 4 about the travails of apostles. Others include *two unknown Christians,* who were delegated for the collection in Corinth (2 Cor. 8:23), and *Epaphroditus* (Phil. 2:25), whom Paul calls "my brother, fellow worker, fellow soldier" and tells the Philippians he is "your messenger" and "minister to my need."

❦ *Finding support.* But my question was still not resolved: *Was Junia actually named as an apostle?* There seems to be stronger support today for adding her to the list of "other apostles," making her the *only* named woman apostle. For example, Eldon Jay Epp, the Harkness Professor of Biblical Literature, emeritus, at Case Western University, recently conducted an analysis of the Junia issue. "The conclusion to this investigation is simple and straightforward: there was an apostle Junia," Epp wrote in 2005. He compiled his findings in a book called *Junia, the First Woman Apostle,* establishing a strong scholarly foundation for the premise that Junia was an apostle.

Further support comes from James G. Dunn, who says, unequivocally, in his *Word Biblical Commentary on Romans,* "We may firmly conclude, however, that one of the foundation apostles of Christianity was a woman and wife." He believes Andronicus and Junia "belonged to the closed group of apostles appointed directly by the risen Christ in a limited period following his resurrection."[2]

Further, the United Bible Societies Handbook Series, an acknowledged authority with a board of respected translators, calls Andronicus and Junia "a male/female team" and says that although some have misunderstood the "Romans 16:7 reference to mean "the apostles know them well," a far more acceptable interpretation would imply, "These were counted as apostles and were well known."[3]

Those statements seem clear-cut. But one thing I learned covering City Hall years ago was that looking for the truth often is like looking at a hologram from different angles. If you asked every member of the council about a particular issue, you would get a dozen different shades of answers. The tough part was determining which view was closest to the truth. Each person, looking at the city from their particular vantage point, saw things through a different filter. What was remarkable about Junia's case was that so many scholars were in agreement that Junia was a female apostle; they just described it with varying emphasis. Here are some examples of what I mean:

• *Amy-Jill Levine,* professor of New Testament Studies at Vanderbilt University, says that although *apostle* was a fairly common term for "someone sent out," it appears Junia and Andronicus were examples of missionary couples like Prisca and Aquila. Further, she says:

> In Acts and in Paul's writing, we see how men and women were
> sent out, and perhaps the women would teach the women and the
> men teach the men. The same sort of thing occurred in pagan tradition and Jewish tradition. But we know Junia and Andronicus were

important because Paul goes out of his way to say "hi." How does he
know them, since he has not been to Rome? He tells us that they
are relatives, although that doesn't necessarily mean blood relatives,
and that they worked closely with him. It would not surprise me if
many of these people in Romans 16 were among the Jews who got
thrown out of Rome by Claudius and returned after he died in
54 C.E. It would not surprise me if Junia and Andronicus were
among the very earliest Christians.

• *Wayne Meeks,* a professor of biblical studies at Yale University,
pointed out to me that Paul sometimes uses the term *apostle* broadly
(1 Cor. 15:7) when referring to key leaders, but "presumably in Romans 16,
he's not distinguishing Junia and Andronicus's apostleship from his own."

• *Craig S. Keener,* of Eastern Baptist Theological Seminary, says that
Paul applies the title explicitly only to a handful of leaders in his day besides
the Twelve and himself (1 Cor. 9:5–6; Gal. 1:19; 1 Thess. 2:6, with 1:1).
Every use of *apostle* in the New Testament, Keener maintains, resulted from
a special commission and message, reflected a ministry that included signs
and wonders, and "broke new ground for God's kingdom." He points out
that the church fathers and most modern scholars take the phrase in
Romans 16 to mean that Junia and Andronicus were "of note among the
apostles," not merely known to them. And he raises the valid question, why
would Paul commend them for something less than what an unqualified
apostle means in every other New Testament instance? Why commend
them for being near-apostles?[4]

• *Bruce W. Winter,* of the University of Cambridge, concurs by saying,
"We would wish for more information, but this ancient snapshot however
indistinct in places, shows that she had a role and it was not a case of
Andronicus simply traveling with a wife who was an appendage."[5]

• *Ben Witherington III,* of Ashland Theological Seminary in Ohio, says
that at the least it would appear that Paul means Andronicus and Junia were
"engaged in evangelism and church planting, and that they were itiner-
ants."[6] Witherington deduces that the fact that Paul says they are "notable"

or "outstanding" implies their work had "borne much fruit." Since Paul adds that they were converted before he was, that would mean they were some of the earliest converts to the church. "By the time Romans was written, they could have had a decade or more of ministry behind them," Witherington suggests.

I wondered whether there might be dissenting views—scholars who are still skeptical that Junia was a female apostle. And I found that there are, to be sure. Paige Patterson, the conservative president of Southwestern Baptist Seminary, believes that an egalitarian agenda is driving the revival of Junia's name and that the scholarship can't be proved.

> There are a number of people with an egalitarian mind-set who want to take a text that you can never be sure about and then build their case on a dubious text. I'm not arguing that Junia isn't a woman. It is very possible she was, but it can't be proved. Even if it is a girl's name, it doesn't mean it is a girl. I was placed in a girl's dorm because my name is Paige, just like a boy named Sue. I've had that all my life. I even had an uncle named Shirley. But the point is that there is no way to establish that Junia was in fact a female. The attempt to make her one of the apostles, based on a suspect text that can never be proved, is an agenda looking for a reason. You've got to remember that just because people are scholars doesn't mean they don't have an agenda.

It seems to me that his words strike to the heart of the matter. Recognizing Junia rekindles the debate whether women should be authorized to preach. Many denominations still do not ordain women as ministers—large groups such as the Southern Baptist Convention, the Church of Christ, the Roman Catholic Church, the Orthodox Church, and the conservative branch of the Presbyterian Church. The men and women in those congregations believe they are being true to the original intent of the church by limiting women's leadership roles. Their faith is unquestionably sincere. The question is, however, Can they keep an open mind to the growing body of scholarship that shows women had a proactive role in the establishment of the early church?

My own sense is that the dissenters may be losing ground in scholarly circles. There are respected conservative scholars who would never be accused of having a liberal, equal-rights agenda, who now support the thesis that Junia was a female apostle. Bishop N. T. Wright, who was named by *Christianity Today* as one of the top five theologians in the world, is crystal clear about the women mentioned in Romans 16: "Paul names them as fellow-workers without any sense they hold a secondary position to the men," he notes in *Paul for Everyone*.

> One of them, Junia, in verse 7, is an apostle: The phrase "well
> known among the apostles" doesn't mean that the apostles know
> her and Andronicus (probably wife and husband), but that they *are*
> apostles, that is, they were among those who saw the risen Lord.
> She has the same status as all the other apostles, including Paul
> himself.[7]

In *What Jesus Meant,* eminent Catholic scholar Garry Wills confirms that a woman named Junia "is called an emissary (*apostolos*), Paul's own title for himself."[8]

As I checked with scholar after scholar around the country, it was apparent that "the Junia issue" is well known among New Testament scholars. Some of the professors even took the politely jaded attitude that "this is not really new."

That's true. Concern about how to interpret the name Junia has seesawed back and forth for centuries. It's not new to the cognoscenti—the academic insiders. But stories about Junia and other women of the early church are just beginning to spread from the seminary libraries to the church lounges. The challenge at hand is to "unpack" Junia's story, extract it from the footnotes and files, and make it available for laypeople to follow more easily.

Is it possible to learn from Paul himself what the real story of Junia is? I wondered what we might discover from a close study of Paul's writing. And I concluded that we can know (or make a good guess about) the following.

- *Relationship of Paul and Junia.* If Paul wrote his letter to the church in Rome in approximately 55–57 C.E., it is probable that he would have known Junia from earlier missionary trips. He may have been imprisoned with Junia and Andronicus in Philippi (Acts 16:23) or possibly in Ephesus (1 Cor. 15:32), where he ran into great difficulty. Clement of Rome later speaks of Paul being in prison seven times, so there would have been multiple opportunities when they could have been incarcerated together. Since Paul describes Junia and Andronicus as "my fellow countrymen," or "kinspeople," they most likely were Jewish. The reference also could mean they were from Tarsus—Paul's hometown in Cilicia (an area of Asia Minor that is now part of Turkey). But most scholars take the word *syngenes* ("related" or "akin to") to mean Junia and Andronicus were Jewish. Philippians 4:22 indicates that Paul had dealings with slaves or *liberti* (freed slaves) of the imperial *oikia* (household) in Ephesus, so Junia and Andronicus could have been among them.
- *Significance of missing information.* Although it is true that we don't have much background information about Junia and Andronicus, we don't have many details about some of the other apostles either. Little is known about James, the son of Alphaeus, and Thaddeus, who are counted among the twelve disciples. Those who discount Junia's apostleship solely because the reference to her in scripture is limited would also have to discount James the Less and Thaddeus, using that logic.

The fact remains that Paul does not stint in his praise of Junia. She and Andronicus are historical figures. They are people Paul knows well and admires. His greeting puts it on record: Junia was among the first believers who fanned out around the Mediterranean to tell the Jesus story; they were the "hands and feet" of early Christianity.

• *Change in definitions.* As the church grew, the term *apostle* came to describe not just the twelve but other key followers of Jesus, such as Paul. Two main qualifications are associated with Paul's claim to being an apostle: (1) witnessing the risen Christ and (2) receiving a divine commission to go forth with the Jesus story.

A more restrictive definition is imposed several decades later by Luke in the book of Acts. According to Acts 1:21–22, those called apostles must have been with Jesus during his earthly ministry, baptized by John the Baptist, and eyewitnesses to the resurrected Christ.

It is also suggested in Acts 1:23 that a new apostle had to be male. But most scholars believe the criteria in those scriptures apply more to the twelve than to subsequent missionary apostles. Using the strictest standards, Paul himself would not qualify as an apostle because he had not been with Jesus before his encounter with the risen Christ on the road to Damascus or baptized by John the Baptist. Paul maintained that his very personal recruitment was sufficient to qualify him. As he said in 1 Corinthians 9:1–2, "Am I not free? Am I not an apostle? Have I not seen Jesus our Lord? Are you not the result of my work in the Lord? Even though I may not be an apostle to others, surely I am to you! For you are the seal of my apostleship in the Lord" (NIV). Some believers may have argued with Paul's position then, but few do today.

Overall, the term *apostle* is very rarely applied in the New Testament to anyone other than the leading messengers of Jesus Christ. The very use of the article *the* in Romans 16:7 to say that Junia and Andronicus were noteworthy among the apostles indicates there was a precise, well-known group of people who had earned that title.[9]

❧

❦ *So what, exactly, did apostles do?* I thought if I knew that, I might be able to visualize Junia doing the things apostles apparently did.

• They were primarily teachers, telling what they had witnessed (John 14:26 and 16:13; Acts 2:37), and they could claim that their teaching should be received as the word of God (1 Thess. 2:13). As Orthodox scholar Kyriaki Karodoyanes Fitzgerald explained to me, "Only those deeply discerning persons who know God, who are invaded by God, were to speak for God, so we know from Paul's praise that Junia was a holy person who could be trusted to speak truth."

- We also know that some apostles had the power of working miracles (Matt. 10:8). They could empower others by laying on their hands (Acts 9:15, 17, 18; 19:6).
- The apostles also had some ability to distinguish between spirits (1 Cor. 12:10) and to forgive sins (John 20:23).
- They could punish (Acts 5:1–11).
- They ordained presbyters (elders) over the congregations that were organized through their ministry (Acts 14:23), and they exercised some jurisdiction over those churches (1 Cor. 5:3–5; 2 Cor. 10:6, 8, 11; 1 Tim. 1:20).
- They could administer the sacred rites (Acts 6:1; 16:33; 20:11).
- They could make laws (Acts 15:29).

The concept of the differing gifts for ministry begins to be explained through the charges to the earliest apostles:

> It was he who gave some to be apostles, some to be prophets, some to be evangelists, and some to be pastors and teachers, to prepare God's people for works of service, so that the body of Christ may be built up until we all reach unity in the faith and in the knowledge of the Son of God and become mature, attaining to the whole measure of the fullness of Christ. (Eph. 4:11–13 NIV)

Note that *apostles* is the term mentioned first; they were worthies among worthies, so to speak. Paul says that the apostles were "set apart" to share the gospel of God. He describes his own Damascus commission as being "called."

How then might Junia and Andronicus have been called?

By sifting through the scriptures, I found that the apostolic mission-aries got their commissions in a variety of ways:

- *The seventy.* Clement of Alexandria said that Barnabas, Paul's coworker, along with Sosthenes and Cephas, were among the seventy disciples mentioned in Luke 10:1 as having been sent two by two to teach. (Some ancient sources use the figure seventy-two.) James the Just, the brother or relative of Jesus, is considered in some traditions as the first of the seventy. Some scholars believe the seventy were also called apostles. The Greek text doesn't use the noun form *apostolos* but rather the verb form *apostello,* which means "to send away"; in combination with the rest of the text, the implication is that they were apostles. Some scholars maintain that the missionary pairs were all male. But perhaps not. The great scholar Origen of Alexandria stated that Andronicus and Junia were among the seventy-two sent out. That view also was given credence by other church fathers.[10]

- *The 120.* At Pentecost, fifty days after the Resurrection, 120 men and women were praying in the temple in Jerusalem. Jesus had advised his followers to wait for the Spirit before venturing out. And sure enough, a violent wind blew in. The columns shook and the pavement shuddered. Tongues of fire rested on those present. The Holy Spirit fell on all the 120 people present, not just the twelve disciples. Each one began preaching in languages that the others could understand. The prophecy of Joel had come to be: "And afterward, I will pour out my Spirit on all people. Your sons and daughters will prophesy, your old men will dream dreams, your young men will see visions. Even on my servants, both men and women, I will pour out my Spirit in those days."

- *Women present at Pentecost.* Scholars Stanley Grenz and Denise Muir Kjesbo note that in Luke's account of Pentecost, "certain women" were present in the upper room, prayerfully waiting for the fulfillment of Jesus' promise of divine power (Acts 1:14). As a result, they were also in that place when the Spirit came and empowered sons and daughters to proclaim "the wonderful works of God" (Acts 2:11). "Luke's inclusion of Peter's sermon provides conclusive evidence that the Pentecost experience was shared by all—both male and female," they say. Women's inclusion has far-reaching implications. It means they also received the Spirit's power, giving them a fundamental responsibility for ministry.[11]

• *The broader Pentecost audience.* Many other early Christians were converted at Pentecost. A crowd was drawn as the Holy Spirit shook things up and the 120 began speaking excitedly. Jews "from every nation" were present for the holy observance of the wheat harvest, but they found a harvest of a different kind. Peter stepped forward to reassure the crowd that the 120 were not drunk, but inspired. He explained the fulfillment of prophecy with the Resurrection of Jesus and urged the onlookers: "Save yourselves from this corrupt generation." Some three thousand onlookers were converted that day (Acts 2:41). It is said in Acts 2:10 that the onlookers included "visitors from Rome" who could have brought the gospel back to Rome with them.

• *The five hundred.* Others saw Jesus after the Resurrection (some five hundred, according to 1 Cor. 15:5) and retold his story as eye-witnesses. By the time Paul wrote his letter to the Corinthians, two decades after the crucifixion of Jesus, he said most of them were still alive, although some had died.

• *The seven.* Early in the Jesus movement, it became apparent that more leaders were needed to manage the growth. The missionary work expanded early. In Acts 6:1–7, we see how the twelve disciples began to feel overwhelmed with the tasks of preaching, teaching, and ministering to the poor and needy. So they deputized seven men to take charge of the work of caring for the poor, in particular the widows among the Greek Jews. The seven were deemed spiritually sound enough for the task and were blessed with a laying-on of hands.

Two of the seven—Stephen and Phillip—went on to distinguish themselves with the very same kind of evangelistic work as the twelve disciples. Stephen, who carried on an apostolic-like ministry of preaching and healing, was stoned to death as a result and became the first martyr of the church. Stephen's eloquent last speech in the face of death is a classic sermon on Christian belief. His dying words, a prayer for himself and his executioners, provided a model for many martyrs to come.

Phillip took the word to Samaria and had the same ability as the apostles to perform miraculous signs to confirm his message. Like Peter, Phillip could exorcise evil spirits, and witnesses told of hearing the sounds of the spirits leave as the subjects were healed. The effect was that people paid much more serious attention to his preaching. It was Phillip who performed the famous missionary act of converting and baptizing the Ethiopian stranger on the road.

❀

Mapping out the sequence of events helped me see the ripple of faith to more believers, but one question seemed to lead to so many others. For instance, I now wanted to know, *Were Stephen and Phillip apostles in practice, if not by title?* Should they be on the apostle list, along with Paul and Barnabas and Junia? I was beginning to see how difficult fixing definitions can get after the fact.

• *Difficulty of definition.* What sets Junia and Andronicus apart is that they were given the title—or designation—"apostle" by their contemporaries, in real time. Romans 16:7 says Junia and Andronicus had become Christians even before Paul, so they may have been among the devout Jews who had traveled to Jerusalem for Passover and witnessed the drama around the crucifixion of Christ. As David Dawson Vasquez, a university director in Rome, told me, there was considerable traffic from the Jewish community in Rome to Jerusalem for religious observance.

Junia and Andronicus could have been among those "visitors from Rome, both Jews and proselytes," who were converted at Pentecost. It's possible that Junia and Andronicus could have been present during those times and would have been emboldened to take the teachings of Jesus to Rome. We know that the Roman church was already well established before Peter or Paul traveled there (Rom. 1:7–13).

• *Difficulty of language.* A key sticking point in the lingering debate about Junia is whether she really was *among* the apostles or was merely *known to* them. The pivotal Greek phrase in Romans is *episemoi en tois apostolois*. The question is whether the phrase, in context, means "outstanding *among* the apostles" or "well known *to* the apostles." Lexical studies show that *episemoi* can be used in a comparative sense ("prominent," "outstanding [among]")—or what is called an elative sense ("famous, well known [to]").[12]

Skeptics say that even if the *en* is used in the sense of "among," it doesn't necessarily mean Junia and Andronicus were esteemed within the group of apostles. Rather, they argue, it could merely mean that favorable *knowledge* of them existed among the apostles. The scholars in this camp would include Michael H. Burer and O. B. Wallace of Dallas Theological Seminary. They argue that Junia was probably a female but not an apostle with a capital *A*. They claim to have examined the usage of *episemoi en* in extant Greek literature (some sixty million words), and their conclusion was that Andronicus and Junia were not apostles but were a nice couple whom the apostles—the leaders of the Jerusalem community—knew and, as Paul implies, approved of.[13]

Respected scholars who take the phrase to mean that Junia and Andronicus were esteemed as apostles include Douglas Moo of Wheaton College, Bart Ehrman of the University of North Carolina, Ross Shephard Kramer of the University of Pennsylvania, and Mary Rose D'Angelo of Notre Dame University. As Margaret McDonald, professor of religious studies at St. Francis University in Nova Scotia, put it, the most straightforward reading of Romans 16 is to understand that Paul is calling both Andronicus and Junia apostles. There is no indication that the role of the woman apostle is diminished. What's more, McDonald writes that we should not underestimate the importance Paul attaches to the designation. "He could defend his own apostleship vigorously and call others false prophets vehemently," she writes.[14]

• *Difficulty of reconciliation.* To be sure, opinions on both sides of this issue can be sharp-edged. In pronouncing that comparisons of Greek translations proved Junia was *not* an apostle, John Hunwicke, head of the Theology School at Lancing College, gleefully wrote this after the Burer and Wallace research was published:

> So, oops-a-daisy, there wasn't a woman apostle after all! And—oops-a-daisy—the NRSV is an iffy translation. Stick with the RSV. And I bet you are wondering why you haven't read all this exciting stuff in the papers. If some new bit of evidence, however dodgy, has just emerged for women apostles, headlines like NEW EVIDENCE FOR WOMAN APOSTLE would have screamed at you from the media. Now that a woman apostle has just smiled the demurest of smiles and gracefully tiptoed out of history, we hear not a word. Funny, isn't it.[15]

But the laugh may be on the naysayers. The majority of scholars with access to the best Greek texts today favor the reading that Junia and Andronicus were esteemed *among* the apostles. The highly regarded New Testament scholar Joseph Fitzmyer, in his *Anchor Bible Commentary,* names ten of the leading Pauline scholars who interpret Romans 16 to mean that Junia and Andronicus were "those of mark (numbered) *among* the apostles." He found only two who held that the phrase meant Junia and Andronicus were merely "esteemed *by* the apostles."[16]

The supporting Bible translations include

"outstanding apostles" (NAB)
"outstanding among" (NASB, NIV)
"prominent among" (NRSV)
"eminent among" (REB)
"of note among" (KJV, ASV, NKJV)
"very important apostles" (NCV)

Aida Besancon Spencer of Gordon-Conwell Theological Seminary has made the grammatical point that "The Greek preposition *en* always has the idea of 'within.'"[17] Distinguished British biblical scholar F. F. Bruce has added that the wording indicates Junia and Andronicus were not just "well known to the apostles," they were "notable members of the apostolic circle."[18] James A. Witmer explains that *episemoi* literally means "having a mark [*sema*] on them" and therefore Junia and Andronicus are "illustrious, notable, or outstanding among the apostles."[19]

• *Preponderance of evidence.* The interpretations certainly add up to someone who bears the label of an apostle. Contemporary and past scholarship, lexical definitions, and grammatical construction all provide strong support that Junia and Andronicus were "regarded as apostles." In fact, it is difficult to imagine why Andronicus and Junia would have been esteemed by the apostles unless they were prominent evangelists.

"Junia was a major Christian figure," insists John McGuckin at Union Theology Seminary in New York.

> She would have been the equivalent of what was called the Arche-synagogue, a leader of prayers in the synagogue. She has made a choice, she has accepted a mission, she is running a house church and helping Paul. Paul affirms her as one who has seen the resurrection of Jesus and has a mission. That makes her a powerful figure.

Others hold that Junia and Andronicus were apostles all right but in a more generic sense. When Paul uses the word *apostle,* says L. Michael White at the University of Texas, he usually means a "missionary," that is, someone sent out to spread the word. In his 1996 commentary on Romans, Douglas J. Moo of Wheaton College agrees that Paul is referring to a woman as an apostle, but qualifies that "Paul often uses the title 'apostle' in a looser sense" to designate a messenger, emissary, or commissioned missionary. He maintains the Romans 16 reference is to a "traveling missionary."[20] Likewise, scholar Garry Wills contends that other than references to "the Twelve," the term *apostles* is a broad term for many "emissaries," including Junia.[21] Such a generic missionary classification would put Junia and Andronicus more in the category of apostle with a small *a*.

Even with that more modest designation, Junia and Andronicus still would have the distinction of having been among Jesus' earliest followers who went out to preach and teach. By the end of the first century, those missionaries began to take on veneration as the "first generation" of the movement, much like our "founding fathers." Using that analogy, Junia and Andronicus certainly would not rise to the level of a Washington, Madison, Jefferson, or Franklin, but they would compare to lesser-known signers of the Declaration of Independence, whose contributions later fell from view. They still would have been in the front phalanx spreading the gospel, standing out enough to be thrown in jail, and being among the most important members of the Jewish Christian group in Rome.

As Jouette Bassler, a respected Pauline scholar at the Perkins School of Theology at Southern Methodist University points out, ten of the twenty-nine individuals that Paul commends in his letter to the Rome churches are women (34 percent). Of the six functions Paul praises the Romans for performing (deacon, patroness, coworker, host, laborer, apostle), only three are performed by men. Yet Paul names seven women in those roles! At the least, this shows that admonitions on later Pauline writings for women to "keep silence" and "not teach or exercise authority over men" were not necessarily the rule in the early Roman church.

"Once you get your mind around the statistics, the whole Pauline mission field begins to change," Bassler says.

Bassler often begins her graduate classes on Paul with Romans 16 as the entry point, rather than verses like Ephesians 5:21 ("Wives, be subject to your husbands, as to the Lord. For a husband is head of the wife as Christ is the head of the Church" [RSV].)

> If you study the names in Romans 16, you make some reasonable
> guess about who was Jewish, who was Gentile, who was slave or
> free, male or female, what their socioeconomic class was. Once you
> look at the roles men and women were playing, you begin to see
> that the traditional picture of Paul was not accurate. He actively
> supported women in ministry.

Further, she said, "Junia is the leverage I use for uprooting, destabilizing the pervasive picture of Paul as an irredeemable, misogynistic figure." She added, with a twinkle in her eye:

> Typically, when we get through the course, there is a string of confessions, usually from the women, that "I've always really hated Paul for his views about women and didn't read him. Now I'm willing to go back and see what he has to say." Other women on the Romans 16 list are important. Prisca is important. She played a decisive and important role. But Junia is the big one if it is true that she was an apostle. It changes things. It changes the way we have to read Paul.

🌿 *Can we know for sure who or what Junia was?* The preponderance of scholarly opinion is that Junia was among the early apostles, a respected missionary figure. Whatever conclusion is drawn about her relevance for women in ministry today, we all owe a debt of gratitude to her and the early believers who planted the faith in Rome. Something had happened to these everyday people—tent makers, tax collectors, fishermen, women of independent means like Phoebe, women who went to jail, as Junia did. Something amazing happened that propelled them across the Mediterranean. They had learned something they had to share. The world has never been the same.

Nor would I ever be the same. I was gaining a new appreciation of what arduous work was done to take the Jesus movement all the way from tiny Palestine to faraway places. I was learning that it required traveling weeks on rough cargo boats, miles by foot, and then witnessing a person at a time, a house at a time.

As I tried to follow the sketchy trail of references to the first believers, I began compiling a larger and larger library about the early church. Soon the books were stacked on my sofa like piles of folded laundry. When I ran out of space on the sofa, I started more stacks on the floor. My two sons watched the pillars of books grow. Finally, they spoke up. "Mother, why do you care about this Junia person? Nobody we know has even heard of her." They were looking at me the same way they looked when I wore something they would be embarrassed for their friends to see me in. I could see it in their eyes: no one else's mother was researching a missing apostle.

The best explanation I could give my sons was that there was an injustice that needed to be made right. "How would you like it if somebody changed your name to a girl's name after you died? What if people thought you were a *girl?*" Hmmm. They nodded their heads in understanding. They didn't say anything more about my Junia project after that.

For better and worse, we now live in a vastly different world than Junia knew. A glance back is healthy. We are barely aware of what life was like a few decades ago, much less what women struggled with centuries ago. We've been rocketing ahead too fast to look back.

For example, when Danica Patrick became the first woman to lead the pack at the Indianapolis 500 in June 2005 and made the cover of *Sports Illustrated,* she was asked in a *Newsweek* interview if she considered herself the "Gloria Steinem of auto racing."

"The what?" she replied. "I don't even know who that is. Is that bad?"

No, not bad. But worth noting, whether you agree with Steinem's views or not. It had only taken one generation to forget one of the primary newsmakers on women's issues for more than three decades, from the 1960s to the 1990s. Imagine multiplying that "generational forgetting" by nearly twenty centuries, and it is easy to understand why people today know so very little about the women at the forefront of Christianity. We have to search for them.

It intrigued me that N. T. Wright, the Bishop of Durham in England and an authority on the life and letters of Paul, said in his writing on men, women, and the church that "we should not be surprised that Paul calls a woman named Junia an apostle in Romans 16:7. If an apostle is a witness to the Resurrection, *there were women who deserved that title before any of the men.*"[22]

And who might some of those other women be? Should other women's names be added to the list, along with Junia's? As I would come to see, the answer is yes and no.

CHAPTER THREE

Was the "Lady in Red" an Apostle?

Lest the female apostles doubt the angels, Christ himself came to them
so that the women would be apostles of Christ and by their obedience
rectify the sin of the ancient Eve. . . . Christ showed himself to the
[male] apostles and said to them . . . , "It is I who appear to these
women and I who wanted to send them to you as apostles."

HIPPOLYTUS, EARLY CHRISTIAN BISHOP AND
MARTYR OF ROME (C. 170–236)

f you accept the premise that Junia could have been an apostle,
then the troublesome question tugs at your sleeve: Is it possible
that *other* women could have qualified for that distinction?

❧ *What about Phoebe?* She is called the *diakonos* of the church at
Cenchreae and is extravagantly recommended by Paul. The Greek *diakonos*
not only can mean "deacon" or "servant" but also "messenger." Paul uses the
term interchangeably with *synergos* (missionary coworker) to refer to the
same circle of people. Couldn't you therefore say that Phoebe is a missionary apostle of the church? She takes Paul's epistle to the church in Rome, so,
in effect, she is fulfilling the function of an official messenger of the word.
And like other missionaries and apostles, she has a letter of recommendation
to show that she is an authentic representative of the core church.

Writing in the early third century C.E., Origen described Phoebe as
being officially ordained. So did John Chrysostom a century later, saying,
"You see that these were noble women, hindered in no way by their sex in

the course of virtue, and this is as might be expected for in Christ Jesus, there is neither male nor female."[1]

Still, it would be a tough sell to include Phoebe. She is not specifically named as an apostle in the New Testament or noncanonical writings.

❧ *What about Prisca?* She helped start three house churches. To appreciate the magnitude of that effort, just imagine starting three churches from scratch in three cities around the world today. Then imagine starting three churches in a time when you could be flogged, stoned, expelled, or imprisoned for doing so.

Prisca is obviously a remarkable woman. But she is not described as an "apostle" in the six times she is mentioned in scripture or by early intellectuals of the church. Junia was. Although the rich details of Junia's work did not survive, you have to assume that there was something even more impressive about Junia and Andronicus that would qualify them, in Paul's eyes, as apostles.

❧ *What about Mary Magdalene?* The next obvious candidate is Mary Magdalene—Mary of Magdala. She is called in early church writings an "apostle to the apostles." A good case could be made that she should be included in the list of "other" apostles, along with Junia.

- She was a loyal supporter of Jesus' ministry to the bitter end.
- She traveled with Jesus from Galilee to Jerusalem.
- She was present at his crucifixion at Golgotha.
- She was the first to learn of his resurrection.
- She was the first to take the good news to the other followers.

Indeed, in Matthew 28 she gets a double commission: the angel first commissions Mary and the other women to tell the "disciples," then Jesus instructs Mary to tell the "brothers." Doesn't that make her the Messenger to the other messengers?

Anne Graham Brock says yes. She contends in *Mary Magdalene: The First Apostle* that Mary Magdalene's apostolic status is not unorthodox at all; it is just as "orthodox" as Peter's, because it is rooted in three out of the four canonical gospels. She maintains that Mary Magdalene is "foremost" of the apostles because she receives the first revelation of the Resurrection, a sort of ur-apostle, the original one.[2] Hippolytus, a conservative priest of the third century in Rome, also designated Mary as the first apostle in his commentary on Song of Songs.[3]

Darrell Bock, professor of New Testament studies at Dallas Theological Seminary, takes issue with that notion of primacy but allows that Mary Magdalene would qualify as one of the "female apostles," the other being Junia. He points out in his book *Breaking the Da Vinci Code* that the phrase "apostle of the apostles" did not appear until the tenth century. Mary Magdalene, Bock says, would fit the category of apostles in the very general meaning of "one commissioned by another." Yet every believer, male and female, Bock reminds, was called to share the gospel with others.[4]

It is probable but not provable that Mary Magdalene went out to spread the message of Jesus. At the end of one version the gospel of Sophia of Jesus Christ, a second-century document, it says the followers on hand after the Resurrection, which included Mary Magdalene, are given authority by Jesus as "children of light," and they go forth in joy to preach.

Harvard professor Karen King says in her book *The Gospel of Mary of Magdala,* "It is Mary Magdalene who plays the role of the prophetic teacher. Not only does she have a vision of the Lord, but she assumes the roles of comforter and teacher to the other disciples, admonishing them to be resolute."[5]

Likewise, Bruce Chilton contends in *Mary Magdalene: A Biography* that Mary Magdalene should regain her rightful place as "one of the prime catalysts and shaping forces of Christianity."

🌼

🌼 *What do we know about the Mary Magdalene of history?* I was driven to find out more about Mary Magdalene because many of the scholars that I interviewed suggested that the fact that she was a member of Jesus' inner circle established a precedent for the inclusion of women. But what we know is sparse. We know she came from the town of Magdala—a small fishing town with a textile factory that probably was something of a backwater. She first appears on the biblical scene in Capernaum, another fishing town on the Sea of Galilee, about seven miles from Magdala. She has apparently heard of Jesus' healing powers and has come for help. He cures her of her "seven demons," exorcising her torments, which are not named but were probably some kind of physical or mental torment. In gratitude, she becomes one of the most devoted followers of Jesus of Nazareth, helping to support his ministry and following him to Jerusalem. Luke confirms that she was one of the women who provided for Jesus "out of their means." There is no indication of anything improper.

We know from scripture that she was faithful to the end, when other followers hid away. The Gospels place her at the crucifixion, along with Mary, the mother of Jesus, and John, the beloved disciple. All the Gospels but Luke confirm her role in the resurrection story. But after telling the disciples what she has seen on that fateful morning, she is never mentioned in the New Testament again. The lady vanishes.

It was St. Gregory the Great who tarnished Mary Magdalene's reputation for centuries with a sermon in 591 C.E. He drew the mistaken conclusion that since Jesus had freed Mary Magdalene from "seven demons," she must have been the penitent sinner who washed his feet and dried them tenderly with her hair. It was not until 1,378 years later that the Vatican officially corrected Gregory. In 1969, the Vatican sorted out the identities of the intertwined Marys among three separate women: Magdalene, Mary of Bethany, and the penitent sinner.[6] But the bad rap against Mary Magdalene persisted.

As the loosely organized network of house churches jelled into a hierarchical organization that mirrored the patriarchal culture of the Mediterranean, the tone began to shift in ecclesiastical accounts of Mary Magdalene's role. Church fathers suggested that the reason Jesus warned Mary not to touch him was that she was not worthy or that she was sent to tell the disciples because she needed their strength. According to Karen

King, references begin to appear to Mary Magdalene as "the second Eve," which would become a reoccurring method of discrediting women in the church, branding them as daughters of the apple-eating Eve, unworthy, unclean, or morally tainted. I was beginning to see a pattern of devaluing women that would color church practices for generations to come.

Over the centuries, very little was taught in Christian churches about Mary Magdalene other than her dubious past.[7] Though the story of the penitent sinner carried an inspiring message about redemption that helped persuade many people over the centuries that they too could be saved, it did a disservice to Mary Magdalene's reputation. Then along came books like *Holy Blood, Holy Grail* and *The Da Vinci Code* and their far-fetched speculation that Mary Magdalene and Jesus could have been lovers.[8]

Yet those sensational best sellers may have missed some tantalizing twists. It turns out there is more than one church tradition about Mary Magdalene's later life. Here are two versions:

• *Version One of Mary's story, in France.* The tradition in France, which was the Roman province of Gaul at the time, is that after the Resurrection, Mary Magdalene and several others were put on a boat without sail or oars by opponents of the Jesus movement. Those who are often listed as being castaways with her include

- Mary Jacobe, Jesus' aunt
- Mary Salome, who may have been the mother of two of the apostles—John and James the Greater
- Lazarus, the brother of Martha and Mary
- Maximin, one of the seventy-two apostles who were sent out
- Sara, believed to be the Egyptian servant girl of Mary Jacobe

The passenger list is an impressive boatload of Jesus followers. Tradition says that they traveled to an island in the mouth of the Rhone River, where they set out to do conversion work. Mary Magdalene is said to have labored many years to convert people in the area of Provence and retired late in life to a cave on a hill, La Sainte-Baume, where she died.[9] The scenario was intriguing because it shows that Mary Magdalene's apostolic work continued. I had never devoted much thought to Mary Magdalene, but as I read, I was struck that so little has been taught in the modern church about these women of the early church. It was as if half the story has been missing.

What were believed to be Mary Magdalene's remains were subject to numerous moves over the centuries, to avoid invaders like the Saracens and disruptions like the French Revolution. In the ninth century, her relics may have been transferred to Constantinople and placed in the monastery of St. Lazarus. During the Crusades, the relics are said to have been transferred to Rome and placed under the altar of the St. John Lateran Cathedral, a high honor indeed. Tradition is that her relics eventually were taken to France, where not one but two churches claim to have her earthly remains. At Vezelay in the Burgundy region, pilgrims come to see a bit of bone that is in a glass cylinder in an underground crypt built by the Benedictines in the eleventh century. At Saint Maximin in Provence, pilgrims come to honor a skull that is in a glass case in a more ornate basilica that was established by the Dominican Order in the thirteenth century. During the Middle Ages, several other churches in the Mediterranean region boasted having the Magdalene's skull. According to Bruce Chilton, author of *Mary Magdalene: A Biography,* what are claimed to be her fingers and locks of her hair were scattered across Europe.

What has complicated the mystery around Mary Magdalene's later days in France is the speculation around the servant girl Sara, who became known as the "Black Madonna." Author Dan Brown contends she may have been the "love child" of Jesus and Mary Magdalene. It's a fantastic leap.

Since the Middle Ages, the Romany people, now known as Gypsies, also have venerated Sara as a patron saint. On May 24 each year, the shrines of the saints at the Church of Saintes Marie are lowered from the high chapel to an altar, where crowds stretch out their arms to touch them. Then the statue of the black Sara is carried by the Gypsies to the sea. On the following day, the statues of Mary Jacobe and Mary Salome, sitting in a wooden boat, follow the same route, accompanied by a colorful procession. After a blessing by the bishop from a fishing boat, the procession returns to the church with much bell ringing and guitar playing, tambourines and singing. No doubt some local health beverages are enjoyed. Then the shrines are lifted back up to their chapel.

The Roman Catholic Church is not entirely happy with this ritual, because the "Black Madonna" veneration has morphed into a cultlike worship by the Gypsies with overt pagan trappings. Sara is often called "the goddess Kali Sara," by the Roma people—a reference to the goddess Kali from India, which is where the Roma Gypsies originated. Somehow the devoted missionary work that Mary Magdalene may have performed over the years gets lost in the spectacle.[10]

• *Version Two, in Rome.* The Eastern Orthodox Church believes a different and even more intriguing possibility. The Orthodox Church states in its historical materials that Mary Magdalene "went beyond her native borders and went to preach in pagan Rome." That postscript came as a startling consideration. The idea of Peter and Paul preaching in Rome, the Eternal City, is a dominant part of church history. But Mary Magdalene? Actually preaching in Rome? It seems an unthinkable notion in the patriarchal church we have come to know. Yet there it was on the Orthodox Church of America's Web site:

> When the apostles departed from Jerusalem to preach to all the ends of the earth, then Mary Magdalene also went with them. A daring woman, whose heart was full of reminiscence of the Resurrection, she went beyond her native borders and went to preach in pagan Rome. Everywhere she proclaimed to people about Christ and his teaching. When many did not believe that Christ is risen, she repeated to them what she had said to the Apostles on the radiant morning of the Resurrection: "I have seen the Lord!" With this message, she went all over Italy.[11]

It is difficult to find any documentation related to Mary Magdalene's supposed sojourn in Rome, but there is a mention in the gospel of Nicodemus, a less than credible work from the fourth century that purportedly was derived from the official Roman reports preserved in the Roman *praetorium* at Jerusalem. The gospel includes the so-called Acts of Pilate, which were claimed to be the record of the proceedings against Jesus of Nazareth. According to the ecclesiastical writer Tertullian, a report of some sort was made to Emperor Tiberius. Tertullian wrote that Pontius Pilate, who by then may have been a Christian in his heart, informed the emperor of the unjust sentence of death of the innocent and divine Jesus.

Chapter 11 of the gospel of Nicodemus also says that Mary Magdalene, weeping about the death of Jesus, who "did ten thousand good deeds," said "Who will let these things be heard by all the world? I shall go alone to Rome, to the Caesar."[12]

The Orthodox Church believes that while Mary Magdalene was in Italy, she did indeed visit Emperor Tiberius (14–37) and proclaimed Christ's story. According to that tradition, she used her position to obtain an invitation to a banquet held by the emperor. In those days, it was customary for guests to bring a gift to the emperor. Mary Magdalene, once a woman of means, had lost much, so she only took the emperor an egg as a symbol of the Resurrection, telling him, "Christ is risen!" The emperor was skeptical of the story. He said he would sooner believe the egg in her hand could turn red than that Christ has arisen from the dead. Supposedly, the egg miraculously turned scarlet before his eyes, the red symbolizing the blood of Jesus Christ.

Today this story is sometimes credited as the origin of the Easter egg. And indeed, it has been the custom for centuries for some Roman Catholic and Eastern Orthodox Christians to end their Easter services by sharing dyed and painted eggs and proclaiming to each other, "Christ is risen!" The eggs became known as "Paschal eggs," a reference to Passover and the lamb slain for the Passover, a metaphor for the death of Christ. That is why some ancient icons depict Mary Magdalene holding a Paschal egg while others show her holding a jar of myrrh, for anointing the crucified Jesus' body.

Fanciful? Yes. Most likely the egg story is a pious legend. But it gives us a colorful rationale for dyeing Easter eggs, which also may have resulted from the Easter fast when eggs were forbidden through Lent. Easter was the time when eggs made their comeback in the diet as a sign of Resurrection.[13]

Still, the Orthodox Church believes that the apostle Paul is referring specifically to Mary Magdalene's ministry in Rome when he says in Romans 16:6 that "Mary has bestowed much labor on us." This is a phrase that Paul sometimes uses to show great effort on the part of an apostolic colleague.

The Orthodox Church further contends that Mary Magdalene remained in Rome until the arrival of the apostle Paul. If so, she would have been a part of the early house churches, along with Junia and Andronicus. After the first court judgment against Paul in Rome, Mary Magdalene is believed to have departed for Ephesus, where she joined Mary, the mother of Jesus, and the apostle John. There, she may have finished her life and been buried.

John McGuckin, professor of early church history at Union Theological Seminary, says that the traditions about Mary Magdalene going to Rome or Provence are largely legendary, even though they pop up in the gospel of Nicodemus and other apocrypha. He explains:

> In the post–New Testament era, there was a burning desire to learn
> more about these gospel characters that now everyone was hearing
> about—while the texts hardly gave them any modeling whatsoever.
> As a result, lots of legends and apocryphal stories were developed
> in the folk imagination, and popular preaching of the second cen-
> tury onwards (the apocryphal gospels). It is in this welter that our

Mary Magdalene traditions grow up, and to that extent, it is very soft history.

"No one can say for sure whether she went to Rome or not," he added. "It is, of course, not impossible, for others did, too—Peter and Paul and others—since Rome was the great magnet of any religious teacher."

As to the claim that the "Mary" mentioned by Paul in Romans 16 might be Mary Magdalene, McGuckin points out, "Mary was a very common Jewish name and Rome was a major gathering point in ancient times. So it is a bit like shouting out in Grand Central Station, 'Is there a John of New York present?'"

Which version of Mary Magdalene's later life should we believe? Number One, in France? Number Two, in Rome? Or neither one? I was discovering that finding out what happened to the women who helped found the early church was like chasing shadows. The best that can be said is that there are multiple indications in the unofficial gospels that Mary Magdalene may have preached and taught until her end. Some traditions have her going to India with the apostle Thomas. Bruce Chilton suggests that she returned to Magdala, where she continued preaching and teaching and healing. He believes she was one of thousands of victims massacred by the Romans in 67 C.E., in reprisal for an armed rebellion.

We don't know any of that for sure, so we have to come back to the writings that have survived, canonical and noncanonical. Establishing whether Mary Magdalene could have preached and taught was important because it would be an analogue for the work of Junia and others.

✤

There are numerous examples in the Gnostic gospels demonstrating that Mary Magdalene was in the "inner circle" of apostles, including

"The gospel of Thomas," in which Mary Magdalene questions Jesus and is among only a few disciples mentioned. Mary and Salome are singled out by name.

In another second-century work, "First Apocalypse of James," it is suggested that James turn to Mary Magdalene and the other women for instruction.

In "Dialogue of the Savior," Mary Magdalene acts as the representative of the disciples in addressing questions to Jesus.

Not only that, in yet another second-century document found near the town of Nag Hamadi in Upper Egypt in 1945, "The Sophia of Jesus Christ," Mary Magdalene is spotlighted as one of the seven women and twelve men gathering to hear the Savior after the Resurrection.

In the *Pistis Sophia,* a third-century text, Mary Magdalene is depicted as a leader among the disciples.

In the gospel of Philip, one of the writings found at Nag Hamadi, Mary Magdalene is mentioned as one of the three Marys "who always walked with the Lord."[14]

Those who would argue *against* including Mary Magdalene in the list of apostles would say that the tradition of calling her "apostle to the apostles" is a meaningless honorific that merely recognizes that she delivered the morning news to the male apostles. Those on her side might respond that, although she was not given the title of apostle in canon scripture, she filled those shoes at important moments.

There is a recurring tension among the early disciples on the issue of gender. Despite the glimpses of leadership attributed to women like Junia and Mary Magdalene, women were not totally accepted as equals by the men around them. Jesus set a powerful example of including women, yet the church was born into a rigid patriarchal culture. Despite Jesus' efforts, some of his key male followers resisted sharing leadership with women.

We see that tension in the Gnostic gospels. Peter is depicted several times as opposing a leadership role for Mary Magdalene. In the gospel of

Mary, Peter testily challenges the legitimacy of Mary Magdalene's claim that she received a teaching from Jesus, saying, "Has the Savior spoken secretly to a woman and [not] openly so that we would all hear? [Surely] he [did not want to show] that [she] is more worthy than we are." However, Levi, another disciple, rises to defend her and the possibility that Jesus might have shared his closest personal insights with believers other than the Twelve. He says, "Peter, your hot temper is always with you, and now you are questioning the woman as though an adversary to her?"

In the *Pistis Sophia,* Peter complains, "My Lord we are not able to suffer this woman who takes the opportunity from us, and does not allow any one of us to speak, but she speaks many times."[15]

In the gospel of Thomas, Peter says to the disciples, "Let Mary leave us, for women are not worthy of life." And Jesus responds, "I myself shall lead her in order to make her male, so that she too may become a living spirit resembling you males. For every woman who will make herself male will enter the kingdom of heaven." In *The Gospel of Mary of Magdala,* Karen King explains that by saying "make herself male" Jesus is suggesting that Mary Magdalene's womanhood is not a permanent impediment to salvation. In a culture where "female" connoted the fleshly body and the "male" symbolized higher values of mind and spirit, females could "become male" by becoming more spiritual beings.

Looking back at the exchanges from the vantage point of two thousand years, we can see there were strong differences of opinion among early disciples about the roles of women, although Jesus held open the door for them. What Junia and Mary Magdalene demonstrate is that Jesus could work through women as well as men. They proved that what really counts is faith, not gender. It reminded me of Supreme Court Justice Sandra Day O'Connor's observation that wisdom mattered more than gender on the high court. As she put it, "At the end of the day, the wise old men and the wise old women usually decide the same way."

When I traveled to Houston to hear Karen King speak about Mary Magdalene, I discovered that women at the Christ Church Cathedral in downtown Houston have formed a "Magdalene community" to carry on the tradition of women spreading the gospel. They call it "Brigid's Place" in honor of a remarkable fifth-century abbess in Ireland. Based on the social concept of equality between men and women, Brigid founded double monasteries where men and women lived in separate quarters but shared the mission of serving God.

For the last ten years, Brigid's Place in Houston has functioned almost like a women's church-within-the-church—a sanctuary for women of all faiths. Many are women who have left organized religion of other types and find spiritual welcome at Brigid's Place. Every July 22, Brigid's Place celebrates Mary Magdalene's feast day by sponsoring top female scholars as speakers. And that was how I came to hear Professor King on a steamy summer evening in Houston.

That particular evening, hundreds of women had trekked across Texas to hear more about Mary Magdalene, the Apostle to the Apostles. Some had even come from neighboring states. You could feel the electricity—a frisson of anticipation—in the audience before the talk. Women of every strata were shoulder-to-shoulder in the wooden pews—middle-aged women in posh St. John knit suits, teens in their flip-flop sandals, and young mothers who looked as if they had just driven a carload full of kids to Chick-fil-A for dinner and were glad to sit still a minute.

As she took the stage, King greeted the audience tongue-in-cheek: "Who would have thought you people in Texas would be so interested in women and heresy?

"When they used to teach about women and heresy, I was told that was redundant. Women have been present and active every century in Christian leadership, but in every century that leadership has been contested," she said. "Recovering those women's stories and voices has been difficult, especially when their names were changed, like Junia's."

There were perplexed looks on the faces of the women in the audience at the reference to Junia. They obviously didn't have a clue who she was talking about. Professor King added that Junia was just as worthy of attention as Mary Magdalene. I smiled to myself as I saw several women in the pews ahead of me turn to the person next to them and mouth silently, "Who's *Junia?*"

I understood exactly how they felt. As I searched for information about Junia, I encountered stories about other women of faith that I had never heard a word about before.

Like Thecla.

When I was interviewing Professor Bernadette Brooten of Brandeis University about apostles, she said in passing, "Then of course, there's the apostle Thecla . . ."

The *apostle Thecla?*

Her tone implied that everyone knew Thecla, just like everyone knows Elvis. I was embarrassed to admit I had never heard of Thecla. The minute I hung up the phone, I started looking for references to Thecla in the books piled on the sofa. And there she was. In book after book. I just had not been looking for her. Like Junia.

Good grief. Was Thecla really an apostle, too? Had her name been erased from scripture, like Junia's? My search for Junia was leading me to much more than I anticipated. As I was learning, there were other women's stories that showed how the church evolved and how women besides Junia struggled to be included. Suddenly, there were new pages to turn.

CHAPTER FOUR

What About Thecla?

On an otherwise ordinary spring day, in the otherwise unnoteworthy
town of Iconium, an otherwise unremarkable young woman named
Thecla was preparing for her upcoming wedding when a
most extraordinary event unfolded.
FORDHAM UNIVERSITY LENTEN SERIES

sk most Protestant women if they know about Thecla, and you
will probably get a blank look. *Thecla?*

Yet virtually every scholar I interviewed about Junia mentioned Thecla in the next breath. If you consider Junia an apostle, you next
have to figure out what to do with Thecla, who was widely praised in ancient times as "equal to the apostles." In many ways, Thecla was as famous
as a rock star in the first centuries of Christian faith. Stories about her were
handed down from generation to generation, gaining embellishments with
every telling, like layers of luster that are added to a pearl that grows to
unrealistic size. We rarely see her face today, but back then, Thecla was a
popular subject for artists. You can find her image in faded frescoes on cave
walls, painted on the peeling ceilings of desert churches, stamped on clay
flasks and oil lamps, engraved on wooden combs, etched into crosses and
medallions, even woven into curtains. Mothers in ancient times named
their girl babies after Thecla. They still do in some parts of the world.[1]

No doubt about it, Thecla (sometimes spelled Thekla) was a great inspiration to women in the ancient world. Early Christian preachers
pointed to her as the role model of chastity for women. St. Ambrose urged
virgins to take Thecla as a model second only to the Virgin Mary. When

Macrina—a renowned sister of the revered Cappadocian Fathers, St. Basil and St. Gregory of Nyssa—was born in the fourth century, her mother had a vision that she was "the new Thecla." St. Jerome likewise wrote that Melania the Elder, a patrician Roman who established a monastery in the fourth century on the Mount of Olives in Jerusalem, could be "the new Thecla."[2]

Even centuries after her death, Thecla's burial place at Seleucia in south central Asia Minor (modern Silifke, in Turkey) was a popular center for pilgrimages. Some pilgrims came from as far away as Egypt. By the fifth century, her shrine—Hagia Thecla—grew to three basilicas, a large public bath and a number of cisterns. The main basilica was more than eighty meters in length.[3]

There were few women back then who could match that popular devotion. So we come back to the question, Who was Thecla?

Was she an apostle like Junia?

Or different?

Thecla did share some attributes with Junia. Both were missionaries. Both may have worked with Paul. But Thecla's story is very different. What little we know about Junia is simple and spare; Thecla's tale is a fabulous, convoluted saga that might be a myth. Or it might contain a kernel of truth. Her name kept coming up as I interviewed New Testament scholars about Junia. At the least, Thecla's story tells us about the difficult cultural climate early women of faith lived in. And then leaves us wondering if she was real.

❦

❦ *Where can we find Thecla's story?* Her story can be found in "The Acts of Paul," which is one of the noncanonical gospels recovered in the desert town of Nag Hamadi in 1945 in Upper Egypt. Sometimes it is called "The Acts of Thecla" or "The Acts of Paul and Thecla." Either way, the story was among the many oral narratives in circulation near the end of the second century.

Thecla's saga brings to mind the old silent movie serial *The Perils of Pauline,* because she is miraculously saved from one predicament after another. The story line is unbelievably fantastic by today's standards. However, in ancient times, which was an age of miracles and visions, it must have been eminently believable. Thecla served as a model for chaste Christian women at a time when there were two preferred options for women: (1) get married, serve your husband, and have a family or (2) stay a virgin, marry the church, and serve God. Thecla was the idealized exemplar of the second option. She was a revered figure, not just for a decade or so but for *centuries.* Indeed, she was such a significant figure in the early Christian church that she was mentioned by Eusebius, the father of church history, as well as St. Augustine and most early church historians.

Initially, Thecla's story was widely circulated from person to person. It was probably written down by an unknown Orthodox Christian from Asia Minor some time between 160 and 190 C.E. The "Acts of Thecla" circulated in many languages, including Greek, Coptic, Ethiopic, and Armenian. The Syrian and Armenian Churches included the "Acts of Thecla" in their early biblical canons. But it is now considered part of the Christian apocrypha. [4]

Her story goes something like this: Thecla was an eighteen-year-old virgin in Iconium, a Roman colony in what is now south-central Turkey. (The location lends some credence to the story, as Iconium is mentioned as a place where Paul taught and suffered persecution in 2 Timothy 3:11.) One day, Thecla overhears Paul preaching from the window of her family home. She is so inspired by Paul's preaching that she clings to the "window like a spider" for three days and three nights, not even taking time to eat or drink. Thecla can't see Paul, but she can hear his preaching about the need to fear only one God and live in chastity. She is captivated. She wants to join him in his missionary work. So Thecla rejects the marriage her parents have arranged for her, which upsets her mother, Theocleia, and outrages her jilted fiancé Thamyris. Seeking revenge, the spurned Thamyris reports the alienation of affection to the governor. As a result, Paul is held for questioning in jail about interfering with Thamyris's wedding to Thecla.

Undaunted, Thecla secretly bribes her way into the jail. She sells some of her jewelry so she can sit at Paul's feet and learn—a reference to the traditional pose of students who study at the feet of rabbis. Thecla's mother and fiancé track her down at the jail. Shocked and appalled that she is on the floor of Paul's cell, they have Paul hauled once again before the governor. Paul impresses the governor with his presentation; as a result, his punishment is comparatively light—he is flogged and expelled from town. Thecla's punishment is more dire. She is sentenced to be burned alive.

Thecla's punishment in the arena is where things get really extraordinary. Thecla is brought in naked and bound to a stake for burning but is saved from the fire when a sudden storm miraculously drowns out the flames with rain and hail. She flees from Iconium in search of Paul and finds him hiding in a cave with a colleague named Onesiphorus and his family. She joins them in the breaking of the bread. Both Paul and Thecla were vegetarians and teetotalers, apparently in the belief that meat and alcohol inflamed passion. Thecla offers to cut her hair like a boy's and follow Paul in his ministry. He exhorts her not to join him, apparently out of concern for her safety on the road. The text says he feared the "the temptation of fornication for a single woman." He refuses to baptize her in order to discourage her. Nevertheless, she follows him to Antioch.

Just as Paul feared, when they arrive in Antioch, Thecla is accosted on the street by a Syrian magistrate named Alexander, who is quite taken by her beauty. When Alexander tries to bribe Paul to hand her over, Paul behaves rather ungallantly and disavows knowing Thecla. Alexander tries to kiss Thecla by force, and she rebuffs him, humiliating him by pushing him away publicly and knocking his crown askew. Angered by the rejection, Alexander has her arrested. Once again, she is sentenced to death in the arena, supposedly for the crime of "sacrilege." Her only request is that her chastity be protected until she is cast to the beasts. Consequently, a rich widow named Queen Tryphaena, whose daughter has recently died, offers to take her in until her execution.

When the day arrives for her punishment, Thecla is brought into the amphitheater and put into a den with a fierce she-lion. The lioness only licks her feet. So Thecla is brought back another day to the arena and stripped naked. Lions and bears are let in to attack her. But the she-lion protects Thecla, attacking a bear and a he-lion instead. Thecla stretches out her hands to heaven in prayer. Then, spying a pit of water, she throws herself in and baptizes herself. The tank is filled with hungry seal-like creatures, but they die and float to the surface. When other wild beasts are set upon her, the women in the arena cry out mournfully and scatter herbs in the arena that seem to put the beasts asleep. Once again, Thecla is spared.

For a third time, Thecla is placed in jeopardy by being tied to a bull, whose genitals are scorched with red-hot irons so that she will be dragged and tossed about. But a mysterious flame cloud covers Thecla's nakedness from the view of spectators and burns off her cords so she is freed from the raging beast.

The drama overwhelms Tryphaena, who faints and is feared dead. This alarms Alexander the magistrate and the governor, since Tryphaena is a royal family member. Alexander relents and suggests the governor spare Thecla. The governor summons Thecla and asks, "Who are you? Why is it that the beasts would not touch you?" She replies that she is a servant of the living God and a believer in his son Jesus Christ, who is the way to eternal salvation. She describes Jesus as "a refuge to the tempest-tossed, a solace to the afflicted, a shelter to the despairing; in brief, whoever does not believe in him shall not live, but be dead forever."

The governor is so impressed that he orders that garments be brought to cover her and announces that he is releasing "pious Thecla, the servant of God." The women in the arena cheer so loudly that the entire city is shaken by their voices. That chorus of support by women in the stands is remarkable. Women had no voice in public affairs at the time. Indeed, women were assigned to sit in the back rows of the arena, along with slaves. Depicting them as defying authority is a significant statement.

After being spared, Thecla returns to Tryphaena's house and converts her and her household. Then, donning a man's cloak to disguise herself on the road, she travels in search of Paul and finds him. Paul takes her to the house of Hermias and hears about her tribulations. Impressed at long last by her faith, he authorizes her to teach the Word. Thecla decides to return to her Iconium to preach and teach. She discovers that her fiancé Thamyris has died, so she is no longer bound by the betrothal. She tries to reconcile with her mother and to convert her to Christian beliefs, but her mother coldly rebuffs her daughter.

❦

In the ancient Greco-Roman world, the concepts of "honor" and "shame" greatly influenced the status of women. In face-to-face societies where great value was placed on how a person was "seen" by others in the community, members were expected to conform to the power structure, which was traditionally dominated by men. Men could obtain "honor" by inheriting social status from a powerful ancestor or by winning respect with military prowess or community good deeds. Men were expected to prove their masculinity and protect their community reputation by defending the chastity of women under their dominance, including wives and daughters. By doing so, a man could ensure his heirs were his own children and could guarantee to a prospective son-in-law that his bride had not been impregnated by another man.

Women were expected to demonstrate the positive sense of "shame" by being modest, reserved, and deferential to the male head of the family. Those virtues helped to preserve her chastity. Women who were "shameless" were those who violated the social norm with promiscuous or rebellious behavior. If a woman lost her chastity, it brought disgrace to the family as a whole. To be shameless was to lack concern for one's family honor and to be insensitive to the opinion of others, causing the family to "lose face."

Seen in that sense, Thecla's behavior—rejecting her arranged marriage, consorting with another man in public—would have been scandalous. What saved her in some eyes (but not her family's) was that she did so in the name of God and made a public display of maintaining her chastity and serving others.[5]

❧

Thecla weeps at her mother's continued rejection but goes on with her ministry of spreading the word from a cave near Seleucia—the same Syrian seaport from which Paul and Barnabas left with John Mark for their first missionary journey. Thecla devotes the rest of her life to preaching and teaching and healing. As Thecla's fame grows, the story says, the devil tempts some local men into trying to seduce her, thinking that her powers are due to her virginity. As the local men try to assault her, God hears Thecla's prayers for help. God helps her escape "miraculously" through a cleft in the rock. Some versions of the story say that Thecla continued her ministry for many more years and lived to the age of ninety, "when the Lord translated her." Others say that she disappeared into the rock as she escaped her attackers, leaving behind only a shred of cloth.[6]

Was this a convenient way to explain why there were no remains, no relics to revere after her death? Was it too unsavory to report that Thecla might have been ravaged by the thugs in her last hour? Did she disappear into thin air? Was she assaulted and killed? Or did she ever really exist at all?

Whatever her finish, people in the ancient world believed that Thecla existed. Some scholars are skeptical now, but back then, generations of people believed in Thecla's story. A church was built over Thecla's cave in 480, and the ruins grew into a basilica complex that can be visited today. According to Nancy Carter of Union Theological Seminary, a church in Antioch in Syria also was dedicated to Thecla in the fourth century.

🌴

What's remarkable about the Thecla saga, picaresque as it is, is that it was so widespread throughout the Mediterranean. The list of Christian leaders who looked upon the Thecla story as genuine is impressive: Cyprian, Eusebius, Epiphanius, Augustine, Gregory Nazianzen, John Chrysostom, and Severus Sulpitius, who all lived within the fourth century.

Although most people today don't realize that it comes from the Thecla story, the physical description of Paul in "Acts of Thecla" has been widely accepted for centuries: "A man small in size, bald-headed, bandy-legged, of noble mien, with eyebrows meeting, and a rather hooked nose. But full of grace, sometimes he seemed like a man, and sometimes he had the face of an angel."[7]

✤

Thecla is not a household word today, but in the ancient world she was a poster girl for the faith. There are multiple examples of art honoring Thecla in Egypt, including these:

- In Rome, scholars found a sarcophagus with a relief showing Paul and Thecla traveling together in a boat.
- At least three places claim to be her burial place: Meryemlik (Ayatekia) Turkey; Maalula, Syria; and Rome, Italy.
- In Maalula, Syria, there is a monastery named for St. Thecla, built near what is said to be her cave. The Syrian nuns continue Thecla's tradition: caring for orphans and assisting those who are poor. Maalula is one of three villages in the world where Aramaic, the language spoken by Jesus, is still spoken.
- A catacomb of St. Thecla can be found on the Via Ostiensis, not far from the burial place of St. Paul, and is mentioned in the seventh-century itineraries to the graves of the Roman martyrs.

Santa Thecla also is the patron saint of Tarragona, Spain, and there are Iberian wall designs from the first century showing Paul preaching to Thecla. In Bede's *Martyrology,* she is celebrated on September 23, which was her feast day in the Roman Catholic Church for many years. Her name was removed from the official calendar in 1969, presumably for lack of supportable evidence that she existed.

The Orthodox Church recognizes Thecla, not only as a saint but as a "protomartyr" as well, and commemorates her on September 24. Because she converted so many people to Christianity, she was sometimes known as "equal to the apostles."[8]

Considering how well-known Thecla was, it is intriguing that her status as "equal to the apostles" has dropped from sight. Recent scholarship has shown that the Thecla cycle was part of the original material in "Acts of Paul," but the story was later removed.

Why?

"Because of its positive portrayal of women and sexual renunciation [the rejection of traditional sex roles]," Michael White says in his authoritative examination of the early church, *From Jesus to Christianity.*[9]

Indeed, there appear to have been attempts to obscure Thecla's role in later years, much the way Junia's role was obscured. One of the foremost Jesus scholars in the United States, John Dominic Crossan, of DePaul University, and Jonathan L. Reed, a leading authority on first-century Palestinian archeology, recently brought to light an attempt to suppress the Thecla story.

In their book *In Search of Paul,* Crossan and Reed tell of a cave that was discovered around 1906, high above the ruins of Ephesus. Just to the right of the entrance are two sixth-century images of St. Thecla and St. Paul.

- Both are the same height, an iconographic sign that they are of equal importance.
- Both have their right hands raised in a blessing gesture, again an iconographic sign that they are of equal authority.[10]

While the image of Paul was left untouched over the centuries, someone later scratched out the eyes and upraised fingers of the Thecla

69

figure, erasing her blessing gesture. Was that just vandalism? Or perhaps a revision by later Muslim occupiers?

If both figures had been disfigured, Crossan and Reed point out, it could be chalked up as a random act of vandalism. But it was only the The-cla figure that was defaced. Paul remains as an authority figure. The woman is blinded and silenced. Crossan and Reed observe that "even the cave's present name, "St. Paul's Grotto," continues the negation of female-male equality once depicted on the walls." Good point.

Today, we can look at the Thecla story on several levels.

If key parts of it are true, it shows that a woman could become a charis-matic preacher and healer during the same time period as Junia.

If it is merely an allegory, it still expresses powerful messages that women of the time were drawn to:

- Thecla defied convention. She did not marry the man her parents wanted her to marry.
- She defied her fiancé. She chose a career of service to God instead of marrying into the most powerful family in her hometown.
- She gave up a position of affluence to live in a solitary cave and bless others.
- She dressed like a man instead of a woman to travel as a public figure.

Were these things that Thecla *actually* did? Or things that women of the time *wished* they could do?

Tertullian, the influential ecclesiastical writer in the second century who often wrote contemptuously of women, claimed the story was a fake. The Carthage church father complained that some Christians were using the example of Thecla to legitimize women's roles of teaching and baptizing in the church.[11]

He claimed that the "Acts of Paul and Thecla" were forged by a presbyter of Asia who "confessed that he did it out of respect for Paul." The presbyter's fraud supposedly was detected, and he was downgraded from his office around 160 C.E. Was Tertullian correct? Or was he trying to counteract women who were using Thecla's story to defend their ability to teach and baptize?

Bart Ehrman suggests in *Lost Christianities* that the stories of Thecla may have been causing problems in the Pauline churches years before Tertullian's accused forger did his work. Ehrman and other scholars say the existence of such stories may have led the author of 1 Timothy, who may not have been Paul after all, to speak out against roles for women in the church and urge readers not to listen to "the tales of old women."[12]

Scholars like Karen King at Harvard think Thecla may have been a real person, "but her story is now obscured by a lot of legend, so historians give her story less credence. The material we have is so covered up with legend that people are dismissive. Feminists pick her up to argue for roles for women in the church, but Mary Magdalene and Junia are much stronger figures and both are in the New Testament, which means they can't be ignored."

Elizabeth Clark, the John Carlisle Kilgo Professor of Religion and director of the graduate program in religion at Duke University, has described Thecla as a "literary character of probably second-century Christianity who comes to be thought of as an actual historical character by the fourth century."[13]

N. T. Wright, the Bishop of Durham in England, also draws the line against accepting Thecla as an apostle. "I don't think any Pauline scholars today would suggest much of a historical core to the Paul and Thecla story," he wrote me. "It's perfectly possible there was a woman named Thecla who was active in the Pauline churches and the stories to which Tertullian refers are manifestly and confessedly later inventions."

That may be the most plausible reading: A devout woman named Thecla may have existed once upon a time, but her story was later embellished beyond belief. Yet even if it is merely folklore, the Thecla story still reflects the social values of the time and provides clues about the world that Junia worked in. Because of the lack of detail about Junia, we have to look to the stories of other women to find illuminating mirror images that help us see what women's lives were like. In that sense, the Thecla saga is a rich parable about the difficulties that Christian women like Junia would have faced:

• *Travel was rigorous for everyone, but particularly dangerous for women because of the risk of rape.* Women out on the road by themselves were assumed to be fair game. Alexander presumed he could make advances toward Thecla because she was on the street instead of behind protective home walls. Not surprisingly, Thecla later dressed like a man to travel to Myra, where she encountered Paul again. Apparently, Peter's advice in the Gnostic gospels that women would have to "become male" to have holy lives was true in the literal and the metaphorical senses.

• *The cultural frustrations of ancient women, who gathered to "network" and share concerns as they prepared the evening meals, are evident throughout the story.* Men are generally opposed in "Paul and Thecla." The women in the arena function like a Greek chorus, cheering Thecla on. When Thecla prepares to baptize herself in the pool of seals, the women weep and beg her not to throw herself in the water. When Thecla emerges unscathed, and other fierce beasts are set loose upon her, the women in the stadium once again voice their protest. They throw leaves, spikenard (a perfume-giving root), cassia (a kind of cinnamon), and amomus (a kind of nard), so that an abundance of perfume fills the arena. It becomes a battle of the sexes, with the men supporting violence in the arena and women using more subtle weapons.

• *Charismatic, wandering women had a somewhat precarious relationship with local communities.* Despite her precautions while traveling and her revered status throughout the region, Thecla ends up being accosted by marauding men in her own cave. Stepping out of the protected boundaries of society carried severe consequences. Junia would have been safer with Andronicus as a companion.

• *Thecla's story was the showcase example of women's asceticism.* As the church struggled with how to handle women and the issue of sexuality, Thecla provided the model of the professional virgin. Withdrawal from society was advocated at the time as a way for women to avoid being a source of temptation for men. Women increasingly were kept behind closed doors. By the third century, Tertullian would write that women should not be seen in public except to visit the sick and at worship.

• *Apostles like Thecla may have had healing powers.* Thecla corrects displaced vertebrae, repairs four broken legs, cures a tumor, remedies a bout of anthrax, restores sight, relieves a kidney malady, and heals an ear infection. She even becomes renowned for being able to make sick animals well. Paul, who likewise heals the lame and casts out demons, suggests that apostles could do so.

• *The popularity of the Thecla story reinforces the possibility that women were apostles in Paul's day.* Even if highly embellished, the widespread acceptability of the Thecla story throughout the Mediterranean shows that the basic idea of a woman being an apostle was not unthinkable. Exceptional women could assume exceptional roles, as they do now.

Still, there is something uncomfortably voyeuristic about Thecla's story and the way it was later depicted in art. Thecla often is shown in artistic depictions with the top of her tunic off and with voluptuous breasts. As researchers like Sarah Barnett of the Anglican Diocese in Sydney, Australia, have pointed out, this was not unusual in the treatment of women martyrs in the early Christian period. Barnett documents that for the few women who were forced to compete as gladiators, their gender influenced how they were presented for the pleasure of the crowd in the arena. One female gladiator, Amazonia, was portrayed in stone as having fought with her breasts exposed.[14]

✤

The execution of female "criminals" in amphitheaters, including Christian martyrs, often took on a sexual tone. For example, at the Carthage arena in 203 C.E., the Christian women Perpetua and Felicitas were saved for the big finale to the games. They were dressed in see-through netting and sent out to do battle with a wild cow. The crowd was horrified to see through the netting that Perpetua was just a young woman and that the slave Felicitas was so fresh from childbirth that milk was dripping from her breasts. The crowd demanded that the women be sent back to be better covered. But their refined sensibilities did not include sparing the young women from death. Likewise, when Blandina was martyred in Lyons, some twenty-six years before, she was dressed in diaphanous cloth as she was tortured to death. And when Agathonike was executed in Pergamum around 249–251, she also was stripped naked.

In Thessalonica in 304, seven women are mentioned who flee from persecution but are arrested in their hiding place. Their crime? Refusing to eat meat offered to pagan gods. Eusebius says that when Potamiaina was martyred in Alexandria in 200, she was tortured, threatened by rape from gladiators, and covered from top to bottom with burning tar. Eusebius also reports eyewitness accounts of agonies endured by women martyrs. Some were torn to bits from head to foot with potsherds. Some were tied by one foot and hosted high into the air, head downwards, their bodies completely naked without a morsel of clothing, "presenting thus the most shameful, brutal and inhuman of all spectacles to everyone watching. Others were tied to trees and stumps—with the aid of machinery, one of each of their legs were attached to a bough, and torturers let the boughs fly back to their normal position, tearing apart the limbs of the victims."[15]

The German scholar Friedrich Augar has documented many cases where Christian women were sentenced to being raped or to serving in a brothel. Even Tertullian complained that Roman authorities had sentenced Christian women to a pimp (*leno*) rather than a lion (*leo*). The threat of sexual humiliation was one way of trying to pressure Christian women away from their faith and toward the Imperial cults. But it didn't work. In 304, a Christian woman named Irene, who had hidden Christian books, in Thessalonica was turned over to a brothel when she refused to sacrifice to pagan gods. She was imprisoned naked in the brothel. But none of the men dared go near her. She was eventually burned to death.[16]

Thecla is given a place among the martyrs, apparently because of her late-in-life assault in her cave by marauders. Some sources consider her in the list of early Christian apostolic martyrs that includes John, Peter, Paul, James, Stephen, Luke, and Andrew. She is honored elsewhere as the first female martyr and ranked alongside her male counterpart, Stephen, the first male martyr (Acts 6:8).

One of the earliest monastics was Amma Syncletica, who was inspired by the example of Thecla. Like Thecla, Syncletica left a well-to-do home to take up the ascetic life in the fourth century. Her sisters and two brothers had already committed themselves to the monastic life, increasing the family pressure on her to marry. Yet she steadfastly refused to do so. In her own writings, Syncletica alludes to the pressures on women of her day: "But even when we confine ourselves in our house, we are not liable to be free from anxiety there." Syncletica renounced her possessions and settled in a cave. She also cut off her hair, a symbolic way of renouncing the secular world.

St. Anthony usually is given credit for founding the monastic movement. However, as Professor John McGuckin points out, that claim overlooks the fact that Anthony wrote that he placed his own sisters in a convent in order to assume a monastic life himself, an indication that women's retreats were already well established.[17]

If you scrape off some of the layers of luster, Thecla's story is a valuable morality tale about a life of chastity and faith. But was she real? Since she was called "equal to the apostles," should she be included on the list with Junia?

The defining test for me was that Paul does not mention Thecla in his numerous letters that were included in the New Testament. Junia was. Even if their paths did cross in Iconium, Paul does not praise Thecla as an apostle. He does praise Junia. Junia may not have inspired the same kind of cult following or contemporary art as Thecla, but then neither did Prisca or Phoebe.

In the final analysis, Thecla's story could best be seen as a helpful parallel to Junia's. Even with its fantastic twists and turns, we can gain insights into the life and times of the early female believers. I still needed to find out how Junia's name got changed to a man's name. What was her life like? What happened to her?

CHAPTER FIVE

A Woman of Her Times

Men should not sit and listen to a woman. . . . Even if she says
admirable things, or even saintly things, that is of little
consequence, since they came from the mouth of a woman.
ORIGEN (185–254 C.E.), EARLY CHURCH FATHER

o see for myself what Junia's world might have looked like, I
scraped together some savings and traveled to Italy. I wanted to
walk where the people of Junia's time walked, see where she
might have lived, find out how she might have looked. We have a tendency
in our high-tech age to see those early believers as somewhat primitive people, denizens of the desert, sweaty, and foreign. For all we know, the apostles all lived in clay houses, like Santa Fe adobes, only with camels and date
trees. The stories of the early missionaries, other than Peter and Paul, are
simply not familiar. Their lives seem very different and very distant from
ours.

So I went to Rome and on to Pompeii and Herculaneum to see what
was left of life from Junia's time that would help me tell her story. Since
Paul wrote his letter to the believers in Rome just two decades before
Pompeii and Herculaneum were buried under ash from Mount Vesuvius in
79 C.E., the ghost towns have the best-preserved examples of how people
lived in Junia's time and frescoes that showed what they looked like.

The sensation of walking through the ruins was like wandering into
a western ghost town where the inhabitants are long gone and the only
sound is the squeak of a broken saloon door swinging. There is quietude in

the excavated cities—a hush, even with herds of tourists clomping through
the abandoned homes in their running shoes.

It took some poking around, but eventually I found the answers to a
series of questions that helped me imagine the world that Junia lived in.

❦ *What would Junia have looked like?* Junia probably had long, dark
hair, perhaps with decorative curls around her forehead—the style of the
time in Rome. In compliance with Jewish custom, she would have worn a
head covering in public. The average height for women was little more than
five feet, so she probably was somewhat petite.

In general, Roman women took great pains with their appearance—
a necessary skill for women who had to please men to survive. Judging
from the cosmetics kits that have been unearthed, women of the time tried
to beautify themselves with creams, rouge, and charcoal for eye shadow.
They used tweezers to pluck their brows and dyes to tint their hair. The
poet Ovid advised women not to let their lovers catch them with their jars
of cream displayed on the table. He also warned them not to let their arm-
pits "reek like a goat" or let their teeth turn black from laziness, but "wash
out your mouth every morning."[1] Since Roman men could divorce women
very easily, the women probably took Ovid's advice to put their best face
forward.

Respectable matrons could be identified by their fine woolen stolas,
while prostitutes wore togas and cropped hair. Women convicted of adultery also were compelled to wear the toga, typically male garb, as a symbol of their "shameless" status.

The stola that married women wore was a long, sleeveless tunic
made of wool that the women usually spun and wove themselves. They
were dyed quite bright colors. Often the Roman women would add a
cloak, or mantle, that draped over one shoulder and could be used as a veil.
There is some pictorial evidence that women wore underwear, at least
some of the time—a simple loincloth called a *subligar*. Women also some-

times wore a band of cloth or leather to support their breasts. Leather shoes were worn outdoors and sandals in the house.[2]

The jewelry that Roman women wore—ornate hairpins, gold earrings, and jeweled rings—would be much in style today. It is telling that the first recorded protest by women in Rome was not against patriarchal domination but against a wartime "sumptuary law" that curtailed the finery that women could display.

It is unlikely that Junia would have been decked out as ostentatiously as the more flamboyant Roman women, who even put pearls—the most esteemed jewel—on their shoes. Dress was determined by class, and because Junia was not a Roman citizen, says Amy-Jill Levine, she would not have worn the same stola as the Roman matron. According to scholar Peter Lampe, she probably would have worn the traditional women's tunic of a Jewish woman from the East who now lived in Rome. And most likely she would have dressed modestly, all the better to seek converts in a way that would not draw negative attention.

At the time, a phenomenon was arising in Rome of the "new woman," which is documented by Bruce Winter in *Roman Wives, Roman Widows*. The "new women" tended to neglect their family obligations and household duties to engage in illicit liaisons. They defied moral conventions with scandalous behavior much like the "flappers" of the Roaring Twenties in the United States. It was during this same period of feminine rebellion in Rome that Christian women were helping organize house churches and were trying to convert their neighbors. Christian women took the lead in calling on the homes of other women, since it would have been highly improper for males to do so. Such evangelizing activities may have aroused suspicions that the Christian women were flouting social conventions, sneaking out of the house like the promiscuous "new women."[3]

That the Christian women were also asking questions at religious gatherings would have been seen as challenging male authority. Under the Mosaic laws, women were not to intervene in public settings or come between two parties in conflict. By Roman and Jewish custom, women were to wear the veil outside the home. Critics who sent emissaries to spy on Christian gatherings could well have reported that Christian women were inappropriately attired and behaved indecently if they did not wear their head coverings. The Christian practice of greeting each other with a "holy kiss" on the mouth, regardless of social status or gender, also would have been considered unbecoming conduct.

❧

The *agape* kiss—the kiss of love—was in stark contrast with public practice of the day in Rome. In the Greco-Roman world, a man was not supposed to be seen kissing his wife, even in front of a slave. And in Jewish culture, the kiss was to be used as a greeting only for the family. Yet the kiss became a standard greeting for the extended family of Christians, an instant fellowship that signaled acceptance and intimacy. The "Holy Kiss" was considered so important in the early church that there are five specific commands in the New Testament for believers to greet each other with a kiss. (See Rom. 16:16: "Salute one another with an holy kiss. The churches of Christ salute you." See also 1 Cor. 6:20; 2 Cor. 13:12; 1 Pet. 5:14; 1 Thess. 5:26.) The custom of a holy kiss[4] is not followed in many denominations today, but Orthodox Christians do greet each other with a kiss on the cheeks (once on each cheek for the Greeks and three times on alternating cheeks for the Russians).

❧

It is highly possible that one of the reasons Paul expressed concerns about how Christian women acted in church services was that he did not want followers of the new Jesus movement, which initially included more women than men, to invite suspicion that they were behaving improperly in public—casting off their head coverings or speaking out of place.

Notably, prostitutes did not wear the head covering of the married woman to signify the husband's authority over her. They cut and dyed their hair. The story even was told that a consul named Gallus divorced his wife because she left the house unveiled, thus allowing all to see, he said, what only he should see.[5] Discarding the trappings of propriety would have invited trouble for the Jesus movement. The Jesus followers were already generating suspicion among Roman authorities because of their friction with establishment Jewish leaders over issues like converting Gentiles to this new way of being Jewish, which was how the followers of Jesus saw themselves at first. Converting Gentiles without requiring circumcision or requiring that they adhere to strict dietary laws was problematic for those who were brought up in the Jewish faith and had been circumcised. On top of that sensitive debate, having Christian women criticized for corrupting the neighborhood would have been a very serious threat.

❋

While I was interviewing scholars in Rome, an incident occurred that brought home to me how unsettling the idea of giving women more of a role in religion can seem, even now. I was having breakfast one morning in the garden of the hotel where I was staying, when a friendly American tourist came over to ask what I was reading. I explained to her that I was doing some research on women in the early church. The tourist was an active volunteer in her own West Coast church and instantly was intrigued by the idea of a female apostle. We chatted for a few minutes, and then she returned to her own table and her husband. From the looks in my direction over their lattes, I could tell she relayed to him what I had told her about Junia and the possibility she was an apostle.

The next morning, her husband made a beeline to my table and announced, "I understand you have been corrupting my wife." I was at a loss for words. Finally, I smiled up at him and said, "Well, I wouldn't put it that way." He was pleasant enough and asked a few questions about where I was going that day and wished me luck. But as he walked away, I sensed that he had said what he really wanted to say at the outset. It would be difficult, I realized, to tell Junia's story in a way that men, as well as women, would accept. In fact, I wondered if that would be possible at all. Christian writer Jill Briscoe likes to say, "Men of quality are not threatened by women of equality." But that may be easier to say than do. Even men of quality can misunderstand.

❧ *How old was Junia when she went to Rome?* If she were indeed present during the ministry or the resurrection of Jesus of Nazareth, then she might have been in her forties or early fifties by the time Paul wrote his letter to the Romans in 56–57 C.E., two decades later. That would indicate she had made it safely past childbearing age. Many women of the time died in childbirth because they were little more than children themselves, and childbirth was often difficult. One woman, whose epitaph was found in the Roman province of Pannonia, was married at eleven, gave birth to six children, lost five of them, and died at twenty-seven.[6] Mortality charts show less than 10 percent of the population lived beyond the age of fifty, so those that survived to their mature years probably were hardy individuals who also practiced careful hygiene.

❧ *Was Junia married?* Most scholars assume that Junia and Andronicus were husband and wife. They point to the parallel reference in Romans 16 to Prisca and Aquila, because the syntax in Greek is identical to the reference to Junia and Andronicus. That is, both references have a greeting, name 1, the Greek word *kai,* and name 2. Critics counter that the same *kai* structure is used to link the two women, Tryphaena and Tryphosa. Still, if those two women are sisters, it is a familial relationship. Because Junia's name was linked to a man's name in the same breath as someone with whom she traveled and was imprisoned, it is most likely that Andronicus was her husband, considering the conventions of the time.

We also can guess that Junia's marriage was a stable relationship because it survived such challenging circumstances. In fact, one of the distinctive features of Junia's story is her enduring "marriedness." She and Andronicus are presented as equals in Paul's eyes. For example, he does not say "Andronicus and his wife"; he says "Andronicus and Junia," just the way he salutes "Prisca and Aquilla." The women are named partners, not anonymous adjuncts. At a time when Paul often was recommending celibacy so believers could focus on their faith, he commends these married couples for their faith. As Marilyn Yalom notes in *A History of the Wife,* a biblical proverb states, "Whosoever findeth a wife findeth a good thing." Junia reaffirms the belief that it is a good thing to have a wife and be a wife.[7]

In the first century, it was quite easy for a Jewish husband to divorce a wife for causing an "impediment" to the marriage. Hebrew law (Deut. 24:1) allowed a husband to divorce his wife if she found "no favor in his eyes" because he had discovered something shameful about her, such as adultery, immodesty, or disobedience; or he could divorce her for burning a meal or if he found a fairer substitute. Barrenness was also grounds for divorce. Infertility generally was considered the fault of the wife.[8] Only on the rarest of occasions could a Jewish woman divorce her husband. It's easy to see how Jesus' outright rejection of divorce would have alarmed many of the males of his day.

Most marriages were arranged. Girls in the Roman Empire were expected to grow up quickly and could marry or become a mother at the age of twelve. A first-century B.C.E. marker found in Rome tells about Aurelia Philematium, who was married at the very tender age of seven and lived to the age of forty.[9]

The forced marriages of young girls before they had reached puberty may well have been one of the reasons that so many Roman women embraced Christianity. While nearly half the pagan brides were under fifteen in the first century, nearly half of the Christian brides were eighteen and over, according to sociologist Rodney Stark. Many prominent women were child brides: Octavia and Agrippina married at eleven and twelve, respectively. Quintillian, who had a famous school of rhetoric in Rome, married a young wife who bore him a son when she was thirteen. She died young, as did their two sons. Tacitus married a girl of thirteen. History does not record how the girls felt about their fate, but Plutarch does admit the custom of taking child brides was cruel and observed the "hatred and fear of girls forced contrary to nature."

❧ *What happened if the child brides got pregnant?* The obvious jeopardy in such marriages was that without effective means of birth control, the young girls got pregnant early and often, frequently dying in the process.

It was Jewish and Christian teaching that it was a sin to kill an unwanted child, but in the Greco-Roman world, the disposal of unwanted infants was quite legal. By law, any female infant and any deformed or weak male infant could be exposed to the elements. That often meant tossing the unwanted babies in the sewer or abandoning them near the public latrines in the hopes that a barren woman might take them in, although typically the infants fell victim to the weather or scavenging animals and birds. Though it was an accepted practice, there must have been some emotional toll for the mothers, even one hurriedly disposing of evidence from an affair.

Abortions prevented some unwanted births but also killed many mothers who were little more than children themselves. The Roman abortion techniques involved ingesting poison in doses that were hoped to be less than fatal, but often were not. Needles, hooks, and knives were used to remove the fetus, which left the brutalized mother susceptible to infection in an age ignorant of bacteria.[10]

Given the harshness of the methods, it is not surprising that abortion was one of the leading causes of death for a Roman woman. As Rodney Stark notes, it was generally men rather than women who made the decision to abort. Under Roman law, the head of the family had the power of life and death over his family, including the right to approve the death of an adulterous wife or to order a female in the household to abort. Emperor Domitian, who is believed to have impregnated his niece Julia, ordered her to have an abortion. She did not survive.[11]

❧ *What was the role of married women like Junia who survived their child-bearing years?* When a woman became a wife and mother, she was called a matron. She was expected to show *pietas,* which was duty, devotion, and loyalty to her family, friends, and the gods. She was always expected to put the male members of her family first and her daughters and herself last of all. We know from Tacitus that the primary duty of the young wife was to focus on the management of the household, seeing to the education of the boys and the training of the girls.[12] For Christian women, the ability to "home school" children was a way of seeing that the next generation grew up in the faith, even if the father was a pagan. The hand that rocked the cradle nurtured the next generation of Christians.

During the Imperial Age in which Junia lived, marriage was not a lifetime union. Roman marriages often were short-lived and ended in divorce. Those in the upper class often married a second, third, or even fourth partner. Those in the lower classes might simply cohabit.

The fifty-seven-year-old Cicero discarded the mother of his children after thirty years of marriage in order to fatten his bank account by marrying the young and rich Publila. Like Jewish men, Roman men could discard their wives with little justification: for going out without a veil, for stopping in the street to speak to a freedman who, supposedly, had an unsavory reputation for attending the games without permission.[13] Serial divorces became such a social problem that Emperor Augustus issued a set of strict morality laws in an attempt to promote more stable marriages. Some of those laws regulated marriage, providing incentives for having children to replenish the Roman ranks and establishing penalties for refusing to do so. Other laws made promiscuity a crime, with a special court to adjudicate matters.[14] However, Augustus was soon embarrassed by his own daughter, Julia. She became a notorious adulteress, carousing nights on end with a bawdy circle of young men.

Legislating morality is always difficult business, but Augustus's attempt failed because it was flawed to begin with and filled with inconsistencies. Courtesans were exempt from the Augustan laws against adultery. Wives were cautioned to ignore the philandering of the husbands, which ranged all the way from encounters with the husband's own slaves to prostitutes and music girls to other people's slaves to unmarried women of other classes to longstanding affairs with higher-class women. The double standard was glaring. Women could be punished for affairs with slaves, while men could not. Augustus had tried to legislate shame into the social code by drawing "bright lines" against runaway adultery, but he lost his credibility when he left Rome with his mistress Terentia. She happened to be the wife of another man. This led to complaints that the emperor punished others while breaking the adultery law himself.

Into this moral sink, the teaching of Jesus Christ came with an astringent clarity. Marriage was for life. Dalliances and divorces were not valid escape clauses. Christianity set a new standard for "holy matrimony." Augustus had tried to enforce fidelity with laws. Jesus wrote it on the hearts of couples that they should be faithful, period.

That's not to say there were not pagan marriages of the time that enjoyed genuine, enduring affection. There are poignant examples in gravestone epitaphs that confirm happy marriages. A Roman butcher noted on the epitaph for his wife that she "was my only wife, chaste in body, a loving woman who possessed my heart, she lived faithful to a faithful husband, equally in her devotion, she never let avarice keep her from her duty."[15]

Women of Junia's time could be playful as well as dutiful. The women celebrated some holidays by washing their hair, a touch that made me smile when I read about it. Pliny tells us that the women chewed gum. Juvenal suggests in his satires that women had dance competitions during some of their secret rites. Unfortunately, much of what we know of everyday women of Junia's time is from their gravestones. One was so moving that it was quoted by the historian Tacitus as an example of the virtuous Roman woman. It said:

> Friend, I have not much to say: stop and read. This tomb, which
> is not fair, is for a fair woman. Her parents gave her the name of
> Claudia. She loved her husband in her heart. She bore two sons,
> one of whom she left on earth, the other beneath it. She was
> pleasant to talk with, and she walked with grace. She kept the
> house and worked in wool. That is all; you may go.[16]

❧ *Was Junia literate?* Most of the scholars I interviewed said the odds are against it, because most women of that era were not educated. As Harvard scholar Karen King pointed out in *The Gospel of Mary,* most people of the time did not read or write. They literally "heard" about Christianity through preaching and teaching. They then practiced Christianity primarily through prayer, singing, and table fellowship, which did not require reading. A large number of people could write their name, having the equivalent of a grammar school education, which would be enough to read receipts or basic instructions. To be able to read and write with proficiency was the profession of scribes. "Even Caesar did not do his own writing," she told me. "He would dictate to scribes."

But if Junia were a freed slave from the noble Junian family, as her name would indicate, it is possible she would have learned some reading and writing skills in the Junian household. Scholars estimate that some 20 percent of the women in Pompeii were literate—a percentage coinciding with the women from important families. It was possible for daughters from the elite and subelite to get an education in the first century. The Stoics had argued the education of women was essential because of the moral element. After all, women could hardly be expected to avoid the cardinal vices if they did not know what the cardinal virtues were.

The rich were educated at home by tutors, who also provided intellectual stimulation to the family at dinners. Daughters participated in this early form of home schooling in enlightened households. Wives also might be exposed to some form of education from their husbands. More experienced women were expected to pass along advice and instruction to younger women. Celsus, a Greek writer who criticized Christians in the second century as a threat to stable communities, accused Christian women of leading children to question authority figures such as fathers and male teachers. The lack of Christian deference to the way things used to be done was alarming to him.

It is often assumed that Junia's contemporary, Prisca, was literate because she came from a noble family and apparently taught Apollos, a gifted preacher. Many of the depictions of the apostle Thecla, who also came from a prominent family, show her with writing instruments. It's possible that some of the women in Romans 16 were literate enough to read the epistles aloud at house church gatherings. Even when reading for themselves, it is likely that women of Junia's time read aloud, not silently as we do now, for that was the custom for many centuries.[17]

❧

Although literate women were the exception rather than the norm, there are some indications that there were female scribes, called *librariae,* who worked for affluent mistresses. Juvenal remarks in his *Satires* that if a husband spurns his wife's advances, her *libraria* will bear the brunt of the spurned wife's anger. The term *libraria* was usually read as *lani pendria* meaning "woolworker," when in fact the reference more likely was to a female scribe. As Cullen Murphy notes, "The underlying reason for the mistranslation in this case, as apparently in others, is a form of circular reasoning: how could the word be *libraria* when we know that women lacked the skills for that job?"[18] Indeed, in other instances, female literacy seems to have been simply suppressed. A letter of Eusebius reveals that women were among the scribes helping the theologian Origen, but Jerome, quoting the same letter at a later time, does not mention the female scribes. One manuscript from antiquity, the fifth-century *Codex Alexandrimus,* which included the Hebrew Bible and the New Testament, contained a rare example of a female scribe's name: Thecla, perhaps named after the popular missionary. Scholars disputed whether a woman had enscribed the code for centuries. Only in the eighteenth century did an investigator accept that the attribution referred to a woman—on the grounds that there were so many mistakes in the manuscript!

❧

❦ *What would conditions in prison have been like for Junia?* Conditions in prisons were extremely harsh. Prisoners often were chained to posts or to guards. Wooden stocks were sometimes used to confine prisoners, and there were few windows. The sexes were not separated, and the lack of ventilation and hygienic facilities, to put it delicately, encouraged rats and disease. Such conditions explain why Christians were often urged to visit fellow believers in prison—and to take food. John McGuckin of Union Theology School suggests that Junia and Andronicus may have survived imprisonment with Paul because they had financial resources. People with money could pay to have food brought in. Carolyn Osiek adds that "how you fared depended on your social network, regardless of your status."

It is possible that fellow believers helped sustain Paul, Andronicus, and Junia while they were in prison. You can see how harsh prison conditions might have been by visiting the Mamertine prison near the ruins of Caesar's forum in Rome. Tradition is that both Peter and Paul were incarcerated there for a time, although it can't be proved. There is a marble column in the subterranean cell, where the apostles supposedly were chained. And if you peer through a grated opening in the floor, you can see a well of water, which supposedly sprang up miraculously so Peter could baptize the jailers who had been inspired to convert.

Whether that story is true or not, Mamertine prison is a grim example of prisons of the day—an underground tomb that was formed by blocks from an ancient quarry on the site. There is no light and little fresh air. Food was lowered down through a hole in the ceiling. Even a few minutes' stay in the small vaulted room gives the sensation of being buried alive twelve feet under the city. One ancient witness wrote, "Its aspect is frightful and repugnant, owing to its state of abandonment, its darkness and the stink." A plaque on the wall tells the fate of prison alumni in blunt terms. Many were *decapito* (decapitated), some were *strangolati* (strangled), and one *morto per fame* (died of starvation).[19]

According to scripture, Paul spent most of his time in Rome under house arrest, chained to a guard, where he wrote and taught. Peter supposedly was imprisoned at San Pietro in Vincoli (St. Peter in Chains) near the Coliseum. Iron chains that are believed to have bound the apostle can be seen there. At the time of his martyrdom, the Esquiline hill site was where the Palace of Justice stood. This was the venue for court hearings, and there also were cells for prisoners. Many Christians were tried on the site. Nearby stood the Templum Telluris, which is mentioned in numerous acts of the martyrs as the place where the Christians were sentenced to death.

❧ *What would it have been like to travel by boat to Italy?* It would have been rough. Passengers had to travel on freight boats, sleeping on the open deck or in cramped, makeshift quarters. Some ships could hold hundreds of passengers; other could hold dozens. The passengers would have had to bring their own food and replenish it at the various ports along the way as best they could. Restrooms? Use your own imagination.

Lionel Casson has written an authoritative book, *Travel in the Ancient World,* that describes travel during Junia's time.[20] Casson points out that vessels were foremost for cargo and carried passengers only incidentally, so they provided neither food nor services. The crews worked for the ship, which meant there were no stewards to prepare meals or to clean cabins. Voyagers brought their own servants to take care of their personal needs and brought their own supplies of food and wine. A few seagoing ships had cabin space for VIPs, but the great majority of travelers simply purchased deck passage. According to Casson, they slept in the open or under small tentlike shelters that their servants put up in the evening. While the crew had first call on the galley, passengers could send their servants down to the galley to prepare food and could purchase fresh supplies when the ship docked in a coastal city.

In addition to a change of clothing, the ship's passengers would have to bring their own bedding. Ships rarely left on a fixed schedule, so passengers were forced to wait for a ship to arrive and for the right wind to depart. Once on board, passengers who could afford reading materials, read.

Others might gamble at games of chance. Some might sit on the deck to chat with the captain. If a storm struck, passengers pitched in to help; otherwise, they might not arrive at their destinations.

Junia probably traveled to and from Rome from the port city of Puteoli, an ancient city on the Bay of Naples. Today the city is known as Pozziuli, and its claim to fame is that it is the hometown of actress Sophia Loren. In the first century, it was the point of arrival for visitors from abroad, including Paul. Travelers disembarked at Puteoli, then traveled by foot or cart along the Appian Way some 155 miles to Rome. The apostle Paul found a Christian community at Puteoli, when he arrived there on his way to Rome, and he stayed seven days with them (Acts 28:13–14).

❧ *How dangerous was it to be a missionary?* We know from the descriptions of the abuse suffered by Paul that apostles were not always well-received. In Acts we learn that merely hosting a controversial missionary in many Mediterranean areas could be dangerous. Paul's host in Thessalonica found himself hauled before city officials on dubious charges when the angry Jewish mob was unable to find Paul. Acts 17:5–9 says:

> But the Jews became jealous, and with the help of some ruffians in
> the marketplaces, they formed a mob and set the city in an uproar.
> While they were searching for Paul and Silas to bring them out
> of the assembly, they attacked Jason's house. When they could not
> find them, they dragged Jason and some believers before the city
> authorities, shouting, "These people who have been turning the
> world upside down have come here also, and Jason has entertained
> them as guests. They are all acting contrary to the decrees of the
> emperor, saying that there is another king named Jesus." (NRSV)

Only after the authorities had taken a "security" from Jason and the others did they let them go.

Paul himself lists the injuries he sustained in his ten thousand miles of travels in Corinthians:

Five times I have received from the Jews the 40 lashes minus one.
. . . Three times I was beaten with rods. . . . Once I received a
stoning [after which he was left for dead]. . . . Three times I was
shipwrecked [and bitten by a deadly snake]. . . . For a night and a
day, I was adrift at sea; on frequent journeys, in danger from rivers,
danger from bandits, danger from my own people, danger from the
Gentiles, danger in the city, danger in wilderness, danger at sea,
danger from false brothers and sisters; in toil and hardship, through
many a sleepless night, hungry and thirsty, often without food, cold
and naked. (2 Cor. 11:24–27 NRSV)

In addition, Paul was imprisoned at least three to four times.
Clement of Rome later says Paul was imprisoned seven times, but he does
not specify where. During his first imprisonment in Philippi, Paul was
stripped, beaten with rods, and locked in stocks. Some Roman stocks were
designed to force a victim's legs as far apart as possible. Indeed, the torture
that Paul experienced in Roman jails may have deformed him, as later
sources described him as having bent legs.[21]

❦ *What was the social and political climate like for women in Rome?* Most
scholars assume Junia was a freedwoman because of her Latin name, but
Amy-Jill Levine reminds us that other Jews in Rome came primarily for
trade, and some followed family members there. Still, Junia's name points
to Roman ties of some sort, which Peter Lampe says would have been her
primary social identification, with her Jewish-Christian background denot-
ing her faith.

Roman women had more independence than Greek women. Women
in the Greek world were literally referred to as "the house" and led a totally
secluded life. They not only took no part in public affairs, they did not
appear at meals or social occasions. There were no laws against wife abuse
in the Greek world. If a man divorced a wife, she was left stranded.

Roman women were beginning to expand loopholes in the first century to find ways around cultural constraints. Roman women could inherit

property and control their dowries. And Roman women often operated small businesses on their own. Opportunities were created when men went off to war. Clay tablets from Pompeii show women borrowed and lent money, although they could not witness documents. Inscriptions also confirm that women were active in commerce and manufacturing and became respected benefactresses.

But you have to ask *which* women gained. Life generally was not better for those without status—the poor, the prostitutes, the freedwomen, or the slaves.[22] The Mediterranean tradition of *pater familias* still was dominant in the first century, which meant women were under the legal authority of men throughout their lives. Roman women were relegated to the private, domestic arena, working inside the home, preparing food, making clothes, providing child care. The men operated in the public arena, engaging in commerce, politics, civic life. Scholar Gillian Clark says the life of homemakers was difficult. They did the spinning, weaving, sewing, mending, cooking, water-carrying, and baby-minding. Just imagine how difficult it was to keep infants clean and healthy on the fourth floor of a walk-up tenement, with the water supply at the end of the street and no washing machine.[23]

In Junia's time, married women wore a cloak or mantle, using the upper part as a veil. The woman's hair was considered her husband's pride, and the veil symbolized the husband's authority over the wife. The removal of the veil by a married woman was a sign of her rejection of her husband's authority and thus withdrawal from marriage. Removing the marriage veil also could be tantamount to signaling you were a prostitute. If a woman were found guilty of adultery, she would have her hair cut off, according to the law.

Even the name *veil* had its roots in traditions of submission to authority. The word *nubes* meant "cloud," but it evolved into the verb *nubere,* "to be married." The word *nuptials* then came to refer to the head of the bride wrapped with a bridal cover, which the ancients considered "clouded over" with a veil.[24]

❦

Women could join some of the same clubs as men. The Rotary-type clubs were called *collegia* and often had a relationship to a trade like weaving or to a particular deity. The *collegia* provided a way for people to gather for eating and drinking, and to ensure that members got a proper burial as a member of the group.[25] Life was brutish and short, so getting a proper burial was a way of ensuring that your life counted.

For the most part, however, law and custom heavily restricted the lives of most Roman women. Proper women were not allowed to recline like the men at dinners. They ate separately, sitting in chairs or in a different area of the room or even another dining room. More women were being allowed to recline at dinners in Junia's day, but artwork still tended to show women sitting apart. In the amphitheaters, women and children and slaves had to sit in the worst seats in the back. Roman women of the time could not vote. They could not declaim in public as men did. They could inherit wealth from their fathers but could not represent themselves in court and had to depend on a male to do this for them.

Some scholars consider Roman women "nameless" because even their names generally were derived from the names of the men over them. Male citizens had three names. Women, however, had only the clan name and the family name.[26] A daughter was automatically called by the feminine form of her father's name, and slave women carried the name of their owners, even after being freed. Junia presumably drew her name from the male head of the Junian clan. Octavia was related to Octavian. Agrippina to Agrippa. Today's equivalent would be like naming a girl Phillipa or Johnette.

Under Roman law, a woman remained under the legal authority (*patria potestas*) of her father until he placed control of her into the hand (*manus*) of a husband. Under a husband's *manus*, the wife ranked only as a daughter in her husband's family, no better than a child. While there were a few elite women who divorced their husbands, women could lose their children if they did so, because the children belonged to the father's family.

Upon marriage, a woman was supposed to renounce her family's gods and accept her husband's gods.[27] The man's gods became her gods, because a family's religion was passed through the males. "Women who rejected their husband's gods in favor of a god called 'the only God' were especially susceptible to a barrage of stereotypical critiques, ranging from gullible fool, to adulteress, to whore."[28]

Yet women were drawn to Christianity because it brought a different kind of freedom. Jesus' teaching was remarkable in that it advised men they had obligations to care for their wives, that marriage had mutual responsibilities. A moral element was introduced to the concept of divorce. It is worth noting that the Samaritan woman that Jesus asked for a drink of water had been divorced five times. Since only men could initiate a divorce in those times, that meant the woman had been abandoned five times, tossed aside for whatever reasons. It was to this woman, so many times rejected by others, that Jesus of Nazareth first revealed he was the long-awaited Messiah. As he instructed her, she carried the news back to her people, becoming the first evangelist.

Jesus also was unique in having women travel with him in his ministry—generally women of some means such as Mary Magdalene and Joanna, the wife of Herod's steward Chuza,[29] plus Susanna, Salome, and Mary. This was in stark contrast to the sequestered treatment of women in Mediterranean society. Jesus treated women a different way and changed the way they saw themselves.

It is understandable why many Roman women were drawn to Christianity before their spouses were. The Jesus movement offered women a seat at the table and a place in the church. And by condemning such practices as abortion and female infanticide, the Christians increased their following among women who were then able to save more of their female babies, who would likely become Christian themselves.[30]

❧ *Which gods would the women next door have worshiped?* Most everyday Roman women worshiped a wide range of Roman, Greek, and foreign gods. Not surprisingly, they showed a special affinity for family gods who protected women during childbirth and children. Since men could divorce barren women for failing to bear children, women were "saved" from divorce, poverty, and shame by bearing children, preferably a male heir.

The deities who tended to the needs of women included Bona Dea, the "Good Goddess." Bona Dea was the goddess of fertility, healing, and virginity. Secret rites in her honor were very private, all-female affairs; not even pictures of men or male animals were allowed at the premises. The words *wine* and *myrtle* were also banned because Bona Dea supposedly was beaten by her father with a myrtle rod after he had gotten her drunk. Wine was served, but it was referred to as "milk," and the jar in which it was served was called a "honey-pot." The sick were tended in Bona Dea's gardens, which contained many kinds of healing herbs and snakes, which were also considered medicinal. In the year 62 B.C.E., the Bona Dea celebration was held in the home of Julius Caesar. His wife, Pompeia, and his mother, Aurelia, were in charge. A notorious Roman politician named Publius Clodius dressed up as a woman and sneaked into the house. He was eventually caught by Caesar's mother and kicked out. The ceremony had to be performed again. Caesar divorced his wife over the incident, claiming that even she had to be above suspicion of scandal. The Bona Dea rites fell into disrepute over the events. The satirist Juvenal suggested that the rites later became nothing but a drunken orgy for girls.

❧

Roman women worshiped more than a dozen goddesses connected to childbearing.[31]

Mater Matuta was an ancient goddess of dawn. The idea of light was closely connected with childbirth, whereby the infant is "brought into the light of the world" when it is born. Originally, only married women were allowed in the shrine. Roman women carried their sisters' children in their arms to the shrine and prayed for their welfare. Under Hellenizing influences, Mater Matuta somehow became a goddess of sea and harbors, and victorious generals brought maps of their campaigns to the temple. But the memory of her earlier function as a goddess of childbirth survived until the Imperial Era.

❦

Legally, women were prohibited from drinking. As the custodians of the domestic realm, they were "keepers of the keys" in their homes, with one notable exception. The husbands held the keys to wine cellars. But according to scholars, women apparently did drink on some occasions anyway, especially at their girls-only religious ceremonies.

❦ *Where might Junia have lived in Rome?* Probably in the *trans Tiberim* ("across the Tiber") area that is called Trastevere today. Peter Lampe of the University of Heidelberg has produced an exhaustive study of property titles and gravestones in Rome that shows some Christians lived in Trastevere, some in the more prosperous Aventine Hill area, others in the Via Appia–Porta Capena area, and some along the Via Salaria—the classic "salt road." But Trastevere was the traditional Jewish quarter and had been so for a century before Jewish followers of Jesus might have migrated there. The cemetery there is the oldest in Rome.[32]

The first settlements of Jews at Rome may have resulted from the conquests of Pompey over the Jewish king Aristobulus in 63 B.C.E. Many Jewish captives and immigrants were brought to Rome at that time. A special district was assigned to them, across the Tiber. Many of those captured Jews later were made freedmen.

Most of the scholars I interviewed agreed that Junia most likely would have lived in one of the Jewish neighborhoods of Trastevere. Because the Tiber river curves around it, the Trastevere area had always been populated by foreigners who were involved in the commerce flowing from the dock area. It was a natural location for craftsmen who needed a nearby water source for their work, like the tanning of hides for tents and shoes. Syrian and Jewish merchants were drawn to the Trastevere neighborhood, as maritime business grew up along the river. Sailors were attracted along with small businesses of tanning, carpentry, milling, and prostitution. It would have been an earthy mix. The residential streets generally were narrow and winding, flanked by multistory lodging houses (*insulae*) that rose as high as seventy feet. More prosperous freedmen would have had more spacious accommodations.

When Peter arrived in Rome, perhaps about 42 C.E., tradition is that he resided first in the home of Senator Pudens on the Esquiline hill and then in the villa of Aquila and Prisca on the Aventine hill. From the Aventine, Peter could have come down to the nearby Trastevere area to preach to the substantial Jewish population. It was from Trastevere that the imperial guard reportedly hunted down most Christian victims for martyrdom.

Today, the neighborhood is one of the most sought-after places to live in Rome. Its quaint cobblestone streets and red brick villas give it the charming, rustic look that guidebooks love. While tourists tramp by in search of historic churches like Santa Maria in Trastevere and Santa Cecilia, residents relax over lunch and a bottle of the local Lazio wine long into the afternoon to avoid the heat of midday. As dusk comes and the temperature starts to cool, starlings begin flying around and over the red-tile roofs in a whirling, swooping bird rodeo. Trastevere has a timeless feel. But there is no sign of Junia. There is no church, no monument in her honor. Yet.

❧ *What would Junia's home have looked like?* Walk through the doorway of one of an ancient *domus* in Pompeii or Herculaneum, and you are likely to be struck by how livable it would be today, except perhaps for the bedrooms and the kitchens, which were small by modern standards and dark, since windows were few. Perhaps that's why people spent much of their time in the open atrium spaces where there was natural light or in the dining room, where there was company.

Houses were built close to the curb, and the streets outside must have bustled and clanged with efficient Roman commerce. The ironmonger, the tavern, the laundry—all were often just a few doors away from residences, not unlike the lower east side of Manhattan, where your neighbor might be a pizza parlor. If Junia and Andronicus had financial resources, they would have lived in a *domus,* a home with a courtyard. The walls most likely would have been painted with the rust-red colors of Indian summer that are still a Mediterranean hallmark. The floors would have been tiled with colorful mosaics. With their graceful lines and elegant atrium fountains, the Roman homes have a tasteful simplicity that *Architecture Digest* would admire.[33]

If Junia had not been well-off and was a member of the working-trade class, she would have lived in yesterday's equivalent of an apartment house, an *insula.* Such tenements were crowded, without personal privacy or toilets other than chamberpots. The wooden, multistory *insula* also were subject to burning down from cooking fires.

Furnishings from that time would have been very comparable to today's home furniture. Romans had stools and chairs for sitting, carved wooden cupboards to keep small objects in, couches of wood and leather to recline on, and mattresses on their beds, with pillows. In the ruins of Herculaneum, you can find a copper bathtub that would be usable today and a cotlike bed that only needs a mattress to host a snooze. Their silver dining ware would be serviceable today.

Meals were an important part of Roman social life.[34] The dining room (*triniculum*), with reclining benches, was the most social room of the home. Even at funerals, relatives and friends observed a meal at the tomb called a *refrigerium,* or funeral banquet. Often they poured food and wine through slots in crypts for the deceased. Such funeral feasts became a standard feature of Christian burials and lasted well into the fourth century. According to some sources, the party scene at funeral banquets could get out of hand as toast after toast was exchanged for the departed.[35]

❦ *What can you see in the ruins about their private lives?* The graffiti on the snack bar walls in Pompeii show that the ancients were as besotted in their search for love as today's soap opera characters. Two fellows named

Successus and Severus wrote on the wall of a restaurant in Pompeii about their rivalry for the heart of a certain slave girl named Iris. Severus scratched a taunting note over the door that Iris did not think much of Successus, who replied, "Don't you try to take over from someone who is better looking than you, who knows how to do it and is better endowed." Severus responded bluntly, "You love Iris but she doesn't care for you." Severus got the last word because the exchanges end there.[36]

❀

By the end of a day walking the rutted streets of Pompeii, the image that stayed with me was of the plaster casts of people who were stopped in their tracks when the volcano erupted. There were a dozen bodies of victims found in the ruins of the public baths alone. They managed to get into the garden before they were overcome by the poisonous fumes. A mother sheltered her baby in her arms. A young girl is turned toward a man who looks as if he is sleeping on his side. She has buried her face in the man's clothing, her head resting on his chest as she clings to him for protection. Even the noisiest tourists got quiet looking at the poignant poses. They were only plaster casts of the shapes of the bodies, but their final positions looked lifelike. "I feel like I ought to cover them with a blanket," the woman next to me said as she looked at the cast of a man who had died curled in the fetal position. I nodded in agreement. The people of Junia's time were beginning to seem more real, not just names in a book, not just desert-y people dressed in long robes, but people who were very acutely like us.

Still, I wondered, what must it have been like for Junia to have been three times an outsider living in the status-conscious Roman society? After all, she was a Christian, a woman, and perhaps a freed slave or daughter of a slave.

✤ *What was the status of freed slaves?* The oldest means of becoming a slave was to be captured, and many people in the Tarsus area were enslaved by Pompey when he subdued pirate activity in the Silicia in 67 B.C.E. Slavery was hereditary, so the child of a slave woman became a slave no matter who the father was.

Under the Roman legal system, a slave did not have a legal family. A sexual relationship with another slave was not marriage but cohabitation. A slave could become free by the act of manumission, whereby the master released the slave from his authority. According to Roman law, slaves that were freed could become Roman citizens, but they had fewer rights than Roman citizens who were born free. The freed slave also still had obligations to the former master, who now became his or her patron.

By the first century C.E., it was estimated one in every three persons in Rome and Italy was a slave. Slaves were field hands, house servants, nannies, nurses, cooks, laundry women, stable boys. Household slaves of elite families enjoyed the best standard of living, although it was significantly lower than that of free members of the *familia*. Work was subdivided on a minute scale—one consul kept a slave whose only job was to brush the man's teeth.

After manumission, a slave could be converted from property to Roman citizenship. Still, manumitted slaves were typically looked down on by the freeborn. Ex-slaves were expected to perform acts of *obseqium,* open groveling in front of their former masters. Whether in public or private, the freedmen were required to lift their hats and drop to their knees in front of their former masters. If she were a freedwoman, Junia would have been well aware of her station in life. As a Jewish Christian, a woman, and perhaps a freedwoman, she was a person circumscribed by multiple boundaries. But she obviously did not let them bind her spirit.[37]

❧

❧ *What was the role of women in the Roman church in those early days?* Women believers played an indispensable role in spreading the word in those rocky early years. Ironically, the tradition of keeping women in the private realm, the home, as opposed to the public square, worked to their advantage as the early congregations moved from synagogue services to private houses. Emperor Claudius had expelled the Jews from Rome in 49 C.E. for their disruptions over someone named "Chrestus." When they were permitted to return, some sources say the Romans authorities forbade followers of Jesus of Nazareth from holding their meetings in synagogues, to avoid more disruptions. Others speculate that those in the Jesus movement shifted to meeting in houses so they could observe the Eucharist as Jesus had instructed them to do. Whatever the impetus, the move from public worship to the private home churches gave women more of a chance to participate. The home was the woman's domain, and many of the early home churches were in homes owned by women.

In his second-century critique of the church, Celsus complains that whenever Christians got children and "some stupid women" in private, they turned them against their fathers and teachers.[38] He may have been partly right. Women did move in and out of the house spreading the Jesus story. And they did encourage people to join without getting proper permission from family figures, according to Carolyn Osiek. She says this in her history of the early church, *A Woman's Place:*

> They did so, it seems, while conducting their daily business. No doubt they sometimes remained largely invisible, but in other cases, they met with real resistance both inside and outside of church groups. This combination of boldness, affront, and concealment is one of the most interesting and little understood features of the rise of early Christianity.

Peter Lampe says that women were the backbone of the church for many difficult years. "The church would not be where it is today without those early women believers. It would have died. It is very obvious," he said emphatically in our phone interview. "When Constantine came into power and Christianity was made the official religion, women in aristocratic families adopted it. It took two or three more generations for the males in the same families to drop their pagan beliefs and become Christians, too. There are several examples in records where the mother and grandmother were Christians, while the males still clung to their pagan religions.

John McGuckin agrees:

The church was threadbare in Rome until the middle of the third century. The church had suffered savage losses, its leaders systematically picked off. Women were in charge of the affairs of the house, which included the education of the children. Women could determine who would cross the threshold into the house. There are writings where the woman of the house insisted someone who was a pagan could not come in. In the early years, this would have been a time when the meetings of the Jesus movement were more like a secret meeting in Stalinist times than an evangelical rally. And that fell within the women's realm. Women could teach and preach in that context, because it was safely within the private realm, not in the public square.

❦ *What would church services in Junia's home have been like?* As organizer of house affairs, Junia would have determined the rhythms of her household and would have helped organize the house church meetings, perhaps in her dining room. Services were held on Sundays and early on acquired the name of "The Lord's Day." Pliny writes to Trajan that Christians met for worship on a "stated day"; other sources describe it as the first day of the week.

In Colossians, it is said the early Christians sang psalms, hymns, and spiritual songs. In Corinthians, there are descriptions of the gifts used in church: prophesy, ecstatic utterance, interpretation, revelations, and teaching. On the walls of the earliest catacombs, Domitilla and Priscilla, you see many fading frescos of *oranta* (Greek for "praying")—women with their arms held up in the air toward God. We know from the writings of Justin Martyr that Christian worship was not dissimilar from today's service. There were readings from the Word, such as Paul's letter to the Romans, followed by a sermon. The people would "rise up" for prayer and share the "kiss of peace" afterward. Bread and wine were shared. Justin uses the term for "thanksgiving" (Eucharist) to describe the sharing of bread and wine and prayer. Those who had the means gave what they could for the orphans, the widows, the sick, the needy—and the "people sing out their assent, saying the 'Amen.'"[39]

According to Carolyn Osiek, a trained person with the skills of a reader might be brought in, so he could read the texts aloud and give a more expansive presentation of the text. A teacher then would work with the congregation to interpret the reading.

Professor Wayne Meeks points out:

> Many early converts very likely were attracted to the movement because they knew someone in it, were connected through some social network to a household that had become Christian, heard the story the Christians were telling and thought it was intriguing, or were curious about the new club that was meeting in their neighborhood and, once they made the connection, found the enthusiasm and the lifestyles contagious.

Life gained more meaning and purpose when it was no longer controlled by fickle gods or "the fates," said David Dawson Vasquez. "The new Christians also were no longer bound by social class. An artisan could have the love feast with a matron from a prominent house. It was shocking and very radical," Vasquez told me. "To say you could be born again in Christ and that God loved everyone the same was a departure. Paul had to try very hard to remind them that the social revolution part of the message was not as important as your relationship with Christ."

Historian Karen Armstrong says that as the Christian movement began evolving into a "great church" that shunned what was not considered mainstream, Christianity became more urbane. It began to appeal more to highly intelligent men who tended to shape the faith along lines that fit with their Greco-Roman culture. She confirms in *The History of God* that the new religion also drew in women because of scriptures that taught that in Christ there was no male or female and instructed men to cherish their wives as Christ cherished the church. Christianity stood in stark contrast to the cults like that of Baal, which had required the sacrifice of the firstborn.[40]

❧ *How many Christians were in Rome with Junia?* The sociologist Rodney Stark calculates in his book *The Rise of Christianity* that the number of Christians in Rome in 40 C.E. was roughly one thousand (accounting for 0.0017 percent of the Roman Empire). The followers of the Jesus movement initially were a tiny minority in a culture awash with gods and goddesses—Greek, Roman, Egyptian, Persian, and more. Three hundred years after the first house churches, there were 34 million Christians. Today there are 2.1 billion. The names of the popular gods of ancient times, like Apollo and Hermes and Venus, are seen today only as names on space capsules, neckties, and broken statues.

Then, as now, the Holy Spirit brought people together. Initially, private homes were shared for congregating; no houses were dedicated solely for services. But by the end of the third century, some homes were turned over to the Christian community for the exclusive use of worship. There were no edifices built solely for worship until Constantine launched a building program in the fourth century. And as churches moved from the privacy of the home, which had been the woman's domain, to the more elaborate public church buildings, women became more marginalized.

❧ *When were women edged out of church roles?* Elaine Pagels maintains that even the earliest moments of the Jesus movement were not a Golden Age of egalitarianism.[41] She views it as "a new, unformed diverse and threatened movement which allowed a lot more fluidity for women in certain roles for a while, in some places, but not in others." Even then, there was resentment, she says, which you see cropping up in some New Testament writers such as Timothy, who says, "Women should be silent in all the churches," and attributes that view to Paul.

Elizabeth Clark, professor of religion at Duke University, concurs that by the second and the third centuries, "as Christianity becomes more

105

established, and a male hierarchy of the clergy is developed, women tend to get more and more excluded."[42]

Including women as ministers increasingly was seen as a characteristic of heretical groups, like the Montanists, whose leaders included two women prophets, Priscilla and Maximilla. They were vehemently opposed and suppressed. There is evidence that some women served as heads of widows' ministries and even as deacons, bishops, and elders. But those roles steadily were diminished. With the exception of some extraordinary women leaders in the monastic community, women were relegated to the margins of Christian governance.

Leonard Swidler tells us:

> The woman deacon of Paul's day became the deaconess of the fourth century, a holy order lesser in status than that of the male deacon. As Christianity moved into the age of the fathers, the status of Christian women became very more restricted. The fathers took a uniformly male superior attitude that often was misogynist. The trend continued into the Middle Ages and up to the most recent times.[43]

❧

- The Council of Nicea, in 325 C.E., decreed that women were no longer to be ordained along with the clergy for leadership roles but were to remain among the laity.
- The Council of Laodicea, in 352, forbade women from the priesthood and presiding over churches. The council also barred women from approaching the altar.
- The Fourth Synod of Carthage, in 398, said women may not teach men in assembly and may not baptize.
- Council of Chalcedon, in 451, ruled that no woman under forty could be ordained a deacon, and then only under close scrutiny.[44]

❧

Considering the difficulty women had getting their voices heard in the ancient world, it is surprising that we have even a sketchy record of their early roles. Those traces in scripture we have confirm that women were part of the original DNA of the Christian church.

Yet the issue of worthiness—who is worthy to speak for Jesus—was an ongoing struggle in the early church. "These were enormously live issues," Pagels told a PBS interviewer.[45] She continued:

> We know that Tertullian, one of the leaders of the church in Africa, spoke about a woman he called simply, "that viper," because she was baptizing people. And he said, "these heretical women, how audacious they are. I mean they teach, they baptize, they preach, they do all kinds of things they shouldn't do." It's horrible, in short. And so we know there was a great deal of ferment in these communities about the role of women. . . . There is not a single woman of renown in the ancient church whose story does not show enormous opposition from some of the men in the group.

What is truly remarkable about Junia and the other women leaders of the early church is how they were able to manipulate the system to do their work. Perhaps in revolutionary times (and the birth of the Christian church certainly was one of those moments) opportunities present themselves to women to become the equals to men, not unlike Rosie the Riveter in World War II. However, when the status quo resumes, women often revert to subservient roles—or are nudged in that direction. In the case of the women of the early church, history shows they were steadily pushed back to the side.

※

Learning about Junia's time had an unexpected effect on me. It brought back memories about women of my generation with a new historical perspective. Many of the cultural and legal constraints of Junia's day, I now realized, had echoes in my lifetime. My female teachers in Texas had to take their teaching contracts home to have their husbands sign for them. By law, only the husband could sign financial contracts, even into the late 1960s, just as Roman women had needed a male to sign business papers for them. Married women as recently as the 1970s could not hold bank accounts in their own names—a modern way of being under the *manus* of the husband.

A prominent female federal judge had reminded me only recently that while Richard Nixon was dueling with the *Washington Post* in the 1970s, the few women who were appointed as judges in the United States could not have been jurors in their own courts because women could not serve on juries in some states. It was an echo of the time when women of Jesus' era could not testify as witnesses.

And yet such conditions existed just a few decades ago. In the same post–World War II era that we like to think of as "modern," with the introduction of home television and cars with air conditioning, American women who became pregnant were expected to stay largely "confined" to their home when they were "showing" as pregnant. Until the status quo was challenged in the "make love, not war" sixties, pregnant women stayed modestly out of view, like the ancient women of the Mediterranean.

Boundaries limiting women have lasted centuries after Junia's day. It was not until the 1970s and 1980s that women gained seats in major symphony orchestras—only after "blind" auditions were added so that the screening committee could not see whether the performer was a man or a woman. Women who pressed to become doctors and lawyers, ministers and mayors in those transitional decades were regarded as somehow "unnatural." Why would women want to do something men had always done—unless there was something wrong with them? The circular reasoning was that God did not intend women to be symphony conductors, Supreme Court justices, newspaper publishers, race car drivers, or ministers because there weren't any before. But we now know better.

I had lived through all those changes since the 1960s, and yet I had never really stopped to think about how the church had provided the primary model that women were to be kept in their place. It was a discomfiting thought.

CHAPTER SIX

What Was in Paul's Letter?

There is no telling what may happen when people
begin to study the Epistle to the Romans.
New Testament scholar F. F. Bruce

unia was turning from a missing person case into a metaphor for the church's checkered history with women. She had become a way to search out the how and why of church bias as well as the who.

To learn more about the context of Junia's time, I revisited the main piece of evidence, Paul's letter to the believers in Rome. What did he actually tell them? What impact did it have? I knew that Romans is considered Paul's *magnum opus,* his longest and greatest theological dispatch. But I was surprised to learn that the letter has played a major role in the lives of many theological giants of the church.

It turned out that Romans itself has been something of a Rosetta stone—the theological key that unlocked an invisible door to faith for a stunning list of church leaders including such greats as St. Augustine, Martin Luther, John Chrysostom, John Wesley, and Karl Barth. Romans transformed their lives. In turn, each of their lives had an impact on women of the church, but not always in a positive way. Each man's life was a microcosm of the church's struggle with women.

And as I would come to see, one of those esteemed men of faith would play a crucial role in converting Junia's name to a man's name.

• *Augustine of Hippo* (354–430). Augustine was the wayward son of a pious woman named Monica in Roman North Africa. Despite her constant prayers for him, he continued a dissolute life, famously praying to God to make him chaste, "but not yet." Augustine's brilliance helped him ascend academically, and he became a professor of rhetoric at Milan, but he continued to think of Christianity as a mere superstition for the uneducated. He regarded marriage as a "covenant with death" and kept a concubine with whom he had a child.

As Augustine recounts in his autobiographical *Confessions,* one day he happened to be idling in the garden of his friend Alypius. The thought of his shameful habits troubled him so deeply that it brought a rain of tears. Augustine fell down under a fig tree and wept, asking himself, "How long, how long shall I go on saying tomorrow and again tomorrow? Why not now, why not have an end to this uncleanness this very hour?"

Then he heard a child's voice repeating a refrain. Children playing in the garden were chanting a Latin chorus from a popular game, "*Tolle lege, tolle lege, tolle lege.*" The words meant, "pick up and read, pick up and read, pick up and read." The refrain stuck in Augustine's mind as he returned to where he had put down a copy of Paul's letter to the Romans just before emotion overcame him. Augustine snatched up the scroll and read in silence the passage where his eyes first fell:

> So quit the evil deeds of darkness and put on the armor of right
> living, as we who live in the daylight should! Be decent and true
> in everything you do so that all can approve your behavior. Don't
> spend time in wild parties and getting drunk or in adultery and
> lust, or fighting, or jealousy. But ask the Lord Jesus Christ to help
> you live as you should, and don't make plans to enjoy evil.
> (Living Bible)

The words cut to his core. Augustine was compelled to turn from the errors of his past toward faith. It was a transformation that would shape Western civilization. Augustine's influence dominated Christianity for centuries, for better or worse.[1]

It was Augustine who built a theological fortress out of the concept of original sin—that Adam and Eve fell from grace, bringing disastrous consequences for the rest of humanity. The blame, Augustine believed, was due to that darn woman, Eve. His theology reflected the bias of his time against women in general. Yet on a personal level, when Augustine interacted with women who were educated, he treated them as equals. He agreed in 395 to become the spiritual director of a woman named Florentina, who had written to him after dedicating her life to God. His rules for women in the Augustine order were almost identical to those for the men.

Still, Augustine remained conflicted about sex most of his life. Having given up his concubine for a life of celibacy, he wrote about "passionless procreation," intercourse to conceive children but devoid of sensual pleasure and any fleshly indulgence. His personal conflicts with biology shaded his theology. He wrote, "What is the difference whether it is in a wife or a mother, it is still Eve the temptress that we must be aware of in any woman. . . . I fail to see what use women can be to man, if one excludes the function of bearing children."[2]

Such views on women still have repercussions today in the perception that women should not hold sacred positions because of Eve's transgression.

• *John Chrysostom* (347–407). Considered the best preacher ever heard in a pulpit, John Chrysostom famously had Romans read aloud to him several times a week to help him stay "centered" in his faith. His Greek name is difficult to pronounce, but it means "golden-mouthed." (It is helpful to say it like "Chris Austom.") Though Chrysostom was only five feet tall, his sermons were soaring works and sometimes lasted several hours. When he was elevated to the position of Bishop of Constantinople, he put an end to opulent banquets for the clergy and cracked down on the practice of allowing clergy to keep women as "spiritual sisters" in their houses. He sold the ornate dishes and furniture in the bishop's palace and distributed the proceeds to the poor and the hospitals. He took care of the church widows, advising them to either marry again or observe rules of propriety. And he preached against the extravagances of the rich, especially rich women who flaunted their finery.

Though some of his homilies showed shades of misogyny, his commentary on Romans is unstinting in its praise of Junia as a brave apostle. Chrysostom appreciated that women could be noble, perhaps because he was very close friends with Olympias, a well-connected widow and deaconess in Constantinople. She was a wise and generous patron for Chrysostom. According to Elizabeth Clark, at Duke University, Olympias had a great deal of property, and it has been calculated that her contributions to the church, figured in today's terms, would amount to something like $900 million.[3] It is understandable why any bishop might have been attentive. Yet it is evident in the seventeen surviving letters from Chrysostom to Olympias that a genuine friendship developed.

It is noteworthy that Olympias served in the church as a deaconess, even before Chrysostom's appointment to Constantinople, establishing a home where she invited other young women to reside to serve God in a special way. Her community became a center of prayer and charity, much like the religious orders of later centuries. An orphanage and hospital were later added. When he was exiled, he advised her to continue to serve the church, no matter who followed him as bishop. But after someone set fire to the church, Olympias was falsely blamed by Chrysostom's enemies. She, too, was exiled and later put in prison. Some of his most eloquent letters were written to encourage her.

Yet as Bishop of Constantinople, Chrysostom was scathing in his criticism of other women as temptresses: "You carry your snare everywhere and spread your nets in all places."[4] He also wrote, "God maintained the order of each sex by dividing the business of life into two parts, and assigned the more necessary and beneficial aspects to the man and the less important, inferior matters to the woman." He warned, "The woman taught once and ruined everything. On this account . . . let her not teach."[5]

Like many church fathers, Chrysostom was of two minds about women, praising exemplary individuals such as Junia and Olympias, yet broadly condemning the rest. The pattern was similar to the tendency of many Americans to like their own representatives personally but disparage politicians in general.

The little bishop was caustically critical of the vanities of women of the time, especially those of the extravagant empress Eudoxia. When the empress had a silver statue of herself unveiled in the square in front of the cathedral, Chrysostom spoke out against the sin of self-glorification. Such frankness got him exiled—twice. During his second exile, the feisty bishop collapsed and died during a forced march in harsh conditions.

• *Martin Luther* (1483–1546). Martin Luther, best known for his role in the history-changing Protestant Reformation,[6] had his faith clarified in a dramatic way when he was visiting Rome as a Augustinian monk and climbed on his knees up the *Scala Sagrada* (sacred stairs) as a testament of faith. While Luther was inching his way up the *Scala Sagrada,* the thought of the scripture from Romans 1:17 unlocked new insights for him: "The just shall live by faith." The original German translation would be more like "We are made righteous by our belief." Although that phrase may not automatically trigger a breakthrough for other believers, the words clicked with Luther in that moment on the stairs and gave him the moral clarity that later would enable him to defy the corruption of the clergy in Rome.

During a visit to Rome to do research, I retraced Luther's steps and climbed the sacred stairs on my knees. The pain was close to unbearable, even though the marble stairs are now covered with weathered walnut planks. After about three steps, I wished that I could turn around and watch the pilgrimage from the doorway. But there was no turning back. There were throngs of believers deep in prayer on their knees behind me, blocking the way back down. The only choice was to go on climbing and get "above" the pain by concentrating on something else, like God. To tell the truth, I prayed for the man in front of me to hurry up. I prayed for the number of stairs to shrink. Glancing at those with heads bowed down all around me, I could tell they were engaged in deeper thoughts, so I prayed to have better prayers. By the time I reached the top, I had gained a genuine appreciation for the centuries of Christians who sought God on their knees. Was it a humbling experience? Yes.

I could see how the experience could have crystallized Luther's theology and his concerns about the corruption in the church. At the time, the clergy had fallen into the practice of selling forgiveness of sins for money. It was called granting "indulgences," but it was religious graft. Instead of doing penance, people were encouraged to make a donation to the church, supposedly to shorten the time they would have to stay in Purgatory. Luther believed that paying a priest for forgiveness was totally unnecessary, because salvation was something between the individual and God. The practice may have been legal, but it was not righteous, he said.

In his preface to Romans, Luther explained that to understand Paul's letter, you must not understand the word *law* as a regulation about what must be done or must not be done, whether your heart is in it or not. Luther emphasized that God judges what is in the depths of the heart.[7] And he recommended Romans as the "chief book of the New Testament," saying, "It deserves to be known by the heart . . . , word for word, by every Christian."

For all his brilliance, Martin Luther nevertheless failed to fully appreciate the role of women in establishing Christianity. Women were not full citizens of Luther's Christianity, despite his call to the "priesthood of believers." He saw women more in terms of *Kinder* and *Küchen* than *Kirche* (more associated with children and the kitchen than with church). He wrote dismissively, "Women are on earth to bear children. If they die in child-bearing, it matters not; that is all they are here to do."

Yet he, too, had an influential woman in his life. His wife, Catherine von Bora, was a nun when she heard Luther's biblical teaching. She and several other nuns at her cloister wanted to leave their captivity in the convent. When Luther was informed, he persuaded a merchant friend to assist him in freeing them. The merchant, who often delivered herring to the convent, concealed twelve nuns in the empty fish barrels in his wagon. Luther helped find homes or husbands for those without families. After two years, all had been provided for except one—"Katie" von Bora. Friends and his father persuaded Luther to marry her. They had six children and raised four orphans. The former celibate monk now praised marriage and the wife who patiently cared for him when he was sick, which was often. In turn, he encouraged her in her Bible study and suggested passages for her to memorize.[8]

Despite his fondness for his own marriage, Luther's views on sex and women remained unflattering. He taught that women were inferior to men and were created to be ruled by men. As proof, he cited the shape of a woman's hips, saying the broad base indicates that God meant for a woman to sit at home. Later it would become evident that Luther's biased view of women may have contributed to one of the fateful changes of Junia's name.

• *John Wesley* (1703–1791). A young, Anglican clergyman in eighteenth-century England, John Wesley was sitting in on a meeting of Moravian Christians on Aldersgate Street, wishing his faith were more alive, when Romans spoke to him. At the time, Wesley was reading Martin Luther's preface to the Epistle of Romans. About 8:45 P.M., as he read how Luther described the change that God works in the heart through faith in Christ, Wesley felt his own heart "strangely warmed." He later wrote that he suddenly felt a new trust in Christ and felt the assurance that his sins had been forgiven. It was a blessed breakthrough. Wesley had failed miserably as a preacher in Georgia because he was so methodical, so regimented that he repelled the very people he wanted to draw to the church. At Aldersgate, he got the pastoral heart that rounded out his intellectual ministry.[9]

At first, his "Methodist Societies" were persecuted by clergymen and magistrates, attacked in sermons, bullied by mobs. Yet they continued their work among the neglected and needy. Unable to preach from pulpits, Wesley started preaching in the open fields and commissioned preaching by church members who were not ordained. It became one of the great features of Methodism that God could speak through lay ministers. It was an act of necessity but proved the point that professional clergy did not have a monopoly on God's word.

Of the men shaped by Romans, John Wesley was the most inclusive for women in his ministry. He had been tutored in his own faith by his devout mother, Susannah. She led family prayers with such insight and grace that when her husband was out of town, one of the servants told his parents, and they began attending her prayer services. The parents told others, who also came, until Susannah Wesley's home congregation grew to more than two hundred, more than the parsonage could hold. She read sermons to them from the library and spoke to them with warmth and devotion. When a local church leader complained to her husband, he wrote his wife to get someone else to read the sermons. She wrote back that there was not a man there who could read a sermon without spoiling it. When the rector insisted on stopping the meetings, Mrs. Wesley replied that he, not she, would have to take responsibility for neglecting an oppor-tunity to do good when they appeared before the "great and awful tribunal of our Lord Jesus Christ."[10]

John Wesley knew from his mother's example that women could be effective messengers of the word. Though he technically did not authorize women to preach at the outset, he did encourage women to be leaders in a variety of ways, and some of his protégées went on to become lay "exhorters." When some followers tried to bar women from a number of activities, he was infuriated. He told them he did "exceedingly disapprove" of their attempts to exclude women from praying, singing, and reading the scriptures at meetings. Wesley encouraged one young woman to minister to the sick, saying that it was still an unfortunate maxim with many that "women are only to be seen and not heard."

Wesley was outraged that women were brought up as if they were "only designed for agreeable playthings!" He said it was not only a deep unkindness but "horrid cruelty; it is mere barbarity. And I know not how any woman of sense and spirit can submit to it." He encouraged the young women to assert the rights that God had given them and urged them not to yield to "vile bondage" any longer. "You, as well as men, are rational creatures," he told them. "You, like them, were made in the image of God; you are equally candidates for immortality; you too are called of God, as you have time, to do all the good you can, particularly to your poor, sick neighbour. And every one of *you* likewise shall receive *your* own reward, according to *your* own labour."[11]

Wesley traveled constantly, generally on horseback, preaching as often as three times a day, raising funds for schools, chapels, and charities. He died poor but left as the result of his labors 135,000 members and 541 itinerant preachers known as Methodists. Today there are more than 30 million Methodists worldwide.[12]

• *Karl Barth* (1886–1968). Swiss theologian Karl Barth rocked European church circles in the 1920s with his commentary on Romans. He dared to challenge the liberalism that had crept into Protestant seminaries in the twentieth century and made a muddle of the Christian message. He posed a very radical question for the modern age: *What if God really exists?*

That changes everything. Or should. Barth showed that modern equivocating and situational ethics look starkly different from a vantage point that assumes, "God is." It was a startling thought for twentieth-century society that was rollicking along, much like children playing while their parents are away, bouncing on the beds and sneaking the Scotch, thinking the adults won't notice. Then suddenly, a key turns in the lock of the door and there is the sound of large footsteps approaching. Once you think about it that way, either you may feel your heart strangely warmed at the thought that God is drawing near, ready to embrace you as one he loves—or you may hear a clock ticking.

When Adolf Hitler came to power in 1933, Barth wrote a pamphlet opposing the plans of *der Führer* to use the German church to legitimize his racist and self-idolatrous agenda. In keeping with his belief in "ethics totally subservient to God," Barth sent a copy of his defiant pamphlet to Hitler himself. Barth later helped form a group of ministers who opposed the Nazi co-opting of Christian institutions. After he refused to pledge his allegiance to Hitler, Barth was deported to Basel, his birthplace in Switzerland.

In later years, when the rest of the world took sides in the polarized struggle between capitalism and communism, Barth saw both ideologies as "idolatrously materialistic." He called for the church to follow its own path of "reconstruction."

Though he had his critics, Barth could not be ignored. With his neo-orthodoxy, he rekindled respect for the basic mystery of faith and for the value of scriptures as a guidepost, starting with Romans. Today he is considered one of the greatest theologians of the twentieth century.[13]

Unfortunately, however, his commentary on Romans totally avoided the issue of whether Paul referred to a woman or a man in Romans 16— a debate of which he surely was aware. Barth had expressed a disregard for women in his writings, insisting that "women are ontologically inferior to men." (*Ontologically* is a word that scholars pull out if they want to say in an intellectually intimidating way that women, by their very metaphysical essence, are secondary to men.) In his *Church Dogmatics,* Barth claimed Paul as his mentor for his views about God's will for men and women, saying:

> The command of God will always point man to his position and
> woman to hers. In every situation, in face of every task and in
> every conversation, their functions and possibilities when they are
> obedient to the command, will be distinctive and diverse and will
> never be interchangeable. . . . Why should not woman be the sec-
> ond in sequence, but only in sequence? What other choice has she,
> seeing she can be nothing at all apart from this sequence and her
> place in it?

Barth's view is somewhat surprising in that he had a long, close friendship with a brilliant woman named Charlotte von Kirschbaum, whose intellect he greatly admired. She served as his researcher, collaborator, and close companion for nearly thirty-five years, living much of that time with Barth and his wife in their home. It was an unconventional arrangement that left some church eyebrows permanently raised.[14] Critics generally agree that Barth could not have achieved all he did without von Kirshbaum's assistance. Yet when it came to acknowledging the roles of the women in the early church, he was silent.

❊

Barth, Wesley, Chrysostom, Luther, and Augustine were each shaped by Paul's letter to the Romans, and each shaped Christianity in turn. But the male-centered culture of their times blinded many of them to the full humanity of women.

The continuing bias against women well into the twentieth century shows what a countercultural move it was for Jesus and Paul to include women in their missions at the outset. What must the early church members in Rome have thought when they received a letter from Paul that was delivered by a *woman?* Apparently, they welcomed both her and the letter, because there is no indication otherwise.

The letter carried a powerful message in pagan times, and it remains a powerful message today. Granted, it is not easy to "unpack" Romans. It has been described as complex as a symphony, perhaps a Mahler symphony at that. Jesus of Nazareth had spoken in simple parables to help the masses understand what faith was all about. Paul gave that message an intellectual framework—an architecture worthy of Notre Dame.

"Romans is the quintessential book of the Bible for theologians," Paige Patterson, the president of Southwestern Baptist Theological Seminary, told me.

> I have always said that if the mythology came about of being
> stranded on a desert island with only one book of the Bible,
> Romans is the one I would want to have. It is not the sweetest, or
> most comforting, or soothing, but it provides the basic information

about what Christianity is all about. It is the closest thing to sys-
tematic theology we have.

It is all there in Romans—the problem of sin, the gift of grace, the
concepts of salvation and justification, the role of the Holy Spirit, the sym-
biotic relationship between faith and works, the role of the church in
world history, the meaning of the Old Testament, the significance of baptism, the need for ethics and Christian fellowship, and more.[15]

Amen to all that. The Christian doctrine was revolutionary stuff.
Throw away your old gods. Associate with the lowly. Hate what is evil.
Serve the poor. Make love not war. Honor marriage. Forget about class
distinctions, gender differences, and family power structures. Take the high
road. Pray for those who persecute you. Seen in the context of the times,
the Christian message was in stark contrast with the secular world. It still
is. The secular world worshiped the pursuit of happiness and power. The
Christian world honored the pursuit of integrity and humility.

One way to appreciate the impact of Paul's teaching in Romans is to
role play the lives of the church members who were saluted by Paul along
with Junia and Andronicus.

That's the technique that New Testament professor Lareta Haltmann
Finger uses with her classes at Messiah College in Grantham, Pennsylvania.
She describes her technique in a 2004 book of essays by scholars from
across the country, in honor of Pauline scholar Robert Jewett.[16]

Haltmann Finger asks her students to create a personal profile for
one of the twenty-nine characters named in Romans 16.[17] Here are some
of her suggested questions:

> Are you a slave or a freed person? What is your occupation? Where
> do you work? What hours do you work? With whom? What are
> your living quarters like? Do you live in an *insula,* an apartment
> house structure with others? Or are you affluent enough to have a
> home with an atrium and space for fellow Christians to break bread
> together? Are you educated? Literate? If you are Jewish, do you still

attend synagogue? Why have you chosen to join a house church? Did you dislike the rules of Judaism? Do you still have friends and family in Palestine?

If you are a Gentile, why did you join a house church? What is in it for you? Were you persuaded by Paul's relaxation of the rules that Gentiles did not have to undergo circumcision? Were you attracted to the stories of Jesus? Do you still participate in other religions? Have your friends and family joined? Were you attracted to the Jewish law and high standard of ethics?

Suddenly, the people in Romans begin to seem more real. It takes work to break open Romans, but it is worth the effort. It takes you back to the beginning of the chain of faith.

It is significant that Paul's letter to the Romans begins with a reference to a woman. Some historians estimate that during the first centuries, more than 60 percent of Christians were women. In the third century, according to Oxford historian Robin Lane Fox, women were still a clear majority in the church. In fact, in 370, Emperor Valentinian decreed that Christian missionaries must stop visiting the homes of pagan women. Too many were converting to Christianity.[18]

Similar percentages hold true today. Generally more women are on the inside of the church than men. According to author David Murrow, surveys show that in virtually every form of church-related activity, women constitute the majority, generally 60 to 80 percent, even though men hold the majority of leadership positions.[19]

Why, I wondered, do women stay when their voices are so little heard by the church hierarchy? Anna Quindlen, who writes with frank honesty about her Catholic faith, noted in her *Newsweek* column, "For those who ask why we stay, I say: because it is our church." She suggests that church leaders who claim they model the male

priesthood after the gender of Jesus should remember that he violated the norms of his time to admit women to his circle. "They
argue they cannot tailor church bedrock to suit social fashion. The
truth is they have tailored the bedrock to suit their blind spots," she
wrote, pointing out that the first words of Jesus at the tomb were to
Mary Magdalene—"Woman, why are you crying?"[20]

When I heard that Jouette Bassler was filling in for Charles Cox, the minister at Grace United Methodist Church, while he was on vacation, I
decided to attend. She had been kind enough to meet with me for an interview while she was on sabbatical, so I wanted to be supportive. Grace
United is a hundred-year-old Gothic Revival church in old East Dallas,
with stained-glass windows that make rainbows out of the light. The sanctuary has a serene feel, thanks to the warmth of old wood railings and
floors. What used to be a silk-stocking church is now an inner-city church
that draws a diverse congregation of recent immigrants, from Nigeria to
Cambodia, along with middle-class neighborhood families. The church is
known for its high quality of preaching and social outreach, with a health
clinic, clothes bank, and ministry to the mentally ill who are homeless.

I had to smile as I spotted Jouette Bassler, sitting in the huge, high-
backed wooden chair reserved for ministers. She's a petite woman, a
grandmother with graying strawberry-brown hair in a pixie-short style.
The minister's chair looked like a throne built for a giant. When she walked
to the pulpit to begin her talk, she apologized that she was more accus-
tomed to giving lectures in classrooms than sermons. And then she went
on to preach a thoughtful, erudite sermon; as fate would have it, the sermon was about Paul and Romans.

Paul, she said, has been described as "a heavy bucket to carry." He is
prickly, she explained, and tends to go off on tangents that seem strange to
us today—going into detail about circumcision, women wearing veils, the

problem of when to eat meat—"issues that are not at the forefront of our lives today."

But, she said, he also leads us to a different and deeper understanding of what it means to "follow" Christ. The best sermon about Paul, she advised, is simply from the words of Paul himself. The scripture lesson for the day, appropriately, was Romans 12:9–21:

> Let love be genuine; hate what is evil, hold fast to what is good; love one another with brotherly affection; outdo one another in showing honor. Never flag in zeal, be aglow with the Spirit, serve the Lord. Rejoice in your hope, be patient in tribulation, be constant in prayer. Contribute to the needs of the saints, practice hospitality. Bless those who persecute you; bless and do not curse them. Rejoice with those who rejoice, weep with those who weep. Live in harmony with one another; do not be haughty, but associate with the lowly; never be conceited. Repay no one evil for evil, but take thought of what is noble in the sight of all. If possible, so far as it depends upon you, live peaceably with all. Beloved, never avenge yourselves, but leave it to the wrath of God; for it is written, "Vengeance is mine. I will repay," says the Lord. No, if your enemy is hungry, feed him; if he is thirsty, give him drink; for by so doing you will heap burning coals upon his head. Do not be overcome by evil but overcome evil with good. (RSV)

She was right. It is hard to top Paul at his best. You could sense the presence of God in the sanctuary that day, not only as the minister read Paul's words but as a young violinist, the granddaughter of a church member, came forward to play Jules Massenet's "Meditation from Thais." During communion, Bassler helped pass the silver tray of tiny wine cups. Later, as the offering was collected, I noticed that one of the ushers, a tall man in a dark suit and tie, had his young daughter at his side as he passed the collection plate. As he moved from row to row, the little girl in a yellow summer dress and white Mary-Jane shoes very politely helped hand the plate down the pews.

I like to think the women in those early house churches would have looked on that scene and approved. God uses the people available to use. Some have been women. As William Booth, who founded the Salvation Army with his wife Catherine as a full and vigorous partner, once said, "Some of my best men are women."[21]

As for me, I was learning that saying yes to faith is nowhere near the end of the journey. Following Jesus requires active, intentional study. It requires looking back as well as looking in. And then doing something.

I was beginning to hope that sharing Junia's story could be my small part in the chain of faith.

CHAPTER SEVEN

How Did Junia Get Lost?

Clever women are dangerous.
EURIPIDES

nce you resolve that Junia was a female apostle and recon-
struct how she might have lived in Rome, the next question
is, How did her story disappear from view? Who changed
Junia's name in scripture? As mystery writers would say, "Whodunit?"

The first person to ink Junia out of Romans apparently was an archbishop in the thirteenth century. His name was Giles of Rome, also known
in Latin as *Aegidus Romanus.*[1]

Giles was the first scholar that can be found who referred to Andronicus and Junia in his commentaries on Romans as "honorable men."
According to Bernadette Brooten, Giles noted that there were two variant
readings of the second name in Romans 16:7: Juniam and Juliam. He preferred the reading "Juliam" and assumed it to be a male name since it
referred to an apostle. Everyone before Giles had referred to the name as
belonging to a woman. For centuries after Giles, the same person was
referred to as a man. Then there was a period of confusion over the gender of the name that has continued until now.

The modern presumption is that Giles was prejudiced against
women's roles in the church by Pope Boniface VIII—a famously corrupt
figure. Pope Boniface so opposed female leadership in the church that he

ordered all nuns be confined to their convents, which limited their influence in the church from then on. Giles's "politically correct" mistranslation
of Junia's name appeared to flow from the papal prejudice that women
were to be kept in their place.

So was Archbishop Giles merely a lackey for Pope Boniface? Did he
use his considerable intellect to carry out the Pope's ill intents?

To a certain extent, yes. But the more I learned, the more I had to
temper my first impression of Giles. Though little known today, Archbishop Giles and Pope Boniface VIII were key figures during a hinge moment for the church, when raw power-politics would lead to the removal
of the papacy from Rome. Pope Boniface became emblematic of the runaway corruption that would lead Martin Luther to break from the church.
And Junia turned out to be a thread between all of them.

The *Catholic Encyclopedia* tells us that Pope Boniface was accused by
King Phillip IV of France of infidelity, heresy, gross and unnatural im-
morality, adultery, magic, loss of the Holy Land, and last but not least, the
death of his predecessor. Granted, the French king had political reasons for
attacking the Pope, but Boniface did not have a good reputation to defend.
He appears to have been uninhibited by a moral code. Regarding adultery,
the Pope reportedly once said, "there is no more harm in it than rubbing
your hands together."[2] During his battle royal with the French king, Pope
Boniface supposedly proclaimed that he would "rather be an ass or a dog than
a Frenchman."[3] When King Philip brought formal charges against Boniface
after his death, five archbishops, twenty-one bishops, and some abbots
sided with the king rather than with their former pope.

The women of the church probably applauded as well. For it was
Boniface who ruled in 1298 that the roles of women in the church should
be even more restricted. The papal bull decreed that all nuns, no matter
what their rank or what monastic rule they observed, were to be perpetually cloistered. Unless a nun became contagiously ill, she could not leave
her monastery or invite "unauthorized persons" into the cloister. In the
past, nuns had been free to go about their own religious business. Now
they would be completely separated and could not come and go as they

wished. This transformed convents into walled camps of women who were answerable to men.

One order of nuns threw the bishop delivering Boniface's decree out of their convent and tossed the edict out behind him, but to no avail.[4] The reason given for the decree was to protect the safety of nuns. Soon afterward, however, many of the presumably safer monasteries in the countryside were closed and relocated to cities, so the stated reason did not seem valid. It was more likely a matter of control. There had been a growing tendency to lock women monastics within cloistered walls in the belief that women would otherwise give in to temptation and compromise the men they worked with. Boniface imposed strict limitations on the conversations a woman could have with outsiders, as well as the rare occasions on which she could leave her convent premises.

⚜

> The belief that virgin women would be a temptation for male ascetics prevailed many years after Boniface's rulings. The Council at Trent in 1545–1563 reiterated with force the earlier decrees that women in religious orders should be cloistered, isolated from the world, and strictly disciplined. Some of those policies lasted well into the twentieth century. In the 1960s, some English nuns were still so isolated that they did not learn about the Cuban Missle Crisis until three weeks after it happened.

⚜

At the time the restrictions were imposed, many of the monasteries were famous for producing their own copyists and illuminators of manuscripts. That meant the nuns and abbesses were literate. They could think and read for themselves. The educated nuns included a contemporary of Giles—the learned Benedictine nun Gertrude the Great (1256–1302) who wrote *Herald of Divine Love*. Gertrude translated Romans 16:7 correctly and cited Junia as an apostle.

Although many nuns and abbesses protested Boniface's restriction, his edict continued in force. It was precisely during this pivotal period, when women of faith were being fenced in, that Giles was helping Boniface write his major opinions. As the pope's ecclesiastical adviser and ghostwriter, Giles would have been complicit in the crackdown on women.

That close connection has contributed to the perception among contemporary scholars that Giles should shoulder most of the blame for eliminating Junia. Ah, but the rest of the story turned out to be more complicated. Giles did change the translation to refer to a man. But so did a series of others after him. Giles was the first, but not the last. Giles was simply the first "zig" toward a man's name in what would become a zigzag of male-female translations over the centuries. Tracking those changes revealed a chain of prejudice that started with the ancient Greek scholars and stretched past Giles. Asking, "Who rubbed out Junia?" became much like asking, "Who killed Cock Robin?" The truth was that a succession of male scholars did Junia in.

Giles, who started the trend, was one of the most influential thinkers of his time, just as the Middle Ages were ending in the thirteenth century and the Renaissance was emerging. Giles may have been a misogynist, but he also was a man of considerable faith and intellect. And he must have been a highly skilled politician. During the same period that he wrote Junia out of history, Giles of Rome got caught up in one of the most dramatic church-and-state showdowns of all time. Many others perished. Giles survived to an old age.

Exactly who was this fellow Giles? It is suggested that he may have come from the powerful Colonna family, because he is sometimes identified as Giles of Colonna. He was sent as a young boy from Rome to the University of Paris to study, so he must have shown early intellectual promise. In Paris, he became a pupil of Thomas Aquinas, whose gentle spirit and brilliance inspired others to dub him the "angelic doctor." Giles once said that Aquinas "put me on the path of truth."[5]

University study was a fairly new concept at the time. Most of the great universities of Europe sprang up during this era. Those new universities became the learning centers of Western civilization: Paris (1150), Bologna (1088), Oxford (1107), Cambridge (1207), Sorbonne (1257), Seville (1254), Prague (1348), Florence (1349), Heidelberg (1385), and Cologne (1388). Higher education moved from exclusively royal and church circles into the urban centers. More professionalism and erudition was becoming necessary in the learned arts, medicine, law, and the clergy, so a system of higher learning was established.

Yet when the core of intellectual life shifted from the monasteries to the universities, there were long-lasting ramifications for women. The contributions that women had been able to make in monastery schools since the early centuries of the church were diminished greatly. Women were banned from the new university system just as they had been barred from the inner circles of the church. Though some wealthy women could find tutoring, they did not have access to the great universities. It would be hundreds of years before women would be accepted in academic life. Even as the twentieth century dawned, women in England could attend college but not receive degrees. In the United States before World War II, only 5 percent of women attended college, and it was rare for a woman to get a degree. Today women account for more than half of college enrollments, but deanships and presidencies are still elusive.

The shift to a university teaching system in the Middle Ages meant that men became the sole purveyors of higher learning. Men had always been the primary writers of history. They had ruled the world of arts and letters, while women were relegated to the domestic domain. Women had educated young children in the home, but as higher learning was institutionalized, men became the only professors.

"Men, now the professional storytellers, wrote the stories of men," Sister Joan Chittister writes in *Heart of Flesh*. "Men made the rules and made rules that benefited men. Men explained the universe. Men interpreted the scriptures. Men wrote the philosophy texts and enshrined the ideas of male philosophers. Men constructed the theologies that maintained the history of women in the churches."[6]

The result was a "textual invisibility" for women. As the church hierarchy debated issues of faith, women had no cultural voice. Women were spoken of, but always from the male perspective. The stage dramas of ancient Greek literature summarized the problem exactly, Rev. John McGuckin pointed out to me: the characters who represented the views of women were using words supplied to them by male authors, for the exclusive benefit of male viewers, and were themselves, as the law required, male actors impersonating females.

That "no girls allowed" climate shaped Giles's view of faith, as did his mentor, Thomas Aquinas.

❦

Aquinas was the youngest son of a count of Aquino near Naples. According to Elizabeth Hallam's account in *Saints,* he secretly joined the Dominican friars, a new order that was dependent on alms for sustenance. This so outraged his aristocratic family that they had him kidnapped and imprisoned for over a year. They were so intent on forcing him to renounce his vows that on one occasion they brought a beautiful prostitute to his room. But Thomas chased her away with a flaming torch. From then on, he shunned women, as a biographer recorded, "as a man avoids snakes." His family finally relented, and Aquinas went to Paris and Cologne in 1238 to study.[7]

❦

Aquinas, the leading theologian of the Middle Ages, did more than any other to harmonize Christian beliefs with Greek philosophy, for better and worse. Aquinas was known in university circles by the sobriquet, "the

Christian Aristotle." Because he interpreted the words of the apostle Paul through the filter of Aristotle's beliefs, the Greek disdain for women seeped into Christian writings. Aristotle considered women as lesser mortals, writing, "The male is by nature superior and the female inferior, the male ruler and the female subject." Aristotle even assumed that a leader among bees must be male, because leadership is a masculine quality.

Following suit, Thomas Aquinas taught in his landmark compendium of Christian thought, *Summa Theologica,* that women "are subordinate both in nature and in purpose." He maintained that women were carnal by nature and "have not sufficient strength of mind to resist concupiscence"— strong sexual desires. [8] In Aquinas's eyes, women were intellectually inferior and morally pliable, which was why they should be subject to men and why they should not be ordained.

That disdain can be traced back in literature to Homer in the eighth century B.C.E. He defined women as inferior beings in both the *Iliad* and the *Odyssey*—two of the pillars of what would become European literature. In the *Iliad,* women were the cause of all the conflict and suffering in life. As one of Homer's characters sneers, "Thou are no better than a woman." Though women like Penelope were honorable and faithful, most of the women in Homer's works are accessories: wife of, daughter of, widow of, concubine of.

❧

The Greeks took civilization to new heights with their thinking on math, science, literature, ethics, and philosophy. But there was a steady drumbeat of condescension toward women in Greek letters:

- Aristophanes had men chant in the comic *Lysistrata,* "Women are a shameless set, the vilest creatures going."
- Aeschylus's character Eteoles harangues women as "intolerable creatures." He swears, "I would not choose to live with the female sex in the bad times, nor during a welcome peace."

The theme of women bringing misfortune was absorbed into much of Greek literature:

- Semonides believed that men had only one chance in ten of obtaining a good wife—a wife who was like the bee, busy and industrious.
- Socrates advocated education for women as well as men, yet he often referred to women as "the weaker sex" and contended that being born a woman is a divine punishment, since a woman is halfway between a man and an animal.
- Plato is also given credit for arguing that women should be educated. However, he said, "Females are inferior in goodness to males . . ."
- The poet Hesiod loathed women as a "snare" for men, calling women a "baneful race" and "a great plague."
- Menandre agreed: "Women are an abominable caste, hated of all the gods."
- Euripides' character Hippolytus vowed, "My woman-hate shall ne'er be sated."

And even the choir in the *Orestes* sang, "Women were born to mar the lives of men."[9]

❧

There were exceptions to that view; philosophical schools like the Epicureans and Cynics advocated equality for women. But their views did not dominate.

The more misogynistic aspects of Greek culture later became intertwined in a fateful way with Christian education in the first European universities. One of the great ironies in that "mixed marriage" was that the pagan writers were required reading in classes that were taught in churches. At the outset, university teaching was conducted in churches, such as St. Julius le Pauvre in Paris and St. Mary the Virgin at Oxford, rather than separate university structures. Peter Abelard established the University of Paris expressly for the church. All the masters and scholars originally were either priests, like Thomas Aquinas, or potential priests, like Giles. They worshiped God, but they also venerated Greek intellectuals.

❧

The Greek myth of Pandora and her box of evils shows how stories about women often were twisted in ancient times to portray women in an unflattering light. The culprit in this case was the eighth-century B.C.E. poet Hesiod. He described women as a "great infestation" and wrote glowingly of a time on earth when men lived blissfully without women. Paradise supposedly was lost when Prometheus stole fire from the gods and shared it with mankind. In revenge, Zeus created the most horrifying punishment possible: women. According to Hesiod, Zeus made an "evil thing"—a woman called Pandora. She was "a beautiful evil, not to be withstood by men"—the original femme fatale. According to Hesiod's version of the ancient tale, when Pandora went to live among men, she was given a gift from the gods—a sealed jar that contained all the misfortunes of existence.

Soon Pandora's curiosity got the best of her, and she broke the seal to see what was inside, thereby releasing sorrow, disease, labor, old age, and conflict on mankind. Only "delusional hope" remained in the jar and was not lost. Unfortunately, Hesiod's myth reinforced the interpretation of the Garden of Eden story that women were to blame for the world's ills. For thousands of years since Hesiod, "opening Pandora's box" has been the catch-phrase for causing problems.

However, the original version of the myth was more positive. That earlier story lost out over time to Hesiod's darker version. According to Gail Thomas, of the Dallas Institute of Humanities, in the earlier version, Pandora was sent to man in good faith by Zeus. Her sealed jar contained not evils but marriage presents from the gods—the gifts of poetry, art, music, dance. Pandora, whose name means "all-giver," opened the jar and released the blessings of life into the world. It was a benevolent gift. But in Hesiod's hands, the myth was twisted into a darker parable.

Vase paintings of the time tend to confirm the more positive version. Pandora is shown rising from the earth in a benevolent pose, not a malevolent one. On one vase she is called "Anesidora, the sender up of gifts." In addition, the jar that Pandora holds open is the *pithos,* or storage jar used by Minoans and Greeks to hold the food from the earth (wine, olives, grain)—not evils or disease.[10]

✤

Giles must have excelled at the University of Paris because he was asked by the French King Philip III to tutor his son. Giles dedicated one of his first major works to that young French prince, who would become King Philip IV. The book, *De Regimine Principum* (On the Rule of Princes), became Giles's best-known book. It was a handbook on good government and was translated into nearly all the languages of Western Europe and into Hebrew, becoming something of a medieval best seller. Unlike the more famous political handbook that would be written two centuries later by Niccolo Machiavelli, Giles's advice book urged kings to be compassionate, to support education, and to employ learned persons to teach their subjects. Giles suggested they strive to be worthy of the title "king" if they did not want to be remembered as a despot or tyrant.

As it turned out, young Philip did not exactly rule by the book. Giles and his royal pupil eventually would be pitted against each other in an epic struggle between the church and the state. That debate was couched in theological terms, but it was mostly about money and power.

When young King Philip inherited the crown of France at the age of seventeen, he inherited a choking deficit as well. There had been eight Crusades launched to recover Holy Lands from Muslims, and they had been exceedingly expensive. One Crusade alone had cost twice the annual income of all France. "Philip the Fair" calculated that it would take more than three hundred years to repay the debts. So he went looking for money.[11]

Philip the Fair got his nickname not because he was a fair-minded ruler but because he was fair to look at—attractive, blonde, and tall for the times. That description might seem a stretch if you look at the cameo-style portraits of Philip that remain; he probably wouldn't be considered handsome by today's standards. But in his day, he was considered *Philippe le Bel*. In actuality, he was ruthless. In order to pay state debts, he began seizing funds from the Italian bankers in Lombard and from the prosperous Jews in France. Then, just as Willie Sutton robbed banks in the Depression "because that's where the money was," Philip went after the resources of the church because that's where the money was. That pitted him squarely against the corrupt Pope Boniface. And the brilliant Giles.

Philip the Fair and Boniface VIII were worthy adversaries. Both were cunning. Both were contemptuous of what others thought. Boniface was a shrewd canon lawyer and knew church law inside and out, which helped him become pope in a most curious turn of events. The church for many years had been manipulated by the powerful clans of Italy—the Orsinis, the Colonnas, the Savellis, the Dukes of Naples and Spoleto. In 1294, the conclave to select a new pope had been stalemated for two years because of the clan rivalry for power. The conclave of cardinals changed venues four times over the two years in an effort to find ground for consensus. A priest named Peter Morone, who lived a hermit's life on a mountain, wrote to the stymied cardinals and implored them to make a decision for the sake of the church. So they took the hermit's advice—and voted for him. To his surprise, the eighty-year-old recluse became the next pope. He was given the name Celestine V.

Pope Celestine may have been saintly, but he was naïve. He was in the wrong league. It wasn't long before he proved ineffectual. In his simplicity, Celestine gave away privileges and tried to make reforms. He ran into balky opposition from powerful corners of the church, and his reform efforts were frustrated. This played to the advantage of the shrewd cardinal named Benedetto Caetani, who had opposed the hermit's election in the first place. Cardinal Caetani privately counseled the beleaguered new Pope and encouraged him to resign from what was obviously a mismatched situation.

It later would be said that the ambitious Cardinal Caetani placed a secret tube into the ceiling of Celestine's bedchamber and spoke into it for three nights, pretending to be God and telling Celestine to give up his position as Pope. When the spooked Celestine did abdicate and issued a *gran rifuto,* refuting his post, guess who was elected as his successor? No surprise there. Cardinal Caetani, the shrewd lawyer who faked the voice of God, became Boniface VIII.[12]

And guess who helped write the church document paving the way for the hapless Celestine's resignation—the first and only resignation in papal history? Giles of Rome, inviting us to question whether he was one of the good guys or one of the bad guys.[13]

One of Pope Boniface's first acts was to place Celestine in custody, supposedly so he would not promote a schism in the church. Boniface ordered Celestine taken to the Abbot of Monte Casino in Rome. On the way there, Celestine escaped and returned to his hermitage. Apprehended again, he fled a second time. After weeks of roaming through the woods of Apulia (in the heel of the boot of Italy on the map), Celestine reached the sea and tried to board a vessel that was about to sail for Dalmatia. But a storm swept him back to shore, where he was recognized and detained. He was brought before Pope Boniface at his palace at Anagni, kept in custody for a while, and then transferred to the formidable Castle of Fumone at Ferentino. There he remained imprisoned until his death ten months later.

Even those who defend Boniface for detaining Celestine as a measure of prudence do not defend the subsequent treatment of the former Pope. The cell where he was confined was so narrow "that the spot whereon the saint stood when he sang Mass was the same as that whereon his head lay when he reclined." His two companions often had to change places because the narrowness of their confinement was so suffocating that it made them ill. The naïve hermit Pope died in the small, stifling cell.

Such chicanery earned Boniface the enmity of the Colonna family, which had supported Celestine and lost influence when he abdicated. The Colonna cardinals—Jacopo and his nephew Pietro—were Roman princes of the highest nobility, with palaces in Rome and in the Campagna region. The Celestine incident and several other turf disputes prompted a deadly feud with the Pope. As part of their ongoing struggle for influence, the pontiff later demolished most of the city of Palestrina, killing six thousand people and destroying the home of Julius Caesar and a shrine to the Virgin Mary in the process. There was nothing naïve about Pope Boniface.

This was the era when popes sold "indulgences" to sinners who needed to buy forgiveness. The profitable practice gave new meaning to the expression, "paying for your sins." And it paid off for Boniface VIII. The second crown of the papal tiara, indicative of temporal power, is said to date from his reign. Boniface reportedly wore a tiara encrusted with jewels that included forty-eight rubies, forty-five emeralds, seventy-two sapphires, and sixty-six large pearls. No wonder the poet Dante portrayed Boniface in his epic *Inferno* as destined for the Eighth Circle in Hell, where hot seats were reserved for those guilty of simony—the buying or selling of sacred things.

Boniface VIII is often credited with instituting the tradition of "jubilees," which brought many visitors to Rome. On Christmas Day in 1300, he announced that anyone who made a pilgrimage to Rome, bringing a needed infusion of money with them, received a full exemption from Purgatory. Boniface had the churches of Rome restored for the Jubilee and, as a great friend of the arts, brought in Giotto to beautify the cathedral of St. John Lateran. Boniface was also a patron of sciences and education and founded the University of Rome (then known as Sapienza).

But Pope Boniface is most remembered for his battle royal with Philip the Fair. And guess who was caught in the middle of the power struggle? Giles, the cerebral teacher from Paris.

Boniface had named Giles Archbishop of Bourges. Perhaps Boniface "owed" Giles because it was Giles who wrote the theological arguments that legitimized Celestine's abdication and paved the way for Boniface's election. The French nobility protested the appointment of an Italian to such a prize French post, but Giles had friends in high places. King Philip approved and maintained the appointment for his former teacher. It was a plum position. St. Etienne Cathedral in Bourges, one of the finest Gothic cathedrals in France, was a beautiful base. It was closer to Paris than to Rome, but Archbishop Giles often was called to the papal curia in Rome to provide intellectual and ecclesiastical heft to church rulings.[14]

When King Philip tried to tax church holdings to pay France's debts, it was up to Giles to craft an argument *why* the church should not have to pay taxes to the king. Faced with a choice between Philip (his former pupil and patron) and the church, Giles chose the church. Although his own Augustinian order had received favors from King Philip, Giles wrote that all government and secular matters must be legitimized by the Pope, as the rightful ruler and judge of the world. Kings answered to the church, not the other way around, Giles argued, and the church answered only to God. Giles's argument became a definitive statement on the relationship of church and state. By daring to defy the king, Giles staked his life on the principle of the supremacy of the church.

History states that Pope Boniface protested King Philip's efforts to dip into church coffers by issuing a papal bull known as the *Unam Sanctum*, asserting the Pope's superiority over secular rulers. Indeed, Boniface proclaimed in the bull that it "is necessary for salvation that every living creature be under submission to the Roman pontiff." That elevated papal supremacy to its historical extreme. Comparisons with Giles's other writings of the time indicate that he was a major contributor to the papal ruling.

When King Philip received the papal bull, his reaction was unequivocal: he defiantly burned the decree in front of his assembled court.

You could say that was a slap at Boniface, but that's actually what happened next in one of the most infamous incidents in the history of the Roman Catholic Church. Two of Philip the Fair's henchmen, Philip de Nogaret and Sciarra Colonna, confronted Pope Boniface in his hometown of Agnani in Italy. They demanded that he resign, like Celestine. Boniface responded he would "sooner die," perhaps a poor choice of words. In the heat of their discussion, Sciarra Colonna slapped the Pope in the face.

Yes, he slapped the Pope in the face! Try to imagine the uproar if a couple of political henchmen slapped the president of the United States in the face in the White House. Then magnify it many times into a public assault on the "vicar of Christ" while he is dressed in papal vestments. Boniface was held captive for three days before the outraged people of Agnani drove his assailants out of town. Boniface was rescued and escorted back to Rome. But the reverberations from *lo schiaffo di Agnani* (the slap of Agnani) continued to be felt.

Not long after the incident, Pope Boniface died somewhat mysteriously, perhaps from shock from the affront. His successor, Benedict XI, tried to mend the schism with King Philip, but he also died "mysteriously" after eating a plate of figs that may have contained poison.

With two popes disposed of, King Philip arranged a deal with the Italian cardinals for a compromise candidate, who would become Pope Clement V. To sidestep the clan wars in Italy, the new Pope agreed to be crowned in Lyons, France. Symbolically, King Philip held the reins for Pope Clement's horse at his coronation, ostensibly in homage to the Pope's greater authority. The roles were soon switched. It was Clement who usually carried out Philip's bidding. When Clement appointed twenty-four new cardinals, twenty-three of them were French, and he relocated the papal residency to Avignon. The "Babylonian Captivity," when the papacy was removed from Rome to France, became a low point in church history. The pervasive corruption of the clergy ultimately would pave the way for Martin Luther's revolt against the church. [15]

With a new pope in place, Archbishop Giles fell into disfavor. Giles prudently kept close to his cathedral base in Bourges. Even so, he was drawn back once again into papal intrigue when a bloody drama occurred that made Friday the thirteenth an ominous date to this day.

On October 13, 1307, King Philip had the leaders of the Knights Templar arrested. They were charged with heresy, which happened to be the only charge that would allow the seizing of their vast assets. King Philip still needed money. The Templars had it.

❦

> The Templars had acted as guardians for more than a century for pilgrims and crusaders. They were the first of the "Warrior Monks." They fought alongside Richard the Lionhearted and other Crusaders. In the process, the knights had grown rich from protection money and banking interests. They were, in a way, the first multinational corporation. The Templars owned the ships that carried Crusaders; they owned farms that produced the knights' horses, and they grew foodstuffs for the journey. Despite church laws against usury, they bent the rules and established a financial empire, becoming bankers to the kings.

❦

You can almost hear the thunder of hoofs across castle cobblestones as the king's riders rode out to arrest the Templar leaders and confiscate their treasures. Just imagine the clash of wills as the proud, powerful knights were brought to heel by the king's men—humbled, killed, or captured.[16]

Once again, Archbishop Giles was caught in the middle. Although many of the other bishops came to the defense of the Knights Templar, Archbishop Giles sided with the king and Pope Clement, an unlikely alliance. Giles was present at the Council of Vienne (1311–1312), in which the Order of the Knights Templars was suppressed. He wrote a tract titled *Contra Exemptos,* claiming the Templars' exemption from Episcopal jurisdiction was the cause of their abuses.

Why did Giles support the king and his pawn Pope Clement? After all, Giles had disagreed many times in the past with Clement. They were not allies. Was Giles trying to save his skin by currying favor? Or was he trying once again to assert the church's primacy over all? More likely the latter, considering Giles's other positions. The high-and-mighty Templars had exempted themselves from church supervision and enriched themselves by charging usury that was forbidden to others. Giles apparently believed that since the Templars were operating outside the authority of the church, they should have to sacrifice to the king instead of the church. But it proved to be blood money.

At the king's command, Pope Clement abolished the order of Knights Templar and confiscated their assets through a papal decree. When King Philip subsequently had Jacques De Molay, the last Grand Master of the Templars, burned at the stake, De Molay is said to have cursed both King Philip and Pope Clement as he burned. De Molay predicted both of his adversaries would die within a year. And indeed, Pope Clement died a month later. King Philip died in seven more months.

Giles outlived both of them. He died at Avignon two years later at the age of sixty-nine. His bones later were transferred to the church of the Augustinian studium in Paris where he had been a revered teacher many years before. An inscription that was destroyed during the French Revolution once marked his tomb. The Augustinians still consider Giles to be their first master teacher. During his lifetime, Giles built up the Augustinian Order in France and upon his death bequeathed a personal library of some eighteen thousand books to the school. The first writers about Giles gave him the title "Blessed."[17]

So the surprise was on me. Giles indeed had eliminated Junia's role as an apostle, but he was not exactly the villain I had expected. He was a highly complex character who used his intellect to support ruthless kings as well as pious learning. He was a bundle of contradictions and conflicts, a good bad-guy.

In a sense, however, that made Giles a fitting symbol of the church scholars who constructed the intellectual architecture that walled out women. Giles, like most of his contemporaries, probably felt he was somehow preserving the sanctity of the church by keeping women at arm's length.

As Elaine Pagels suggests, most men of their time just did not see women as part of the ruling structure of the world. They never thought to even question the subordination of women. Church leaders over the years drew broad conclusions from isolated scriptures and failed to look closely at how Jesus actually treated women. If church intellectuals like Giles had been inclined to look, they would have noticed that time after time, Jesus entrusted his message to women.

❦

The inclusive example set by Jesus was overlooked by later church leaders:

- He often traveled with women who supported his movement with their own funds, women such as Mary Magdalene, Susanna, Salome, and Joanna, the wife of Herod's steward Chuza.
- He taught women like Martha's sister Mary at a time when women did not study with rabbis.
- He reached out in compassion to the "woman with issue of blood," when no one else would dare do so.
- He trusted the woman at the well to tell others who he was.
- He trusted Mary Magdalene to take the news of his resurrection to his disciples at a time when women were not accepted as witnesses in courts.

❦

Archbishop Giles ignored those examples when he assumed that a woman could not have been an apostle. That does not mean Giles's faith was questionable, rather that he was very much a product of his times when it came to putting women in their place.

One of Giles's famous treatises was on the issue of whether male and female parents both played a role in conception. Giles rejected any valuable role for the female. He declared that the "female sperm," or vaginal secretion, had a subservient role to that of the male sperm—a role that was helpful, but not necessary to procreation. Such analysis endured for years in the thinking that "she is having *his* baby" instead of "she is having *their* baby." Placing the female parent on the same level as the male parent would have been unthinkable for Giles.[18]

&

In a hunter-warrior world where "might meant right," women were devalued as slower, weaker beings. Without the scientific knowledge that would come centuries later, men did not even value the role women played in reproduction, assuming that only males had pro-creative power. The Greeks believed that male semen contained tiny human beings that had been formed in a man's head—a belief that led to the Greek "headship" concept of male authority. Traces of the concept can be found today in debates about whether a woman can be allowed authority over a man.

Aristotle said a woman was inferior, like an infertile male, because "she lacks the power to concoct semen." Centuries later, Thomas Aquinas would write, "Woman is defective and misbegotten, for the active power in the male seed tends to the production of a perfect likeness in the masculine sex, while production of woman comes from defect in the active force." In other words, women were a mis-take of nature, a malformed version of men.

It was not until 1827 that a Prussian-Estonian embryologist named Karl Ernest von Baer discovered that women produced the egg—ovum—that needed to be paired with a sperm to produce an em-bryo. Though little noted today, that discovery was a watershed moment for women.[19] It established that women were co-creators, not just convenient nests. Later discoveries confirmed that *both* the male and female contributed half the material needed to create life. It meant women counted. But in Giles's day, the woman was consid-ered merely an incubator for the male life-force.

Though undoubtedly devout, Giles was a classic example of the intellectual who is so focused on the cerebral side of religion that he misses the compassionate spirit of it. Giles was so intent on his legalisms that he did not see the injustice of subordinating half the human race. Such scholarly myopia is like someone who memorizes the score to the opera but misses the tragedy of the story. Giles reportedly spent quite a lot of time debating with Henry of Ghent about angelic motion, questioning whether the time in which angels existed was a succession of instants or more like the chronological time that we know. It was something of a twist on the rarified debates over how many angels could dance on the head of a pin. Giles tended to win such intellectual contests, but he was fallible and in one treatise mistakenly attributed the view to Augustine that Adam had not received grace before the Fall.[20]

In Junia's case, Giles apparently made the mistake of not keeping in mind the earliest translations of her name, the views of the early church fathers, and the example of Jesus. As a result, Junia disappeared from print for hundreds of years.

I couldn't help but wonder what Junia would have to say to Giles about his role in writing her out of scripture. What would a meeting between the two of them have been like?

Junia had honed her Christianity in prison. She taught in small house churches illuminated by oil lamps. She had traveled across the Mediterranean.

Giles had honed his faith in libraries and cathedrals. He taught in prestigious universities.

Yet I suspect that even with Giles's superior book learning, Junia would have an edge on him. Why? She must have been in the Holy Land when everything started. She also would have been in Rome when Peter and Paul were. She was on the scene. She helped start the church. Giles merely read about what happened and debated about it.

From the vantage point of centuries later, we can see how the prejudice that was brewing in the church of Junia's day became solidly entrenched in the church of Giles's time.

Pagels suggests that as the church membership in Rome became
more affluent and upper-class, it took on the attitudes of the older Greek
culture, which long had assumed men were dominant and women were
subordinate. In the dualistic Greek mind-set, the spirit world was more to
be admired than the fleshly world, which Plato compared to a white horse
and a black horse. Women became emblematic of the dark undertow of
sensual temptation. The Greeks saw female sexuality as a threat that had to
be controlled, subordinated, restricted. The Roman Christians carried on
that viewpoint.

Soon Christian writers like Tertullian were condemning women as
"the devil's gateway." Eschewing carnal life with women was required for
holiness. Spiritually, rejecting women was fashionable. Physically, it proved
more difficult to stay away. Although priests were allowed to marry for
many years and popes often had mistresses and illegitimate families,
church leaders continued to struggle with reconciling their human biology
with their religious beliefs.

❧

A telling example of the increasing church prejudice toward women
can be seen in the evolving attitudes toward menstrual blood. Originally, blood was considered the seat of life. Early ritual laws that
women were not to be touched while they were shedding blood may
have been based on the holiness of blood and regard for the mysterious process of life. Historian Karen Armstrong has said that sexual
intercourse during menstruation originally was forbidden not because a woman was to be regarded as dirty or disgusting but to pre-
vent a man from taking his wife for granted. She points to ancient
quotes that warn because a man may become overly familiar with his

wife, and thus repelled by her, the Torah says she should be *niddah*—sexually unavailable—for seven days after menses, so she will be "as beloved to him as on the day of marriage."[21] But eventually, the laws segregating women during menses led to the isolation of women. The laws excluded women from participating in the priesthood, from entering the sanctuary, and from offering sacrifices. Leviticus (15:19–24) was cited as a justification because of its host of rules for the woman's menstrual period, decreeing that a women was unclean for seven days, anyone who touched her was unclean until evening, and anyone who had intercourse with her was unclean for seven days.

Rather than being seen as miraculous vessels of life, women came to be seen as befouled by the reproductive process. Jewish women, like Bathsheba, took ritual baths to purify themselves after their periods. The idea that women needed purifying after menstruation or birth was carried over into Christian practice, although the commandments for a man to take a ritual bath to make himself more holy before going to the synagogue on a festival day were not. According to Martha Ann Kirk of the University of the Incarnate Word, during the first century, it was said that women in their periods would turn wine sour, make crops wither, dry seeds in gardens, cause the fruit of trees to fall off, dim the surface of mirrors, dull the edge of steel and the gleam of ivory, kill bees, rust iron and bronze, and cause a horrible smell to fill the air. By the Middle Ages it was said that dogs who tasted the blood would become mad, and their bite become poisonous, as in rabies.[22]

Kyriaki Karidoyanes Fitzgerald says that there was an ancient church tradition that someone who was "unclean" lacked the presence of the Holy Spirit. Somehow that concept over time was commingled with the tradition that women were "ritually unclean" during menses. The tradition that evolved whereby women were excluded from the sacraments as well as the altar was a misinterpretation. She says the saying of St. Cyprian of Carthage aptly sums up the situation: "A custom without Truth is merely an ancient error."[23]

Yet prohibitions against the participation of menstruating or pregnant women in public worship remained in canon law in the Roman Church until the sixteenth century, and records show some women were barred at the door of the church. During the reign of Pope Paul V (1605–1621), the ritual of "churching" a woman was instituted to purify her after giving birth and before the baptizing of her infant. Some English women who gave birth during the 1950s spoke of being unwelcome in the homes of relatives and friends until they had gone to be "churched." In the United States, the "churching" service remained in the prayer book of the Episcopal Church until 1979.[24]

As the monastic movement in the Christian Church grew, a corps of bachelor priests increasingly had the power to define women's roles. Not surprisingly, in the eyes of the celibate church brethren, the ideal woman was a virgin. Sex was considered unseemly and worse. Though children were necessary to carry on life, having engaged in sexual relations carried a taint. Those who wanted to protect the Virgin Mary's status as a virgin even decreed she had delivered through her ear, so as to avoid the taint of a vaginal birth. Jerome, who produced the Latin Vulgate translation of the Bible, once proclaimed that the only saving grace of even marital sex was that the union might produce "more virgins." Such distorted notions of sexuality continued to warp the church view of women for many years.

By Giles's medieval era, the church had become so controlling about sexual relations that it decreed that sex was to be indulged in solely for the purpose of procreation and not for pleasure, even in marriage. Certain sex positions were prohibited, as well as masturbation, the use of aphrodisiacs, and oral sex, any of which could incur a penance of three years. According to British historian Alison Weir, people were not supposed to make love on

Sundays, holy days, and feast days, or during Lent, pregnancy, or menstruation. People were led to believe that if these rules were disobeyed, deformed children or lepers might result.

Medieval women in Giles's time were treated as minor children, with no legal or property rights. Under the laws codified by Emperor Justinian, women were stripped of all voice in legal matters. They were even forbidden to represent the rights of their own children in court. By law, they could be beaten by their husbands for "domestic chastisement." Rape was considered minor theft—a property crime rather than assault.

Education of women was discouraged. The size of a woman's brain and her uterus were believed to be related; that is, the more a woman learned, the less available she might be to bear children who were necessary to carry on the work and lineage of the family, so learning was not wasted on women.[25] It was a classic Catch-22. Women were not educated, so men believed them to be stupid. Because they were considered stupid, they were not given much education.

Considering that cultural context, it is understandable that Giles could not fathom that a woman could have been an apostle. With the stroke of a pen, he added an *s* to her name and made her a man.

#

What is little known is that women of Giles's time tried to resist the cultural restrictions that bound them. What may have been the first Christian women's liberation movement occurred toward the end of the Middle Ages.

In the twelfth century, there was a significant migration of single women into communes outside of church control. What prompted the women to seek group homes? There was a shortage of males for husbands. The death toll from the Crusades had reduced the pool of marriageable men. At the same time, the only other option available to women—to live in the convent—was restricted. Entry into the church cloister required donation of a "dowry," which many women could not afford. Left with no other options, thousands of women from France to Belgium banded together in communal groups. They lived together and did good works, providing health care and assistance for the needy, without direction from the male-dominated church. They came to be called Beguines, probably because of their encouragement from a French priest named Jacques Begue.

One of the most famous Beguines was Mechthilde of Magdeburg, who left her noble home in Saxony to become a Beguine in the spiritual community. A mystic who recorded her experiences in a book of revelations, she spent many years in prayer, simple labor, and service to the poor in the Beguinage. During the 1260s, when opposition to the Beguines from church authorities became intense, she entered a convent. Her revelations are considered to be among the most forceful and poetic of women's writings to have survived from the Middle Ages.

Church authorities initially had tolerated the women's communities, but faced with unorthodox movements on several fronts, the church cracked down on the Beguines. And they cracked down hard, accusing the women of heresy and illicit sexual acts. Ultimately, the Beguine movement was suppressed, and the compounds were shuttered.

Today, most women have never heard of the Beguines or their attempt at independent ministry. However, remains of some of the compounds from Giles's time are still standing in parts of Europe.[26]

I was beginning to see how prejudice against women had been institutionalized in the church over the years. What continued to perplex me was how the translation of Junia's name took a series of twists *after* Giles.

The famous King James Version of the Bible—one of the most widely read translations of all time—correctly presented Junia's name as a woman's name in the seventeenth century. Yet by the twentieth century, most Bibles inexplicably reverted back to the man's name.

Junia had resurfaced—and then disappeared again.

CHAPTER EIGHT

Which Bible Can You Believe?

*Don't be put off by some translations, which call her "Junias,"
as if she were a man. There is no reason for this except the anxiety
of some about recognizing that women could be apostles, too.*
N. T. WRIGHT, *Paul for Everyone*

he discovery that Giles of Rome had switched Junia's name to a man's name was not the end of the story. Far from it.

What had puzzled me for months was how the King James Bible showed up in 1611 with the correct woman's name. How did the English scholars suddenly get the name right when the wrong name had been in vogue for three hundred years after Giles?

Even more perplexing, why did the *wrong* male name—Junias—pop back up again in most of the twentieth-century Bibles? The erroneous translation came back another three hundred years later, like the proverbial bad penny.

Granted, tracking down the provenance of Bible translations is not something that most believers have the time or inclination to pursue. That would be a bit like a dedicated natural foods consumer trying to find out about the milk in the carton (which farm supplied the milk, whether the cows grazed on pesticide-free grass) to make sure that it is really organic milk. Most of us just trust the labels. But as the Junia saga shows, the subtext of translations does have ramifications. Most believers today grew up reading Bibles that did not have Junia's name in them; consequently, most

153

don't have a full picture of the roles of women in the early church. So we have to ask, Why?

Just as there were unlikely "villains" who changed Junia's name to a man's name over time, it turned out that there also were unlikely "heroes" who got it right. Oddly enough, all their lives were interwoven. Their stories were entwined with not even six degrees of separation from one life to the next.

❧

Originally, Christianity relied on a loose conglomeration of Greek manuscripts but aspired to be considered a "religion of a book" that would be authoritative in every word, all the better to deter heresy. In the late fourth century, Pope Damasus I commissioned his secretary Jerome to produce an authorized version. Jerome was a provident choice. He had the best classical education and was a phenomenal worker. It is said that his translation of Proverbs, Ecclesiastes, and Canticles from the Hebrew was done in three days. His commentary on Ephesians was written at the rate of a thousand lines a day. By 400 C.E., he had produced a standard Bible in Latin, which made it possible for everyday Romans to have access to the Bible. The name *Vulgate* came from the fact that Latin was the common (vulgar) language of the people. The Latin Vulgate became the official Bible of the Roman Catholic Church until 1530. The Vulgate was regarded as an infallible, divinely inspired text. It served as an inspiration for countless paintings, writings, and hymns.

To the point of this book, Jerome correctly identified a female apostle in Romans 16:7. Although he used the variant name "Juliam" (Julia), that was accepted as a female name.

Over time, however, many human errors accrued in the Vulgate text, as the manuscripts were hand-copied year after year. Later scholars would discover thousands of errors in the Latin text when compared with Greek manuscripts.

According to historian Alister McGrath, some of the Vulgate errors had actually influenced church policy:

- Jerome's version of Matthew 3:1–2 reads, "In those days, John the Baptist came, preaching in the wilderness of Judaea, and saying, 'Do penance, for the kingdom of the heavens is close to hand.'" This became a scholarly basis for the church's doctrine of penance—outward signs to repair sin; in fact, subsequent scholars would say the proper translation is "repent"—a more inward process.
- The Vulgate version of Luke 1:28 also contributed the idea that Mary, the mother of Jesus, was without sin, which influenced the concept of the Immaculate Conception. The Vulgate translated the phrase describing Mary as "full of grace," leading to Mary being considered as sinless as Christ, when the more accurate translation would have been "favored one."[1]

The link between the Vulgate, Junia, and modern translations is the Dutch scholar Erasmus. The great humanist of the sixteenth century deserves a good share of the credit for bringing Junia's name back to light. Desiderius Erasmus produced a landmark Greek version of the New Testament in 1516 that had a ripple effect through the centuries. Erasmus was at the forefront of the movement to study early sources in original languages. Their slogan was *Ad fontes* ("to the sources").[2] Erasmus also was a champion of translating the Bible into ordinary speech. In the preface of his Greek translation, he explained:

> I totally disagree with those who are unwilling that the Holy
> Scriptures should be translated into everyday languages and read
> by unlearned people. Christ wishes his mysteries to be made
> known as widely as possible. I would wish even all women to read
> the gospel, and the letters of St. Paul. I wish they were translated

into all the languages of all Christian people—that they might be
read and known not just by the Scots and Irish, but even by the
Turks and Saracens. I wish that the farm laborer might sing parts
of them at his plow, that the weaver might hum them at his shuttle,
and that the traveler might ease his weariness by reciting them.[3]

It was a noble thought—but a very dangerous thought.

A century before, Oxford theologian John Wycliffe had tried to
make the Word of God available to the average person. Wycliffe reasoned
that Jerome's Latin scriptures did little good for the average man, because
by the Middle Ages, only the clergy could understand Latin. He translated
the Vulgate Bible that had dominated church teaching for a thousand years
into the native tongue of the English. Outraged Catholic Church authorities in England brought Wycliffe to trial several times for having the audac-
ity to tamper with God's word in Latin. Led by Cardinal Wolsey and the
Lord Chancellor, Sir Thomas More, they outlawed the reading of his hand-
copied Bibles. Wycliffe, protected by influential friends, died of natural
causes, denying the authorities the chance to punish him. Church councils
still refused to let the matter rest. Thirty-one years after Wycliffe's death,
they ordered his body exhumed and burned, adding insult, since they
could no longer injure him.[4]

❦

Less well known than his controversial translation of the Bible is John
Wycliffe's role in the Lollard reform movement. The movement
started from Wycliffe's writings, which placed an emphasis on the
inward aspects of religion and the mystery of grace, as compared
with the material power of the church in Rome. The Lollards were
lay preachers, or mummers, who strolled the English countryside
preaching and teaching. Personal faith and study of the scriptures in
vernacular readings were central issues, along with equality of the
sexes. The Lollards supported women preachers. The church accused

the Lollards of heresy and cracked down on several Lollard uprisings, burning offenders at the stake. Afterward, only licensed preachers were allowed to preach after passing a test of orthodoxy. Translating any portion of scripture into English was forbidden.[5]

Seven decades after Wycliffe's death, something happened that revolutionized Bible translation and accelerated the spread of Western thought. A printer in Mainz, Germany, named Johannes Gutenberg figured out how to print text with movable type. Gutenberg's first work in 1456 was a Bible, but he played it safe by printing Jerome's old Latin Vulgate translation instead of a contemporary translation. Gutenberg, who needed money to help with drinking bills, also sweetened his income by printing the "indulgences" that the church was selling to finance the reconstruction of St. Peter's Basilica.

Then Erasmus came on the intellectual scene. Like many of the scholars who played a role in the translation saga, Erasmus was a gifted misfit. He was born the illegitimate son of a priest and a physician's daughter. Despite his birth circumstances, his parents made sure he received a good education in monastery schools. Erasmus was admitted to the priesthood and took monastic vows but never seems to have been a working priest. Indeed, he directed some of his sharpest criticism against the institutional church. While professing to still believe in the tenets of faith, Erasmus challenged the church hierarchy in Rome to clean up and reach out. Like Giles, he studied at the University of Paris, then the center of scholastic learning in Europe. He taught Greek at Cambridge University for a time but, as a lifelong contrarian, preferred the role of an independent scholar.[6]

• *Junia resurfaces.* It was at this point, at the beginning of the 1500s, that connections began forming that would influence Junia's visibility for the next few centuries. During this pivotal period, Erasmus played a role in three of the most historic translations of scripture: his own Greek New Testament, William Tyndale's seminal English translation of the New Testament, and Martin Luther's great German translation. Two of them got Junia's name right. One did not.

• *Textus Receptus.* Erasmus helped fuel the church reform mood in Europe in the sixteenth century by writing *Handbook of the Christian Soldier,* which became a best seller in several languages. The book called for the laity to play a larger role in the church, rather than be spoon-fed Latin scriptures by clergy. Erasmus did not want to eliminate the clergy, according to historian McGrath. He believed that clerics would still play a role as educators and worship facilitators. But in his vision of a future church, the laity would gain more power by becoming more knowledgeable about the Bible. To do that, they would need to be able to read scriptures for themselves.

Erasmus produced a Greek translation of the New Testament. He had hoped to correct the errors that had accumulated over the years in copies of Jerome's Latin Vulgate, yet he ended up producing errors of his own. His first edition in 1516 was done hastily. Erasmus's publisher was prodding him to hurry so he could beat out a rival Spanish edition. Erasmus finished the work in less than one year—a remarkable achievement—but he was criticized for making numerous errors in the process. Erasmus spent the next twenty years of his life correcting the first edition. Most of his initial errors were minor, but he would live with endless criticism as a result, mocked as "Errasmus."

The later, amended editions of Erasmus's translation would become known as *Textus Receptus,* or "received text"—a name drawn from an introduction stating that readers now had a "text that all could receive." For the next 250 years, variations of the *Textus Receptus* were the standard Greek source for the Bible.[7]

But the *Textus Receptus* was not without controversy. Critics complained that Erasmus had left out the verse 1 John 1:17—a verse reinforcing the doctrine of the Trinity. It was a serious charge. It implied that

Erasmus was denying a core tenet of the church. Erasmus reluctantly added the words, "in heaven, the Father, the Word, and the holy ghost; and these three are one. And there are three that bear witness in earth." According to F. F. Bruce, author of *History of the English Bible,* those words were not part of the original Greek text or the early Latin Vulgate. Apparently, Erasmus was pressured by some elements of the church to insert support for the concept of the Trinity, and he did.

Though later Protestant critics would discount Erasmus's work because he was a Roman Catholic, the truth was that he hoped to reform the Roman Catholic Church from within. Toward that end, Erasmus doggedly denounced what he considered the extra-scriptural practices in the church—the invocation of the saints, reverence for relics, enforced celibacy, prayers to Mary. He argued that buying indulgences and making pilgrimages in hopes of gaining grace were worthless. He acknowledged that fasting, prescribed prayers, and the observance of holy days should not be neglected but said they did a disservice to God when believers focused their efforts on the trappings of religion and forgot charity. He was both reviled and respected for saying so. Pope Leo X, who admired Erasmus's work if not all his views, offered to make Erasmus a cardinal, but he refused, saying he would not compromise his conscience.

Because Erasmus and Martin Luther were contemporaries and correspondents in the early 1500s, staunch Catholics condemned Erasmus as a "Lutheran at heart" and a dangerous subversive. While he was not a Lutheran, he was in sympathy for a time. Yet by choosing to follow his own independent path to reform, Erasmus ended up vilified on one side by Catholics as a traitor and on the other side by Lutherans as a coward. Described as vain, cold, and often sarcastic, Erasmus generated mixed feelings, even among those who admired his intellect.[8]

Yet because he relied primarily on Greek sources rather than corrupted Latin texts, Erasmus did get Junia's name right as a female apostle. In fact, Erasmus added a specific note to his 1516 translation that the *Andronicum et Juliam* cited in Latin Vulgate versions should read "Junia." He noted that Paul gave the woman named "Julia" her own place later in

Romans 16. Erasmus also added a postscript to his 1527 translation that a very old codex provided by the church of Constance had agreed with the Greek manuscripts that he had consulted on Romans 16:7.[9]

The influence of Erasmus's translation was enormous. Even though most people did not read Greek, scholars and clergy did. His Greek translation became the foundation for many of the key New Testament translations of the era—English, French, Dutch, Swedish, Spanish, Danish, Czech, Italian, and Welsh. Martin Luther used the second edition of the Erasmus New Testament for his great German Bible. William Tyndale used the third edition for his breakthrough English Bible, which formed the core of the King James Bible. Erasmus's *Textus Receptus* became the dominant Greek version of the New Testament for nearly 250 years and did not lose its position until improved translations were published in the late 1880s.

• *Tyndale Bible.* William Tyndale came to Cambridge just after Erasmus left and was greatly influenced by the Dutch scholar's writing. Tyndale was inspired by Erasmus's arguments for a more personal faith—a faith that is a direct relationship between the individual and God, not one mediated by church hierarchy. More than that, Tyndale agreed that vernacular scripture would bring God's word directly to more people. Tyndale, fluent in eight languages, began the ambitious project of translating the New Testament directly from Greek sources into English, bypassing the flawed Latin Vulgate.

English translations still were banned by church authorities in England, so Tyndale fled to Germany to continue his work. There he met with Martin Luther, the tempestuous German reformer. Luther had recently completed his translation of the New Testament into German. Inspired by Luther's work, Tyndale pressed on with his English translation, using Erasmus's second edition of the Greek New Testament as a primary guide and Luther's German translation as a partial guide. He made the first English translation from Greek sources rather than Latin interpretations of Greek scriptures. With his crisp, simple English, Tyndale set the tone for the King James translation and many other English translations for centuries afterward. For good reason, he is considered the father of the English Bible. We can thank Tyndale for graceful phrases such as, "When I was a child, I spake as a child, I imagined as a child," "Eat drink and be merry," "salt of the earth," the "powers that be," and "our Father which art in heaven."[10]

And because he relied to a great extent on Erasmus's Greek translation, Tyndale got Junia's name right.

In keeping with his mission of taking scripture out of the tight grip of the clergy, Tyndale deliberately replaced key words in hopes of shifting the balance of ecclesiastical power: he used *congregation* instead of *church,* *elder* in place of *priest,* and *repentance* instead of *penance.*[11]

His work proved his undoing, however. Cardinal Wolsey had lost his position when the Church of England broke from Rome, but agents of the Church were still on the hunt for Tyndale. While Tyndale was living in Antwerp and working on his translation of the Old Testament, he was befriended by an Englishman named Henry Phillips, who claimed to have an interest in talking about faith with Tyndale. It was a lie. In truth, Phillips was a spy who betrayed Tyndale. Church agents kidnapped Tyndale and tried him for heresy. He was condemned to death, tied to a stake, strangled, and burned. His dying words were a plea for the Lord to open the eyes of the king of England to the need for an English translation. They proved prophetic.

It was not long before King Henry VIII of England, emboldened by his break from Rome, decreed that an English Bible be placed in every church and be available to everyday people. The Bible that the king approved was cobbled together by Miles Coverdale, using Luther's new German version, the old Latin Vulgate, and Tyndale's New Testament.[12] A hodgepodge of translations soon flooded the country, which prompted King James I to commission an "official" English version that was based on the best available scholarship. A blue-ribbon committee of fifty-four scholars from Oxford and Cambridge worked for seven years to produce the majestic King James Version (KJV), sometimes called the Authorized Version (AV). The AV dominated the Western church and literature for the next four hundred years.

Large sections of the KJV scholars' work were drawn from Tyndale's version. As a result, the King James Bible had Junia's name cited correctly, while less scholarly versions remained in error. Following the biblical manner of charting family trees, you could say that Erasmus begat Tyndale and Tyndale begat the KJV, with Junia included all the way. But there was a divergent branch to the tree.

• *The German Lutheran Bible.* Because they were frequent correspondents about the problems in the church, Luther urged Erasmus to join his reform movement. But Erasmus preferred to keep his status as an independent provocateur. Luther went on to complete his German translation of the Bible, relying considerably on Erasmus's Greek translations. Luther's German Bible would become one of the highest achievements in German literature.

Unfortunately, Luther ignored Erasmus's use of the feminine name Junia in Romans 16. He chose the male name, *den Juniam.* He may have been influenced by a 1512 commentary that listed a male "Julias," according to Bernadette Brooten.[13] Later, Luther would embellish his own mistake by writing in his *Lectures on Romans,* "Andronicus and Junias were famous apostles," claiming that Romans 16:7 said, "Greet Andronicus, the manly one, and Junias, of the Junian family, who are men of note among the apostles."[14] Luther's words, though in error, carried much weight. From Luther's time forward, German versions of Junia's name were consistently masculine, along with many Dutch and French editions.

❧

Luther made other changes to scripture: he removed seven books from the Old Testament, which is why Protestant Bibles are seven books shorter than the Catholic Bibles. (He included those omitted books in the Apocrypha as an appendix and called those writings "useful and good to read.") He also pared down the list of sacraments from the seven observed by the Catholic Church for centuries (baptism, confirmation, penance and confession, the Eucharist, anointing the sick, holy orders, marriage). Luther began his book titled *The Babylonian Captivity of the Church* by arguing that there should only be *three* sacraments—baptism, confession, and the Eucharist—because Jesus had commanded those three.

However, further along in the book, Luther decided that since confession need not be made to a member of the clergy to be valid, confession did not need to be included as a church rite. That meant that by the end of his book, he maintained there were only *two* sacraments—baptism and the Eucharist. That's why many Protestant churches do not have an individual confession process. But those who just read the first part of Luther's book would have thought confession was a sacrament. Those who read the last part would have thought there were only two.[15] As Virginia minister Ken Collins points out in his study on sacraments, Luther's shrinking list is a fine demonstration of the value of proofreading.

The effects of Luther's mistaken reading of Junia's name were multiplied over time. According to British scholar John Thorley, subsequent translations of Romans leaned to the masculine interpretation of Junia's name because of Luther's influence, which was why the male name cropped up again in English translations in the 1800s.[16] Other scholars, such as Luise Schottroff, Eldon Epp, and Bernadette Brooten, agree that you can connect the dots between Luther's wrong translation and many that followed. Though there were a few zigzags back to the female name after Luther's 1522 German translation, the male name became the norm well into the twentieth century.

• *A partial explanation.* The continued use of the male name Junias in modern times is perplexing. There was little scholarship to support the male usage. Why did so many Bible publishers stick with the wrong name? More Greek manuscripts had become available; it was easier to compare notes with other scholars with modern technology. What took so long to discover the Romans 16 mistake?

To find the answer, I hired one of the top divinity students at Perkins School of Theology at Southern Methodist University—Nathan Wood— to help me work through the myriad translations one by one. We met for dinner near the campus and plotted how to track the twists and turns in Junia's name. He was young and earnest—a dedicated believer, part-time minister, and talented student of Greek. I was a graying veteran of the newspaper world, a professional skeptic as well as a serious believer, so we made a good research team. After nearly two years of working on the Junia issue on my own, usually late into the night after work, it was a tonic to hear from Nathan what he was discovering in the theology school library. He had found an ancient reference to Junia as a saint. He did multiple data-base searches for Junia's name and confirmed that the female name was in use in Ephesus, Didyma, Lydia, Troas, Bithynia, and Rome during the first century, but there was no such use of a male name Junias. The male name was simply not a bona fide name. We were on the march.

Then something unexpected happened.

Eldon Epp, former head of the religion department at Case Western University, published a book called *Junia: The First Woman Apostle*. When I first heard about it, I was crestfallen that someone had published Junia's story first. I thought about abandoning my own effort, because my motivation mainly had been that Junia's story be brought to light. It didn't matter to me who did so, as long as it was done. Then I realized that Epp's book was a marvelous gift, an academic blessing. It would provide a firm scholarly foundation for Junia's existence. It would plow the way. And indeed, it did. Epp had compiled detailed charts that tracked the translations of Junia's name from Erasmus's 1516 translation up to *The New Living Bible* translation in 1966. And in the process, he solved the mystery for me of what had happened to Junia's name after Giles and Luther.

Here's what, apparently, had caused Junia's disappearance during modern times. Publishers of standardized texts in Greek that are used by ministers and scholars included the female name Junia from 1898 to 1920. But something happened in 1927. The influential Nestle translation changed to the man's name—Junias—with no notes of explanation. Other major translations followed like orderly dominoes: Merk, Bover, Nestle-Aland, Kilpatrick, Tasker, United Bible Society. All changed to the male name.[17]

What most churchgoers may not know is that a very small number of companies produce the master translations of the Greek New Testament. Those master translations take into account what the majority of the thousands of Greek manuscripts show when it comes to a textual variation like Junia's name. A "critical" edition attempts to re-create the most plausible rendering of a scripture, taking into consideration many kinds of references before settling on the most credible wording.

The two most influential publishers of critical texts today are Nestle-Aland and United Bible Society (UBS). In an attempt to provide the best possible critical texts, Nestle-Aland and UBS rely on committees of top Bible scholars rather than one individual scholar. The idea is to bring multiple voices to the translation table, which is a fine idea, except that for much of the twentieth century they were all male voices. In 1927, those committees selected the male name of Junias for Romans 16, with virtually no scholarly basis for doing so. Like Giles and Martin Luther, they apparently assumed it must be a male name because *women could not have been apostles.*

That view was repudiated sixty years later, when the New Revised Standard Version of the Bible, which generally gets high marks for its scholarship, published the female name—Junia—in 1989. The Nestle-Aland master translation followed suit by changing to the correct female name in 1994. Epp reports that New Testament scholar Bruce Metzger, writing for the committee, explained that some members still considered it unlikely that a woman would described as an apostle, but others were impressed that (1) the feminine name occurs more than 250 times in Greek and Latin inscriptions, whereas the male Latin name is found nowhere, and (2) even when Greek manuscripts began to be accented in ancient times to show the difference between feminine and masculine forms, early scribes preferred the feminine name Junia.[18]

The Nestle-Aland, along with the subsequent UBS change in 1994, helped trigger a return to the female name. Since 1995, most of the critical texts and the leading Bibles have used Junia's name in Romans 16, including the New American Bible, the Revised New English Bible, the New Revised Standard Version, the Oxford inclusive, the New Living Translation, and Today's New International Version. Junia seems finally to have arrived in her rightful place.

❧

• *Search for "best source."* After tracing all the zigzags in Junia's name, what remained troubling for me was that the Bible translations over the years were so riddled with errors. A lot of human frailty was evident between the lines. The thought bothered me. How are we to know which one of these very human interpretations of God's word to believe?

Scholars struggle with the same dilemma. For centuries, they have been searching for the "best source"—a manuscript that is closest to the words of the apostles with a complete, pristine, authoritative text. It is a little bit like the search for the lost Ark of the Covenant, Noah's Ark, and the Holy Grail. The idea is that finding irrefutable, tangible evidence will prove that the stories in the Bible are true. Finding an uncorrupted manuscript would accomplish the same thing, resolving once and for all the discrepancies in scraps of scripture.

So far, what was lost is still unfound. The paper trail still is scattered in bits and pieces. That means we have to continue piecing together fragments of scrolls in hopes of figuring out what really was said and done two thousand years ago.

As Epp points out, since we lack a perfect manuscript, we have to draw from some 5,600 Greek manuscripts. What we call the New Testament is actually a patchwork text that includes at least one-third of a million variant readings.

Because of recent scholarship, we now have much more accurate texts than ever before. But the dispute over Junia's name is but one small example of how errors can become institutionalized, and even "group-think" by learned committees can be wrong. How do you know what is *really* the "gospel truth?" How do we know which version to believe? In many ways, it is a matter of sheer faith. There are some things beyond words—soul truths. Believers are called to trust but verify, to borrow the Cold War phrase. It is incumbent on believers to do some detective work themselves, applying the hermeneutics of suspicion, like turning over the package to check the contents on the label.

❧

Many Christian believers assume the first books of the New Testament were contemporary reports, written shortly after Jesus' ministry, like newspaper accounts. The truth is that the Gospels and Epistles were written down several decades after Jesus' death. A generation had passed. To further complicate matters, the Gospels and Epistles were written down in a language that Jesus didn't speak. Jesus spoke Aramaic. The oldest copies of scriptures quoting him are in Greek. That compounds the difficulty of having a verbatim record.

❧

Examples of translation inconsistencies abound:

• Several verses in Matthew and Mark were not in the earliest texts of the New Testament and appear to have been added by later copyists. They include Matthew 17:21, Matthew 18:11, Matthew 23:14, Mark 7:16, and Mark 9:44 and 46.

167

• Though he got Junia's name right, Erasmus passed along several errors from corrupted Greek texts that diminished the roles of women in the early church. Following an erroneous source, Erasmus put Aquila's name ahead of Prisca's in Acts 18:16 and credited the house church in Colossians 4:15 to "Nympha," saying the church was in "his house." Later scholars, who had the use of additional Greek manuscripts, would see that Prisca's name should have been first in that instance and that a woman probably hosted the Colossian church.

• Bruce Metzger writes in his *Text of the New Testament* that an anti-feminine bias crept into Western texts in numerous places. In Acts 17:4, words were changed so that women are not referred to as "prominent in the community" but as "wives of leading citizens." That is, they do not have status of their own right, but their status is derived from that of their husbands.

• In Acts 17:12, early Greek translations said that at Beroea, those who responded to the teaching of Paul and Silas included a considerable number of "Greek women of the better class, and men also." Later the scribe of the Codex Bezae version did not approve that women were given precedence over men and altered the sentence so as to read "a considerable number of men and women of the better class."

• The story of the woman caught in adultery in John 8 is a dramatic morality tale, but it was only added to later versions of the Gospel. It was not present in early manuscripts.[19]

✤

The challenge in deciphering translations is made more difficult by the way ancient manuscripts were written. The earliest scriptural references to a female apostle are contained in papyri from the eighth to the thirteenth centuries, known as No. 40 and 46. One refers to *Junia* and one to *Julia,* but both names are feminine. The text is written in all capital letters with no spaces and no punctuation. That would be like writing

SENDGREETINGSTOANDRONICUSANDJUNIAMYRELA
TIVESWHOWEREINPRISONWITHMETHEYAREPROMINEN
TAMONGTHEAPOSTLESANDTHEYWEREINCHRISTBEFORE
IWAS.

Uncials (later scribal compilations of papyri) are also written in all caps but with some spaces, so they are more legible. But some of the uncials had accented words, and part of the controversy over Junia's name has stemmed from how the name was accented. If there had been a circumflex (^) over the *a* in the Greek name "Iounian," it would have indicated a man. If there had been an accent (') over the *a,* it would have indicated a woman. It was up to the scribe to get it right. Most early scribes chose the female name.[20]

To talk to scholarly sources closer to the scene, I tried many times to get an interview with someone associated with the Vatican in Rome; I worked through the U.S. Embassy, the Friends of the Vatican, and the Vatican information office. After many months of unsuccessful calls and e-mails, I was, finally, referred to the Pontificio Instituto Biblico, which is where Vatican scholars study. Jean-Noel Aletti, the dean of the faculty, graciously invited me to lunch in the refectory. As it turned out, the resident expert on Paul was in Northern Italy the week I arrived in Rome, but Professor Aletti was well-versed in New Testament exegesis, and he offered to gather several other scholars for lunch.

Finding the Institute in the labyrinth of cobblestone streets of Rome was a challenge, but the address proved to be not far from the famous Trevi fountain. The Pontifical Institute is considered an extraterritorial part of the Vatican, since it is in a different location from the St. Peter's Basilica complex. It is an imposing burnt-orange structure, with giant wooden doors that are taller than many houses in the United States.

Dean Aletti was waiting to greet me and swung open the door. Dressed casually in a sport coat and knit shirt, he could have passed as a businessman instead of a Vatican scholar. Yet stepping into the high-ceiling halls of the institute was like stepping back through time to Old World universities. There is a tranquil garden at the center of the cloister, with a fountain and a poetic-looking orange tree. The halls had the paper-and-glue-and-ink smell that is the same in schools everywhere. Likewise, lunch was cafeteria-style—pasta, salad, fish, wine on plastic trays—but very tasty. This was Italy, after all.

True to his word, Aletti had gathered a group of institute professors. Surrounded by male scholars at the table, I had the feeling that this was what it must be like to have lunch at the Elks Lodge. I had envisioned a defensive or hostile reaction from the church scholars, but the institute professors exuded a gentlemanly curiosity about my topic. As it turned out, studying the women of the church was not high on their list of scholarly pursuits. It was like asking them what they thought about hormone replacement therapy. It wasn't an issue they were inclined to pursue. But they apologized for not being able to be more helpful, and they recommended a half-dozen authors who might be.

We talked through lunch about the early house churches and where the early martyrs might have been hastily buried. Essentially, the Vatican professors echoed what I was hearing from other scholars in the United States.

When it came to the problems with inaccurate translations, they were sympathetic. "One of the first things you learn when you get here is that nothing was written by the person you thought," one chuckled. Aletti added that an ancient saying is that "the translator is a traitor." He added, with a shrug, "You do the best you can and keep on believing." It was an appropriate note to end on.

❦

Believers are warned not to add or take away from scripture several times in the Bible (Revelation 22:18–19, Proverbs 30:6). What is important to remember in Junia's case is that placing Junia's name in Romans 16:7 is not an addition; it is a restoration of wording that was wrongly changed.

• *New approach to scripture.* You can believe that scripture, overall, is inspired by God, as I do, but leave room for the possibility that translators and printers make mistakes. Instead of insisting, "God said it, I believe it, that settles it," most believers can acknowledge that human error and church politics crept into translations over the years. This is not to say that we should chuck the Bible in the dumpster or haul all the copies off to Half Price Books. As a journalist, I know that even if a detail is wrong, a story can still be essentially true. A house fire that was reported to have occurred on Adams Street, for example, may have actually happened on Abbott Street, but it was still true that a house burned to the ground and a family was devastated. Even though the King James Version also contained many errors, it has inspired Christians for centuries because the essential truths have proved enduring.

The Junia controversy forced me to give more thought to how to best resolve discrepancies in scripture, large and small. In sorting them out, perhaps it would help to keep in mind the guideline of St. Augustine: All scripture, properly interpreted, should lead to greater love of God and neighbor. This puts verses that condone slavery, for example, in a different light. We know better now. God gave us an internal plumb line to discern what leads to greater love—or not.

By its very nature, the Bible is pluralistic. The name comes from a Greek plural noun—*ta biblia*—meaning "books." There are four versions of the Gospels and two accounts of creation. There are different versions of the resurrection story, with varying numbers of women at the tomb. There are several lists of the twelve disciples, with variations in the names. The Bible offers a lifetime of ways of looking at things and pondering them.

To paraphrase the way Sarah Lancaster put it in *Women and the Authority of Scripture,* the Bible contains a rich diversity of material. It does not fit easily together. Some of it, in fact, may appear contradictory. The value of the material is not in merely accepting it without question. The value is in thinking through the material. It presses us to rethink our assumptions, our actions, our own relationships.[21] As my young colleague Nathan put it, the Bible teaches us how to think, not what to think.

Faith often requires reading between the lines. Wesley scholar Albert C. Outler coined the expression the "Wesleyan quadrilateral" to describe the way that John Wesley arrived at theological conclusions.

1. Scripture—reading the Bible
2. Tradition—interpreting the scripture through the lens of two millennia
3. Reason—applying rational thinking to the issue
4. Experience—what one has learned through a personal journey in Christ

Scripture always was the primary source for Wesley, but it was read through the filter of church history, mature reason, and life experience.[22]

A technique like Wesley's is helpful in reconciling scriptures like Psalm 137:9, which declares, "Happy the person who seizes your children and smashes them against a rock." Or Leviticus 17:11, which forbids eating meat with blood in it. Such scriptures have to be situated in their own time and place. Those are examples of Bible people groping to find their way, stages in the process of becoming God's people that are long behind us. The challenge of comprehending goes on. History still is being revealed, and so is scripture.

Another technique for reconciling interpretations is modeled on the structure of a tricycle: the text of the scripture serves as the large center wheel of the tricycle that pulls you forward. The two side wheels that balance the center wheel are your own reason on one side, the church teaching and tradition on the other. If we consider Paul's supportive words about women in Romans 16 as the center wheel, then we must balance the church teaching that turned against women in later centuries with our own reason on the other side.

What are we now to make of scriptures in which Paul cautioned women to cover their heads and pipe down during services? Some detective work is instructive:

• *Wearing a head covering* (1 Cor. 11:10). Seen in context, we learn that for Jews, worshiping without one's head covered was regarded with keen disapproval. Unbound hair in public was a sign of sensuality, even grounds for divorce. Times have changed. Most women do not wear a veil to church anymore. But note that Paul says women should cover their head "while praying or prophesying." This is tantamount to saying women can prophesy in church, a powerful gift that includes preaching, so it is unlikely that Paul intended women to be mum spectators at worship services. At a time when the young church was under scrutiny, he may have just been trying to keep women from appearing louche by community standards.

• *Keeping silent* (1 Cor. 13:34–35). Again applying context, it is worth noting that whenever Paul established a church, he insisted that women be educated in the faith. And indeed, he says in 1 Timothy, "Let a woman learn," which would have been a departure from Jewish and Greek practices. It is possible that women who were unaccustomed to learning from ecclesiastical lectures in a church setting would not have known how to comport themselves. Paul counsels them to learn "in silence with all subjection," with a word that means being responsive to the needs of others, but learning nevertheless.

• *Prohibiting women from teaching men or exercising authority over them* (1 Tim. 2:12–14). "But I suffer not a woman to teach, not to usurp authority over the man, but to be in silence. For Adam was first formed, then Eve. And Adam was not deceived, but the woman being deceived was in transgression" (KJV). This passage seems to contradict women who spoke for God in the Old Testament, like Deborah, Miriam, and Huldah. It does not fit with Paul's own practice of supporting women house church leaders or Prisca's tutoring of Apollos. Women instructing men might have outraged men in the Hebrew culture at that time, but that doesn't mean it should two thousand years later, when women teach everything from calculus to golf swings to scuba diving.

More scholars now believe the instruction was specific to problems in Ephesus, which was plagued with pagan cults like the worship of Diana and the false doctrines of some Gnostic sects. Gnostics had been turning the creation story upside down to say Eve was created before Adam.

❦

The "Eve issue" begs to be examined because of the importance attached to gender roles. Some denominations say that because Adam was made first, he is superior to Eve, and that is God's natural order of things. By that same thinking, some scholars rebut with a wink, pigs and cows and bugs would be superior to man, since they were created earlier. And remember, in the first creation account in Genesis, God created male and female at the same time.

The second account in Genesis says that God sensed that Adam was lonely and created woman as a "helper" for him. Subsequent generations interpreted that to mean a subordinate assistant. The actual Hebrew phrase is *ezer k'neged. Ezer* can be translated as "partner" as well as "helper," and the word does not connote an inferior status, according to scholar John Temple Bristow.[23] In fact, when it is not referring to Eve, it appears seventeen times in the Old Testament, and each time it refers to God. Furthermore, in reference to Eve, God qualified the word with *k'neged,* which means "equal." He made Eve an equal helper or partner, not to serve Adam but to serve *with* him.[24]

The text of 1 Timothy 2:12 is often used to bar women from public ministry because they supposedly are more easily deceived than men and susceptible to false teaching. Yet in Romans 5, Paul blames Adam for the Fall in the garden and says sin entered the world through one man. He goes on to explain in 1 Timothy 2:14 that Adam gets the blame even though Eve sinned first because Eve was deceived but Adam was not deceived; he had been forewarned and still chose to do wrong.

❧

Once you put scriptures in the context of the time and place, you can see that the Bible has absolute truths (thou shall not kill) that endure over time, as well as relative statements—teaching that was given relative to a particular time, place, and situation, like 1 Corinthians 11:14, which says a man is dishonored or shamed if he has long hair. If it were an absolute truth that women cannot teach men, then we would have to reexamine our entire education system, as well as our Sunday school classes.

What began to bother me more and more as I turned back toward Junia's time was the message between the lines: that women by their very essence were not eligible for sacramental roles. By excluding women from church leadership roles, women in effect were told they were not as holy as men, not capable of bring "an outward and visible sign of an inward and spiritual grace." If that really were true, I found myself wondering, what would that say about God? What kind of God would listen to men but not to women? Would a just and true God say half the population was less worthy to speak for him because they had a pink blanket on the crib when they were born? Or was that something that mortals decreed?

In the Benedictine Order, I am told, the brothers always approach the altar in twos. They bow first to the altar, to signify that God is present in that place. Then they turn and bow to each other to signify that God is present in each other. Is God not present in each woman as well as each man? Are we not all "words of God"? Can we not all speak of God? This was the real heart of the matter that Junia had led me to.

Following the trail of translations had taught me that the historical setting of the scriptures should not be ignored. Where there are conflicting scriptures defining roles for women, it would be unjust to uphold a doctrine built on one view and ignore countervailing evidence.

As I had discovered, that's exactly what happened in Junia's case. But questions still remained unanswered about what Junia's ultimate fate might have been. Was she killed in the persecutions against Christians? Did she die of old age? Or disease? There was no map to tell me where Junia might be buried, but there were several possibilities to follow, even if it meant looking underground.

❧

Because of human error, numerous typographical errors have occurred in Bible translations over the years, including a prominent error from the 1631 King James edition: "Thou shalt commit adultery" (Exod. 20:14). Here are some others:[25]

"Know ye not that the unrighteous shall [*instead of* shall not] inherit the kingdom of God" (1 Cor. 6:9).

"Printers [*instead of* Princes] have persecuted me without a cause" (Ps. 119:161).

"Go and sin on [*instead of* no] more" (John 8:11).

"The fool hath said in his heart there is a [*instead of* no] God" (Ps. 14:1).

"Let the children first be killed [*instead of* filled]" (Mark 7:27).

❧

176

CHAPTER NINE

The Saints We Left Behind

The real mark of a saint is that he makes it
easier for others to believe in God.
ANONYMOUS

aints. The church initially used the term to refer to all the early stalwarts of the church, then elevated the rank to recognize those who had led an exceptionally holy life. Was Junia among them? Establishing whether Junia was a saint became important not only to show that she was real but also that she was uncommonly holy.

I had hoped that finding where early Christian leaders were buried would help establish Junia's place in their firmament. The search led me to new clues about what happened to Junia as well as a new appreciation of the saints whose stories have been confined to waxwork museum status. The necropolis underneath the Vatican seemed a good place to learn.

As we stepped down the stairs into the "city of the dead," a glass door slid out from behind a wall and closed off the way out behind us. It was the kind of hidden door you see in James Bond movies. The British agent is usually trapped inside with the villains. In this case, the passage was sealed to keep microorganisms and other unwanted visitors out of the necropolis. As the door glided by with an electronic purr and clicked shut behind me, I suddenly remembered that I get claustrophobic in tight places with stale air. But it wouldn't do to turn back. Junia would not have been claustrophobic,

I told myself. Besides, I'd come too far to miss seeing the mausoleums where some of the early Christians were buried. St. Peter is believed to be entombed in the innermost walls. So I kept climbing down the brick stairs, past crypts that had been designed to look like little marble houses. They had stone windows, terraces, lintels, doorposts, and thresholds. But the stone doors had not been opened for centuries.

It had taken some rigmarole to get on the list to tour the excavations under St. Peter's Basilica. Security was extraordinarily tight. Multiple layers of metal detectors have been in place since the terrorist attacks of September 11, 2001. But it was worth the hassle to walk back through time to a place where some of the Christians martyred by Nero had been buried. Perhaps Junia would be here.

Over the centuries, as new buildings were constructed on the Vatican site, the family crypts that once lined the road by Nero's Circus were covered up. Thanks to recent excavations, however, you can descend below the main floor of the magnificent basilica and walk down, down, down the ancient brick streets in a descending spiral to the burial sites of the first century. While we were several stories below the ground level, looking at ancient tombs in quiet awe, thousands of tourists were jostling their way through the majestic marble halls above us, digital cameras clicking away.

Twenty centuries ago, the same Vatican area was a marshy zone, with snakes that were said to be big enough to swallow a baby and mosquitoes that carried fevers. The most hospitable ground was where St. Peter's Basilica was later constructed, on the site of Agrippina's imperial gardens. Her brother Caligula began the construction of a circus there that was later completed by her son Nero; it was something of a family affair. Nero's Circus had a track for chariot races that was 600 meters long—as long as six football fields.[1] Many of the early Christians who were killed by Nero died at the track or the adjacent gardens, including Peter, the impetuous fisherman who became the rock of the church. Tradition has it that Peter asked to be crucified upside down, to distinguish his own death from that of Jesus. It is believed that the bodies of the martyrs were buried hastily in graves close by that were covered by stones or tiles.

The specific burial area is called "Field P" for *Campus Petri,* after St. Peter.[2] Tradition is that a host of other martyrs were buried in the same general area, but as our Vatican guide said with an expressive palms-up gesture, "Who knows?" In that dangerous time, no markers were erected. There was a conspiracy of silence among Christians to safeguard their own. It would be more than a hundred years after St. Peter's death before a "funerary aedicule"—an opening framed by two columns—was built against a red-plastered wall to mark the spot of Peter's burial. Christians called such decorative grave markers "trophies," in keeping with the belief that the deceased had triumphed over the trials of this world and had gone to a better one. Excavations in the vicinity have uncovered the graves of other Christians who may have been prominent figures in the early church and were given the honor of being buried near St. Peter.

Near the red wall is the hiding place for what are believed to be the remains of St. Peter. Behind some bricks, archeologists have found what they think are the bones of the apostle, wrapped in a purple cloth that is interwoven with a gold thread. Is it really Peter's grave? Some say no, but the circumstantial evidence—the location, a bit of graffiti with part of Peter's name—seems to support that it is.[3] As is often the case when it comes to locating the graves of the early apostles, Peter's final resting place remains uncertain. However, history is still being revealed. As recently as 2005, Vatican archeologist Giorgio Filippi found what appears to be the tomb for St. Paul near the basilica erected in his honor, St. Paul Outside the Walls. The graves of other apostles might yet be discovered.

We have a few clues. In ancient times, Pope Zephyrinus (199–217 C.E.) was provoked by the heretic Proclo, who had boasted that the tombs of the apostles were in Asia Minor, to say that he had been assured in words handed down by the historian Eusebius that the apostles' remains were in Rome. "I can show you the trophies of the apostles. If, in fact, you go out towards the Vatican or along the Via Ostia, you will find the trophies of those who founded the Church."[4]

Although the common assumption is that the early Christians were all buried in the catacombs, those grave colonies did not develop until around the second century. The Roman custom of the time was to bury the dead outside the city walls. The Christians of Junia's era in the first century most likely would have been buried (1) above ground, in shallow graves at the execution sites of Nero's Circus and gardens; (2) in crypts outside the city limits along the roads leading to Rome (like the Via Appia Antica, Via Salaria, and the Via Ostia); or (3) near house churches supported by well-to-do patrons, such as the Priscilla family cemetery. The richer families preferred to lay their loved ones in marble sarcophaguses or in terra cotta caskets located under the floor.[5]

Due to their belief in the resurrection of the body, the early Christians chose to bury rather than cremate their dead, which was the pagan Roman custom. Inhumation required more space than cremation, however. Real estate for resting places was scarce, so deeper underground burial places had to be excavated. The catacombs were created when enterprising Christians tunneled underneath graves on the surface to place other burial niches below them.

One of the things that struck me as I visited catacomb after catacomb looking for traces of Junia were the many little niches for children. Since there was a 40 percent infant mortality rate, many small slots are grouped around the larger crypt niches, many barely big enough to slip a shoebox inside. The average life span at the time was thirty, so death loomed close at all times. One way Christians stood out among the pagans was that they brought a different attitude to the Roman funeral rites. The Christians declared the deaths of loved ones as *dies natalis* (day of birth)—the first day of eternal life. In that same spirit, the Christian burial areas were called "dormitories"—a temporary sleeping place while awaiting resurrection.[6]

Pagans believed in survival after death, but it was survival in the underworld without much meaning. Heroes might go to the section called Elysian Fields; villains were dispatched to a dark hole called Tartarus, deep under the land of the living. The Romans believed that as soon as the dead were forgotten, they were absorbed into nothingness. You can tell by the inscriptions on their tombs that the deceased desperately wanted to be remembered.[7] They believed that as long as someone could look on their graves, read their names, and remember their earthly images, they would survive. When all memory was lost of them, they believed they faded away forever. That's why pagan Romans left large legacies to ensure that their heirs (or at least hired hands) would come each year on their anniversary, light a lamp, or make a sacrifice at their tomb—all in order that they would not be forgotten. Christians believed in a more hopeful afterlife. They believed that you died to this world so that you might rise anew and be in the company of saints. All faithful believers were regarded as saints in the early church, not just the martyrs or ascetics. Saints were people belonging to God, and they were urged to live lives befitting their position.

❧

Occasionally, you will find gravestones in the catacombs with the word *Depositus,* sometimes abbreviated as "Dep" or simply "D," marking it as a Christian grave. *Depositio* was a legal term used by lawyers, meaning, "the giving on deposit." Christians used the word to designate that the dead were consigned to the earth just like grains of wheat and would be restored to life in the future.[8]

❧

One reference has been found in one of the oldest catacombs to "Amplias," who may be the early church member commended by Paul in Romans 16 along with Junia. It was a common slave name, however, so we cannot know for sure. There are no known traces of Junia and Andronicus in the Rome cemeteries, but since Junia's name has been lost for so much of the time, archeologists probably haven't been looking for her. In the meantime, every time a parking lot is excavated in "The Eternal City," the past comes back into view. Last year a two-foot-tall bust of the Emperor Constantine was found in a sewer. Nero's fabulous golden palace, Domus Aurea, has only recently been reexcavated and opened to tours. Word of Junia may yet surface.

181

How might Junia have died?

Very few people of the time lived beyond the age of seventy. Because of health risks and the waves of persecution against Christians at the time, it is doubtful Junia would have lived to a very old age. Since the Orthodox Church has listed Junia as a saint and a martyr for many centuries, we can assume that she died while working for her faith. She is depicted in church icons as holding the cross of the martyr. We know that she was in Rome at the time Paul wrote his letter to the Romans (55 C.E.). If she were still there when Paul was martyred (67 C.E.), she would have been in jeopardy during the reign of Nero.

When much of Rome was burned in 64 C.E., Christians were wrongly blamed. The Christians, who were already considered a suspicious cult, were persecuted horribly by Nero.[9] They were tortured in the arenas, crucified, and burnt like human torches to light the night. Could those Neronian martyrs have included Junia? I did not find any mention of Junia's name in public accounts of the martyrs, but many historians cautioned me that the absence of her name doesn't mean that she was not martyred at the Circus, like Peter. The honest truth is that no one knows for sure. She could have been. It is equally possible that she might have perished with Andronicus while taking the message of faith to far-flung areas that were in need of salvation but did not welcome it.[10]

The historian Tacitus says that Nero eliminated a "vast multitude" of believers in Rome.[11] Most scholars that I interviewed believe that description may have been exaggerated. Edward Gibbon, in his *History of the Decline and Fall of the Roman Empire,* estimated that the whole might amount to 1,500, "an annual consumption of 150 martyrs."[12] Roman Catholic records indicate that several hundred Christians were killed during Nero's reign, in which case, the numbers would have included many of the well-known leaders. Tradition is that Prisca and Aquila were among those martyred leaders.

We know from Tacitus that the persecution of Christians was vicious, even by Roman standards: "Covered in the skins of wild beasts, they were torn by dogs and, at the sunset, burnt alive like torches."[13] Nero offered his gardens for such spectacles and dressed up as a charioteer, as if the killing were a game in the Circus. Sometimes he circulated with the common people or reclined on a couch, while the Christian victims were massacred.

The modern image of the narcissistic Nero was established firmly by British actor Peter Ustinov's brilliant portrayal in the 1950s movie *Quo Vadis?* Ustinov was memorably mad in the movie, but the life of the real emperor was much more sordid. Nero was a crazed composite of the very decadence that the Christians hoped to remedy.

In fact, it's helpful to look closely at the emperor's life to see exactly what the early Christians in Rome were up against. Nero was the son of Emperor Claudius's fourth wife Agrippina. She was the scheming sister of the mad Emperor Caligula. Agrippina had been married at the age of thirteen to Gnaeus Domitian Ahenobarbus, described by historians as depraved, dishonest, and usually drunk. He died of dropsy (edema) overseas when their son Nero was three.

While her brother Caligula ruled, Agrippina reportedly was so promiscuous that she even prostituted herself at an imperial brothel. Her behavior became so outrageous that her brother sent her into exile, where she was forced to dive for sponges like a peasant to earn money. When her elderly uncle Claudius became emperor, she ingratiated herself as his mistress, persuading him to marry her and adopt her son, whose name was changed from Lucius Domitius Ahenobarbus to Nero.

It was not long before Claudius's own son Britannicus died, supposedly at Nero's hands. Agrippina then killed Claudius by feeding him poisoned mushrooms. The way had been cleared for Nero to inherit power. Young Nero began his sadistic reign at the tender age of sixteen.

In his *Lives of Twelve Caesars*, Suetonius gives a vivid description of Nero: "He was of almost normal size but had a spotted and foul-smelling body, his hair was fair and his face was more attractive than graceful. He had blue eyes and a very weak chin, big neck, prominent belly, delicate legs and excellent health."[14]

The name Nero meant "strong," but the callow emperor was intimidated for much of his early reign by his overbearing mother. At first he seemed a model ruler, supporting good laws, providing ample numbers of circuses for the people.

Because Nero had no previous record of animosity toward Christians, leaders such as Prisca and Aquila may have been encouraged to return to Rome when he assumed power after the death of Emperor Claudius. Claudius had exiled the Christian sect in 51 C.E., but Nero presented a more benevolent image, thanks to Seneca's tutoring. In the end, their hope of finding tolerance in Nero's Rome was misplaced. According to tradition, Prisca and Aquila perished in the general persecution that occurred around the year 64.[15]

It wasn't long before Nero proved one of the most troubled teenagers of all time. He neglected his state duties to seek applause on the stage and in Circus races. He began indulging his greed, his lust, and his craving for wine—a fatal combination. Maliciously, he ordered the murder of his mother's lover, Pallante.

Sensing she was in jeopardy, Agrippina was said to have made indecent proposals to her own son in an attempt to regain his favor. Nero tried poisoning her three times, but she survived. He arranged for the ceiling panels in her bedroom to fall on her, but the plans fell through instead. Finally, he arranged to have her drowned at sea in a boat that had been rigged to break into two parts. The comedy-of-errors scheme didn't work, as Agrippina's maid was bludgeoned to death by mistake; some fishermen saved Agrippina. She did not survive a centurion who caught up with her when she landed on shore.

The blood on Nero's hands included his nineteen-year-old first wife, Octavia, who was also his sister by adoption. She was, by most accounts, virtuous but childless. She was found tied up in her hot bath with her veins slashed.

Nero's mental instability grew with his homicides, and he often woke up screaming from nightmares. In his paranoia, Nero began a political purge, condemning senators, army officers, and his advisers to be killed as traitors. It was said that he kicked his pregnant second wife, Poppaea

Sabina, to death in a rage when she scolded him for coming home drunk. His next wife, Statilia Messalina, was replaced by Sporus—a castrated young man who reminded him of Poppaea. Nero married the boy Sporus with the ceremonial bridal veil and treated him as his wife, parading him about on a litter with the finery of empresses.

Nero also took advantage of the destruction caused by the great fire of 64 C.E. and constructed on the burnt-out land his elaborate "Domus Aurea"—a Golden Dome of soaring vaults filled with art treasures from around the world, an indoor waterfall, and a rotunda with a revolving floor on ball-bearings.[16] It was a memorial to wretched, megalomaniacal excess.

Ultimately, Nero's excesses exhausted the state treasury and the patience of the senate. The senators sentenced him to death as "an enemy of the state." Nero escaped on horseback but, spineless as ever, asked a servant to slit his throat for him. A notoriously untalented musician and actor, Nero had the hubris to whine in his last moments, "What an artist dies with me."[17] He was thirty-one years old. His cruel legacy included the crucifixion of St. Peter and the beheading of St. Paul.

Nero's persecution not only cost the early church many of its top leaders, it established the precedent for subsequent persecutions. If Junia were not among Nero's victims after 64 C.E., she would certainly have been well aware of the cruelty being inflicted on believers around her. There are some mentions of specific female victims in writings over time: Tacitus writes about the trial of Pomponia Graecina, a woman of high rank, who was accused of "foreign superstition" and handed over to her husband as judge for trial. She died for her faith before the Gospels of the New Testament were even written.[18] Pliny the Younger writes about two maidservants who were tortured because they were "ministers." Clement wrote that the apostle Peter's wife was martyred before him during the Neronian persecutions. Some believers were exiled, like Flavia Domatilla, the niece of a Roman consul, who was sent to the island of Pontia.[19] It was a dangerous climate. Rome had become a blood-soaked culture, which made the Christian message of brotherly love all the more radical.

• *Why did Nero single out the Christians for persecution?* At first, Romans tolerated the emerging Christian movement, thinking that the believers represented just another sect within Judaism. But by the summer of 64 C.E., when the nine-day fire destroyed most of Rome, Roman authorities had come to believe that Christianity was a distinct, minority religion and regarded the followers with growing distrust. Emperor Nero took advantage of this suspicion to shift blame for the fire from himself to the Christians. A rumor had spread that Nero had ordered the fire to clear the way for a glorious new city that he planned to call Neropolis. Tales spread that as the flames soared, Nero "fiddled" with glee on his lyre in his palace, which probably was not so. Tacitus reported that "to suppress this rumor, Nero fabricated scapegoats—and punished with every refinement the notoriously depraved Christians."

• *Misunderstanding of Christian beliefs:* The Romans often misunderstood Christian beliefs, assuming wrongly that the Lord's Supper was a cannibalistic feast, for example. The first persecution of Christians took place, Tacitus explained, to punish Christians not so much for the fire but for such shocking antisocial behavior.[20]

Although the actual number of Christians martyred by the Romans may have been relatively small, the majority of men who were executed were officials, including bishops, as those offices developed. That a very significant proportion of martyrs were women has led some scholars to believe that they must also have been regarded by the Romans as holding some sort of official standing. This is consistent with the fact that the two young women mentioned by Pliny, who were tortured and then probably executed, were considered ministers.

The gruesome treatment of Christians was immortalized in the story of Blandina, who was tortured from morning until night in the arena yet would not betray her faith. She insisted, "I am a Christian, no wickedness is carried on by us." When led into the amphitheater to die, according to the writer Eusebius, Blandina was bound and suspended on a stake and exposed to the assaults of wild beasts. Still alive, she was brought back another day for more torture, along with a young boy named Ponticus. Force was used to make them swear by idols, but when they held firm, the crazed crowd supported round after round of horrible torture for them. The young boy, comforted and supported by Blandina, steadfastly refused to swear by pagan gods, and died. Blandina was scourged, exposed again to the beasts, subjected to flames, and finally thrown into a net and cast before a bull that tossed her battered body around and about the arena. At long last, she, too, died. According to Eusebius, "Even the Gentiles confessed that no woman among them had ever endured sufferings as many and great as these."[21]

• *Women "becoming male."* The account of another martyr, Perpetua, helps explain the curious references in early church writings about the need for females to "become male" to be saved. Thanks to what is purported to be her prison diary, we have a rare first-person account of what it must have been like to be persecuted by the time of the third century.

Perpetua was still breast-feeding when she and her pregnant slave woman, Felicity, were imprisoned and executed in Carthage. According to her account, her father tries to convince her to recant to save her life. She tells him that it is God who now rules her life, not him. She is baptized in prison and becomes emboldened to demand better conditions for her fellow prisoners. She has a final prophetic dream that she is going to the arena to die but that when her clothes are removed, she discovers she is a man.

In antiquity, according to British scholar Marianne Dorman, the male body was considered the norm and the strong woman was described as "becoming male." The phrase later would be applied to virginal women who had not been penetrated. The act of "becoming male" for women indicated that the carnality of Eve had been left behind and a new, more masculine person was produced. This dream convinced Perpetua that she would prevail in the arena. In a way, she did. She asked for a pin to fasten her disheveled hair, so she would not appear unseemly at her end. She

187

announced to the crowd, "Thou art judging us, but God shall judge thee"—a final challenge to the imperial powers. As she was dispatched, she bravely guided the wavering hand of the novice gladiator to where to strike deep, or so the tradition says.[22]

❧ *Why were Christians punished so severely for not swearing by Roman gods?* After Augustus's death in 14 C.E., he was declared divine. After that, all emperors were considered divine and many insisted that they be worshiped as gods. Not to give homage to the divinity of the emperor and the Roman gods meant invoking their wrath. By not participating in the celebrations of the gods, says David Dawson Vasquez, the Christians aroused concerns among their pagan neighbors that they would bring the displeasure of Jupiter on everyone. For the sake of their own health, safety, and prosperity, the Romans wanted the Christians to follow the accepted order.

Christians did pay taxes, served in the military, and obeyed the Roman laws, but they were counseled by their leaders not to attend the blood sports of the gladiator arenas or decadent theater shows. With their emphasis on family values, modest dress, and right living, the early Christians must have stood out in Rome like an Amish sect in New York City. Some aroused suspicions by refusing to buy meat that had been sacrificed to the gods. Because of their aloofness and "secret" worship services, Romans started singling them out as the culprits when things went wrong. Tertullian, writing in about 196, said:

> The Christians are to blame for every public disaster and every
> misfortunate that befalls the people. If the Tiber rises to the walls,
> if the Nile fails to rise and flood the fields, if the sky withholds its
> rain, if there is earthquake or famine or plague, straightway the
> cry arises, "The Christians to the lions!"[23]

Early Christians also were very suspect in Roman society because of rumors they were magicians as well as cannibalistic and incestuous. How did such bizarre misconceptions get started? Wild rumors of cannibalism apparently were triggered by the repetition of the phrase in communion ceremonies "Take and eat, this is my body broken for you." Scriptures calling upon "brothers and sisters" in the faith to greet one another with a "holy kiss," usually on the mouth, were misinterpreted as incestuous. Because Eucharist ceremonies were open only to baptized Christians, the secrecy led others to suspect the worst.[24] "When Christians had a communion meal together and called it an *agape* feast, a love feast, their neighbors misunderstood and thought it was a wild party," explained Vasquez.

One of the lingering suspicions was that Christians practiced magic. The intonation of baptism rites and the Eucharist were misinterpreted because they sounded a lot like chants used by Roman magicians. In fact, the Latin phrase *Hoc est corpus meum* (This is my body) was later adapted by magicians as "hocus pocus."[25]

❋ *How did Christianity spread, despite such suspicion and the series of persecutions?* It took many years to persuade early skeptics that Christians were moral, upright citizens who even prayed for the emperor. What ultimately convinced the pagans was that the followers of the Jesus movement practiced what they preached. They provided food for the hungry, shelter for the homeless, comfort for the sick and dying. They took in abandoned children. As time went by, it was not the brave way that Christian martyrs died that so impressed other Romans; it was the uncommonly kind and generous way they lived. According to *Christian History,* some early Christians even offered to sell themselves into slavery in order to spare others. Clement confirms that some members of the church delivered themselves into bondage that they might ransom others. Some provided food for others with the price they received for themselves.

Author Rodney Stark also points out that there were at least two great plagues in the first three centuries of the church (between 160 and 250) that were instrumental in the young church's growth. When the plagues came, the Christians stayed in cities to minister to the sick and dying while others fled. Dionysius, Bishop of Alexandria, writing about the response of believers to the plague of 250 says, "Most of our brother Christians showed unbounded love and loyalty, never sparing themselves and thinking only of one another." The heathens pushed the sufferers away and fled from their dearest, "throwing them into the road before they were dead," according to Dionysius. In contrast, Christians provided food and water to those too weak to care for themselves. Stark estimates some 80 percent of the Christians survived the plagues, compared to only 25 to 50 percent of the general population. Surviving pagans developed a more favorable opinion of the caretakers whose God had watched over them. Christian numbers grew. During Junia's day in Rome, there were probably only 1,400 Christians. Two hundred years later, there were more than a million. Three hundred years later, there were 33 million.[26]

Dallas Willard, author of *The Divine Conspiracy,* says that the reason Christianity survived and spread is that the early Christians manifested a quality of love and intellect that was unique. As he put it, Christianity spread for basically the same reason Palm Pilots and iPods spread: "People found it good and helpful."[27]

❦

❦ *Do we know what happened to Andronicus?* The Orthodox Church of America tradition is that St. Andronicus later was made Bishop of Pannonia (modern Hungary). The church Web site says that his preaching took him and St. Junia far from the boundaries of his diocese, where they converted many pagans "to the knowledge of God, many pagan temples closed, and in their place Christian churches were built." Another Orthodox Web site calls Junia "assistant of Andronicus" but goes on to say that "they both possessed the power of Grace to work miracles through which they drove out demons from men and healed every type of disease and illness." The Orthodox readings in honor of the couple say both Andronicus and Junia suffered martyrdom for Christ.

The Orthodox history says:

> In the fifth century, during the reign of Emperors Arcadius and Honorius, their holy relics were uncovered on the outskirts of Constantinople together with the relics of other martyrs "at the Eugenius gate." It was revealed to the pious cleric Nicholas Kalligraphos that among these martyrs were the relics of the holy Apostle Andronicus. Afterwards, a magnificent church was built on this spot.[28]

Alas, the church was later destroyed, so there's no grave to visit today. The end of the apostles remains clouded by uncertainty, but it seems likely from the Orthodox Church descriptions that Andronicus and Junia died in hostile circumstances. Their unknown fate is like the fallen soldiers who are honored with anonymous memorials that are inscribed, "A Comrade Known Only to God." If Junia and Andronicus perished some distance from Rome in relative anonymity, it could explain why a cult did not develop around their ministry at the time and why they did not become more prominent in church history.

Their ministry is remembered today on the feast day of May 17 by the Orthodox Church. Were Andronicus and Junia also recognized by the early Roman church as saints? It is possible, but it is difficult to find earlier references to the couple as saints because there was no "official" list of saints during the first one hundred years of the church. The practice of venerating saints evolved over time. The organized church lists of saints did not begin until the ninth and tenth centuries. Some of those lists included Junia. A reference to Junia and Andronicus as saints can be found as far back as the tenth century in an Orthodox menology (a calendar of saints' days). The menology of Emperor Basil Porphyrogenitus says of Andronicus and Junia: "Having with him as consort and helper in godly preaching the admirable woman Junia, who dead to the world and the flesh, but alive to God alone, carried out her task."[29]

The fact that Junia and Andronicus are mentioned in a tenth-century menology is a good indication that they may well have been on earlier lists of saints that are no longer available and would have been considered saints before the Roman Catholic and Orthodox churches split. John Barnett, a New Testament professor at St. Vladimir Orthodox Theological Seminary, says it is probable that Junia and Andronicus were on earlier lists because the Orthodox, Coptic, and Armenian churches carried over most of the saints that were honored before the schism with the Roman church in 1054. Over time, he said, the Roman tradition for honoring saints became more "top down" than in the past and tended to venerate the ascetic monastic saints over the married "host of witnesses." That would help explain why married couples like Junia and Andronicus, as well as Prisca and Aquila, faded from view.

If you look today, you won't find Junia in the current lists of Roman Catholic saints. You can find St. Waldo—a hermit who lived in a tree hollow. And you can find St. Aldalbert, St. Egwin, and St. Josaphat. Other figures from the early church, including Prisca, Phoebe, Barnabas, Epathroditus, Silas, Mary Magdalene, and Mary Salome, are recognized with feast days. Even the wily Pope Boniface VIII is honored as a saint by the Roman Catholic Church. But not the highly praised Junia and Andronicus.

❧

In the early years of Christianity, the followers of Jesus looked to the martyrs as examples of sacrificial faith. Rather than mourning their deaths as terminal, as the pagans did, the believers were comforted, if not joyful, that their comrades had gone to heaven, where they would be at peace with God forever. In that sense, the day of the saint's death was considered a birthday and observed as a "feast day"—a day of celebration. Practically all martyrs were considered saints, though official honor required the authorization of the local bishop. Sainthood initially rested on popular acclaim, and many early cults of martyrs were based largely on oral traditions. After the fourth century, the local bishop would approve new cults if sanctity was evinced by holiness of life or miracles. By the year 1000, papal approval was increasingly required for veneration of new saints.

Rigorous legal procedures were put in place over time to screen candidates for the list, called the "canon." In 1969, the Roman calendar was reformed, and the number of feast days cut back. A core group of several thousand saints was selected for universal veneration. Some saints were restricted to local recognition and others were dropped, ostensibly for lack of evidence.[30]

It was a relief to discover that Junia had been recognized for centuries as a saint by the Orthodox Church. It was more confirmation that she really existed. In the official Greek Orthodox Church icons of saints, Junia is seen standing at the side of Andronicus, her head properly covered with a veil, a purposeful look on her face.

Regardless of our religious denominations, the saints have always had a mystique, a power over our imaginations as extraordinary, supernatural beings. But when you examine their stories, you appreciate that the saints were mostly very ordinary people who made a moral effort to walk with God.

It was fortunate that the small group that I toured the necropolis with included William Frank and his wife Therese Frank, who both were teaching at the University of Dallas campus in Rome. Going through the necropolis was a sobering experience, because it took us breathtakingly close to the roots of faith. It was helpful to compare notes with the Franks for a few minutes afterward in the fresh air of the sun-drenched Bernini plaza. As we talked about the sacrifices of many early Christians, Therese Frank, who teaches theology, mentioned that the day before, several of her students had expressed shock to learn that while St. Catherine of Siena is buried in a church in Rome, her head and a finger are enshrined in her hometown of Siena, more than one hundred miles to the north. That struck them as "gross." Therese Frank explained to the young people that while the ancient tradition of revering relics of saints, even severed body parts, may seem barbaric today, it was a way of reminding believers that "these were real people, not a myth."

That noble sentiment was spoiled when hucksters in the Middle Ages started faking relics of the saints and hawking them to make a profit. As a result, at least two heads of John the Baptist are revered in separate churches. The local joke is that one was his head when he was a young man and one when he was a mature adult.

By the 1500s, Erasmus would complain in exasperation:

> What would Jerome say could he see the Virgin's milk exhibited
> for money . . . the miraculous oil; the portions of the true cross,
> enough if they were collected to freight a ship? Here we have the
> hood of St. Francis, there Our Lady's petticoat, or St. Anne's comb,
> or St. Thomas of Canterbury's shoes . . . and all through the avarice
> of priests and the hypocrisy of monks playing on the credulity of
> the people.

Erasmus viewed the veneration of relics as mere superstition. Better to imitate the virtues of the saints than to pray to their paintings, he advised. As he put it, "Do you want to honor St. Francis? Then give away your wealth to the poor, restrain your evil impulses, and see in everyone you meet the image of Christ."[31]

It's understandable why the Protestant reformers would leave behind unseemly practices like selling saints' relics and buying indulgences when they separated from the Catholic Church in the sixteenth century. The veneration of the Virgin Mary was left behind as well. The reformers worried that respect for Mary had turned into adoration that was dangerously close to idolatry. The idea that believers needed the saints or the Virgin Mary as mediators between them and God was offensive to the Protestants, because it was central to their faith that you don't need a mediator for a personal relationship with God.

"That suggests some inadequacy in Christ if you need another mediator, something lacking in Christ. It is a distraction that says God the Father and his incarnate Son are not good enough if you need all these adjuncts," Darrell Bock explained to me between his classes at the Dallas Theological Seminary. "It's as if you had direct access to the President of the United States—then why take your concerns to his mother or the secretary of defense?"

True enough. But by de-emphasizing Mary, Protestants left behind the primary feminine image of faith. As Beverly Roberts Gaventa of Princeton Theological Seminary says, "We can't just bring her out for Christmas Eve and put her back away on the twenty-sixth." Mary's steadfast faith deserves better.

And by discarding the saints, Protestants lost almost all the other early role models for women. As a Protestant, I had never thought much about the saints, other than a certain St. Nicholas at Christmas. I was not familiar with the stories of women saints. To put their stories of faith in context, I bought some jogging shoes at one of the many shoe shops on the Via del Corso and headed out for the churches in Rome that honored the memories of martyred women.

• *St. Cecilia.* There was St. Cecilia's church, built on the site of her family home in Trastevere, where she was condemned to die by suffocation. When the stifling heat did not kill her, executioners attempted to behead her. She survived three blows, and because the law forbade striking more than three blows, she was left dying for three days on the floor of her home. As she lay dying, countless people who came by to comfort her were inspired to convert by her brave example of grace in suffering. Today Cecilia's courage is remembered with an eerily beautiful statue of her lying on her side as if she were sleeping, her head twisted slightly sideways by the blows of the executioner. Her slender arms and delicate hands, a young girl's arms, rest at her side.[32]

• *St. Catherine.* At St. Clement's Basilica, near the Coliseum, you can see a series of fifteenth-century frescoes of St. Catherine of Alexandria, who was believed to be an exceptionally learned noblewoman. Because she protested against the worship of idols and the persecution of Christians, she was ordered by Emperor Maxentius to defend herself before fifty philosophers. She made such a brilliant defense that the philosophers were converted. Maxentius then tried to seduce her, but she replied that she was betrothed to Christ. The emperor sentenced Catherine to be tied to two-spoked wheels that would stretch and tear her apart as they turned. Yet the wheels broke instead, the story goes, and Catherine was freed through the intervention of an angel. Her captors resorted to beheading her.

I would later find out that Catherine of Alexandria was removed from the official list of Roman Catholic saints in 1969, along with Thecla, because there was no proof they had existed. Some scholars, like Kyriaki Karidoyanes Fitzgerald, believe there is a truth to Catherine's story. The Orthodox Church still recognizes her as a saint. Fitzgerald says there was a wealthy woman who was exiled around the time of Catherine's believed tribulations who could have been the basis for the story. Although the name Catherine has not been traced, it could merely have been taken from the Greek Katarina, meaning "one who had purity of heart." The official position of the Roman Catholic Church now is that Catherine was apocryphal. But perhaps her story was just highly embellished, like Thecla's. It remains intriguing that church men and women of long ago believed a woman could outdebate philosophers. They believed it so deeply, in fact, that they enshrined artwork in her honor in St. Clement's Basilica, one of the oldest and holiest sites of the church.[33]

• *St. Catherine of Siena.* The Roman church does honor another Catherine—St. Catherine of Siena, who is a Doctor of the Church and Patron Saint of Italy and Europe (c. 1347–1380). The full-length tomb sculpture of her in Rome shows a slender woman with a slightly long, thin face and straight nose. You can see that this was a very serious woman. Catherine nursed the sick and established hospitals throughout Italy. She preached openly, sometimes to crowds of more than one thousand, at a time when society frowned on women in public advocacy. Unafraid to take on the authorities, she campaigned against corruption in the church and lobbied forcefully to have the papacy returned to Rome from Avignon, where it had been moved after Pope Boniface's power struggle with King Philip.[34] Catherine wore herself out with her work and died at the age of thirty-three.

• *St. Agnes.* And then there is St. Agnes, who was barely thirteen years old when she refused an arranged marriage to the son of a Roman praetor, saying she was dedicated to Christ. She was condemned to stand naked in a brothel, possibly near Domitian's stadium. Her nakedness was miraculously covered by her hair and a dazzling cloak. She was condemned at the stake but escaped the flames. She finally was beheaded with a sword and was buried in the Via Nomentana. Because of her chastity, she became the patron saint of young girls.[35]

Of the many saints whose stories you encounter in Rome, these four stuck in my memory. Perhaps because there were elements of the stories that still could be inspiring for women today.

Modern women who have watched friends wither from cancer can understand St. Cecilia's dying example and remember what it means to show faith to the end.

St. Catherine stands out for having the courage to articulate her faith publicly. Though some women might not identify with the story of her torture on the wheel, the truth is that they probably know some friends who have been broken on the modern equivalent of the "wheel of life"—depression, divorce, disease, disappointment, the deaths of loved ones. It takes a strong core of belief to survive in the face of so much pain.

It's more difficult to identify with Catherine of Siena's often austere, self-denying asceticism. But her lifelong care for the sick is admirable, as is her courage in getting involved in church politics. She spoke truth to those in power, something all too rare in the church today.

And St. Agnes? She is a reminder that sometimes your strongest witness is simply to say no, you will not do as others insist you do.

The lives of early women of faith deserve remembering, like Junia's. They kept faith alive. Honesty challenges us to look back at the lives of these forgotten women, tell their stories again, learn from them what we can. The Romans had it partly right: people are not forgotten so long as their stories are told.

Historians tell us that over the last ten centuries, since the High Middle Ages, when the patriarchal church was solidly entrenched, relatively few women have been named to sainthood. Most of those who are celebrated date from earlier periods in which the recognition of sanctity rested on popular acclaim rather than on a canonical process. Between 1000 and 1900, according to Philip Sheldrake, about 87 percent of saints were men, 13 percent women. What's more, he notes, only a little progress has been made in recognizing women saints. In this century, 25 percent of those canonized have been women, 75 percent men. [36]

In his compendium, *Lives of the Saints,* Richard McBrien, professor of theology at Notre Dame, likewise observes that not only have fewer women than men been recognized as saints but women saints do not have as significant a place as men in the church's liturgical and devotional life.

- Only forty-one of the daily commemorations on the General Roman Calendar or the Proper Calendar for Catholic Dioceses in the United States are women saints, and twelve of those are related to Mary.
- Some fifty-two liturgical celebrations of male saints are ranked as "obligatory memorials," compared with only twenty-three for female saints, five of which are Marian.
- There are sixty-six "optional memorials" for male saints, compared with thirteen for female saints, again with three Marian.

McBrien agrees that in such subtle ways, "the tradition has destroyed and continues to destroy the memory of women" and points to the many women who were traditionally mentioned in the Roman Canon of the Mass, such as Perpetua and Agnes, who are now "bracketed," which means that they effectively are left out of the central prayer of the Mass.[37]

"If the names of women who ministered in the early church seem unfamiliar, part of the reason is that they are rarely included in the lectionary readings we hear at Mass," says Barbara Reid, a professor of New Testament at Catholic Theological Union in Chicago.[38]

Junia's name, she says, is included in the lectionary scripture reading of Romans 16, but it was mistranslated as a man's name in 1970 and has only recently been corrected in the lectionary. The verse is scheduled to be read every other year on Saturday of the thirty-first week of the year. Only one woman who ministered in the early church is found in a Sunday reading—Chloe—who may have been head of a house church in Corinth.

Other denominations have not fared much better in commemorating women of faith. In the Episcopal Church, there are 127 celebrations honoring men, in comparison to 18 commemorating women. In the Lutheran Book of Worship, women make up about 15 percent of the sanctoral cycle.

Once you start looking, it is apparent that many of the female "saints" of the early church are missing from view.

As my search for Junia went on, I began receiving unexpected feedback from friends who were following my research progress. A college vice president confided to me over lunch that she had never told anyone before, but she likes to imagine the Holy Spirit is a feminine presence, because it makes her feel more connected to her faith. Perhaps that's in keeping with the tradition that wisdom, called Sophia in ancient times, was considered a feminine presence. Or perhaps it is just another way of expressing that some women feel left out of the equation. The very structure of religion tells women who they are and tells men who women are, as well. No matter how you dress it up in ecclesiastical jargon or rationalize that God meant for men and women to have "complementary" roles, it comes down to saying women are "assistant persons" in some church eyes.

Another thought-provoking response came from a business friend, who e-mailed me that his head was now in a knot over Junia and her identify theft.

> My church and I have always taken the Bible as literal truth. Over
> the last thirty years, I have found where I disagreed or did not
> understand, things worked out best if I accepted and obeyed. The
> Pauline injunction of women not having authority over men has
> never been questioned—even by my wife, who gets pretty prickly
> if she thinks she or our daughters are being treated as anything but
> equal partners in our journey through life. I am, rather grudgingly
> at times, acknowledged as the spiritual head of the family. This is
> always done in a manner that makes me rethink everything I have
> "decided" to make sure it is fair. More often than not it results in
> my doing it the way my wife first suggested. Therefore, I have
> never felt my position very elevated.
>
> Now the whole deal is up in the air! Now I suspect all of the
> Pauline injunctions limiting the role of women in worship, teach-
> ing, and administration. I thought that Christ put them in there
> because he knew how lazy men are, and by prohibiting women
> from certain tasks, the men would have to do something besides sit
> in the pews and snore. I have always thought crusaders for women's
> rights as poor girls who couldn't get a date to the prom. Now I
> have plenty of things to think about for the next few weeks.

Important as it is for men to be spiritual leaders and set an example for a godly family, I wondered if it would be more important for them to be spiritual *partners*. Opponents of the ordination of women often argue that it will threaten the family, by reducing male authority. But wouldn't it strengthen the family to have more mutual cooperation and consideration rather than domination? Wasn't mutual submission what Paul was saying? Wasn't what Jesus modeled what is today called "servant leadership," not domination of others? So it seemed to me, but I wondered if I could possibly make that point without sounding strident or antifamily or antiman. I was learning that we are all called to holiness, whether male or female, to be invaded by God, to become more of the person God is calling us to be. As one scholar said, it is a sin to know the truth and look the other way. Yet a number of people, perhaps because they are afraid of engaging with this issue, have kept quiet.

CHAPTER TEN

Finding Junia

*It takes some extra examination to find the numerous women who
worked side by side with Paul and the other "well-knowns." Possibly we
are slow to notice their names because our own culture has trained us
to see women more in strictly family roles than in ministry roles.*

WINNIE CHRISTENSEN, BIBLE TEACHER AND AUTHOR

I didn't quite understand why, but I felt drawn to the little church in Rome that is named for St. Prisca. Perhaps I was drawn because Prisca is mentioned more times than Junia in the New Testament and figures repeatedly in the spread of Christianity. Perhaps it was because she was a contemporary of Junia's and they would have known each other in the small Christian community of Rome. Visiting Prisca's namesake church might be as close as I could get to a tangible memorial to Junia and the women of Romans 16.

The search for St. Prisca's church turned out to be a frustrating exercise, although in the end, it was enlightening in ways I did not expect. According to my Michelin guide, the church was one of the first places of Christian worship in Rome, with remains of an early house of worship, as well as a second-century Mithraeum, where the Persian god Mithras was worshiped. Tradition says that Prisca was baptized there by St. Peter himself. It also says that she was the first woman to suffer martyrdom in Rome. But those accounts may be scrambled. Some sources believe the early martyr was actually Prisca's teenaged daughter, who had the same name.

We do know that Prisca helped start churches in Ephesus, Corinth, and Rome. We know that she risked her neck for Paul and that she helped

203

tutor the gifted preacher Apollos. Bishop Chrysostom named her the sole tutor. Some believe she might have been the author of Hebrews. So you would think the church called Santa Prisca in Rome would be a place of special remembrance—a place where the Christian faithful could honor brave founders of the Christian church.

But you would have to think again. Finding traces of Prisca turned out to be just as elusive as finding Junia, even though Prisca was much better known.

❦

Did Prisca write Hebrews—a letter to encourage Christians whose endurance is wearing thin? The author, who seems to have a pastor's heart, helps them see where their Christian journey is taking them and how their lives relate to those who have gone before. Because it ends like a letter and mentions Timothy, some were led to believe it was written by Paul. But it is written in a different style than Paul's letters; it is not his voice. The final greeting sent by "those from Italy" (Heb. 13:24) has suggested the recipients were in Rome.

Scholars have guessed that the identity of the author might be Apollos, Barnabas, Priscilla, Luke, or Epaphras. Tertullian said it was Barnabas. Origen said God alone knows who wrote Hebrews, but it might have been an unknown disciple of Paul's. Others have said the very loss of the author's name lends credence to the idea that it was written by a woman. Some scholars point to the sympathetic treatment of women like Sarah in the text as a clue. The *Women's Bible Commentary* suggests that while the highly educated Prisca would have been capable of writing such an epistle, it may not be so because most of the imagery is male, few women are mentioned, and the author is referred to by the male article. However, that could mean it was written by a man or by someone who wanted to be seen as a man. And some suggest it could have been a team effort by Prisca and her husband, Aquila, since the author (or authors) moves easily from first-person singular to first-personal plural, as married couples often do.[1]

❦

The map in my guidebook was somewhat limited and so was the Rome street signage, so I spent several hours walking around the Circus Maximus area and around the Aventine Hill on a hot and humid October afternoon, trying to find the church of St. Prisca. I wore blisters on the bottoms of my feet and, to my surprise, on the tops of my feet. I asked directions four times and was courteously directed four different ways. Nobody on the busy streets around the Circus Maximus seemed familiar with the church.

Finally, I found my way up the steep Aventine Hill to the street where Prisca's church was supposed to be. It turned out to be a pleasant residential area, a welcome relief from the blaring traffic around the ruins of Circus Maximus at the base of the hill. At the top of the Aventine, there were stately homes, majestic umbrella pines that were three stories tall, and a gentle breeze. Children could be heard playing on a school playground—a sound that is the same all over the world. The neighborhood had a pleasing feel. I asked a businessman walking by if he knew where the church of St. Prisca might be. He looked at my Michelin map with some disbelief. "I've walked down this street for more than a year and I have never seen it or heard of it," he said, handing back my guidebook. "Sorry." I decided to give up.

I was walking gingerly back down the hill when I passed by an elderly nun walking the other way. She was stooped a bit with age, but she was climbing the hill with determination in her sturdy black shoes. We smiled and nodded at each other. It took me a few steps down the hill before it dawned on me: "She's going to the church." It was a Nancy Drew moment. I turned around and followed the little nun up the hill to some stairs that

I had not seen from the street. There it was. St. Prisca's church was just a few yards from where I had shown my map to the man on the street! The church was set back from the pavement, behind a retaining wall, so it was partially obscured from pedestrian view—hiding in plain sight, I thought, just like the references to Junia in the Bible.

I followed the stooped-over nun through an iron gate into a large open garden and watched her disappear quickly down some stairs and through a basement door into the church, like the white rabbit in *Alice's Adventures in Wonderland*. As I started to follow her down the stairs, a workman with a dark moustache suddenly appeared in the doorway and looked angry. "No, no," he waved me away with the shovel in his hands, indicating I could not go in because the church was closed for repairs. *"Per favore!"* I begged him, explaining I was leaving the next day. He wouldn't budge. I walked away, deeply disappointed. I still felt a compelling need to get inside the church and see where Prisca may have been baptized and where her family home may have once stood. I realized I would have to make another trip. And so I did.

When I returned to Santa Prisca eight months later with one of my sons, I found a modest church sanctuary that was visibly in need of restoration. Rolled-up carpets and folding chairs were stashed in front of side altars. The architecture of Santa Prisca certainly was not on the level of the graceful Santa Sabina down the street. Still, there was something about the time-worn Santa Prisca that attracted me. The caretaker sweeping up in the sanctuary was surprised when I asked if there were any pamphlets about Santa Prisca, as if to say, "You want a brochure about this place?" When I persisted, he motioned me to wait while he walked back to the office in the rear of the church and pulled a desk chair over to an antique armoire. He stepped up on the chair in order to reach the top of the armoire. After feeling over his head around the top, he found a small stack of pamphlets that had been stashed up there. They were held together with a rubber band. He peeled out one to give to me with a polite smile, put back the chair, and showed us the door. There were no other visitors in the church. It was midday, and he was locking up so he could go to lunch.

For the next few months, I read everything I could on Prisca and what is supposed to be her church. The official story from the parish is that the Titulus Priscae was built at the end of the fourth century, after Constantine had made Christianity the official religion of the empire.[2] Yet there are two competing claims for the namesake of the church. One is that the church was named in honor of Prisca, a young virgin and martyr. That's the official namesake on current church records. The other claim is that the church was named after the Prisca and Aquila mentioned in Romans 16. Mercy. Which version was true?

❧

In the beginning, the faithful tended to gather in the homes of wealthy Roman Christians. After the legalization of Christianity by Constantine, the house churches (*domus ecclesiae*) became the property of the Christian community. These church buildings were identified by a wooden plaque (*titulus*) above the front door, so they became known as *tituli* in honor of their original owners or honored martyrs. There were twenty-five *tituli* in the early church. Those twenty-five original "parish churches," including Santa Prisca, still exist and can be visited by pilgrims.[3]

❧

Constantine's edict of 313 mandated that basilicas be built on the remains of the earliest Christian cemeteries or on the *tituli* and dedicated to saints and martyrs. That reinforces the notion that the site of Santa Prisca was known to be a sacred site in the first centuries of the church. Santa Prisca is a small church but deserves to be called a basilica because of its structure. It has three naves supported by fourteen columns. Just below the present presbytery of the basilica is a ninth-century crypt used by Christians for worship. The arched room is not grand, but it is covered with colorful frescoes of St. Paul and St. Peter, giving it the feel of hallowed space.

The Prisca basilica was damaged by Norman invaders in 1084 and over the centuries has been restored many times. Those renovations have reduced its original beauty, to put it politely. Old stone flooring was removed, along with two splendid balustrades at the top of stairs leading to the crypt. Today the church is squeezed between two larger buildings that protrude on either side. One is a hotel called the Domus Aventine. Someone walking down the street, as I did, could easily see the three-star hotel sign and miss the modest church next to it.

The Augustinian fathers who came to supervise Santa Prisca in 1934 began searching for the famous "house of Aquila and Prisca" by excavating under the foundation. Instead of the house, they found a pagan Mithraeum from the first century. The Persian practice had been brought back to Rome by soldiers and was popular among men. The barrel-shaped Mithraeum contains a corner where animals were sacrificed.[4]

It was a disappointment that the excavations by the Augustinian brothers did not uncover the ancient house of Prisca and Aquila. However, a house and what appears to have been an early Christian chapel reportedly were found quite close to the church during earlier excavations. Between wars and hard times, record-keeping has been erratic. A manuscript kept at the Bibliothèque Nationale in Paris gives an account of the discovery in 1776 of the ruins of a Roman house and Christian oratory close to St. Prisca. But this ruin was unfortunately destroyed, and no trace of it remains. An ancient Christian glass also was found in long ago excavations, with etchings of St. Peter and St. Paul, confirming that this was an early worship site but not who the owners were.[5] Still, the parish history maintains to this day that the first basilica was built next to the site of Aquila and Prisca's home. It has been established that Christian worship took place there at an early time, as ancient terra-cotta lamps with the *chi-rho* monogram have been found.

🌸 *What can we learn from the artwork in the basilica?* Artwork in the basilica honors both the Prisca namesakes. An altarpiece painted by Domenico Cresti (1560–1636) shows Prisca, wife of Aquila, receiving baptism from St. Peter. A seventeenth-century fresco on the wall of the presbytery, by Anastasio Fontebuoni, depicts the martyrdom of the Virgin Prisca.

So was the Aventine house church named after the young girl who was martyred? Or the couple in Romans 16? Here's what we might surmise.

- *The case for Titulus Prisca.* At present the Acta Sanctorum tells of a thirteen-year-old girl who was imprisoned during Emperor Claudius's reign for having refused to worship the statue of Apollo. Because she would not renounce her Christian faith, she was whipped and thrown to the lions in the Circus Maximus. Instead of attacking her, the lions supposedly laid down at her feet. The young girl was imprisoned again, whipped, and tied to the stake. But the flames left her unharmed. One legend has it that the girl was taken to the Via Ostiense and beheaded. Her body was buried in the cemetery of Priscilla on the Via Salaria. Toward the end of the fourth century, Pope Eutychianus transported the young St. Prisca's remains to the oratory of the Aventine church. During the reign of Pope Leo IV (847–855), her remains were moved to Santi Quattro Coronati but soon after were brought back to the Aventine church, where they are preserved in the ninth-century crypt. The feast day of the church's patron saint is celebrated on January 18, which is noted in early martyr's calendars as the date dedicated to the martyr Prisca.[6]

- *The case for Titulus Prisca et Aquila.* A reference is found in the eighth century to *Domus o Titulus Priscae e Aquilae.* The Vatican Code 1193 has the same citation. During the twelfth century, the Abbott of the Benedictines who officiated at the church was called *Prebyter Abbatie Priscae et Aquilae.* That title remained until the end of the eighteenth century and is recorded on an engraved stone plaque that the Augustinian fathers placed in the entrance of the sacristy in 1734. No mention is made of Prisca, virgin and martyr. The Acta Sanctorum states that Aquila and Prisca were martyred and buried in the Cemetery of Priscilla on the Via Salaria, together with Prisca, virgin and martyr. Archaeologist Giovanni Battista de Rossi, who examined the Priscilla catacombs where both of the Priscas reportedly were buried, has stated that the martyr was the young daughter of Aquila and Prisca who was martyred before them, around the middle of the first century. In the eighth century, the remains of Prisca and Aquila also were transported to the church of St. Quattro Coronati, to protect the relics from desecration by the Saracens.

Prisca appears to have been a Roman, and by the precedence of her name over that of her husband, it is often assumed that she was of a higher position and that the house on the Aventine was her property. Some historians speculate that she was related in some way to the aristocratic family of the Acili Glabriones.[7]

Aquila was known to be a Jew from Pontus, near the Black Sea in what is now northern Turkey. He may have been taken to Rome as a slave and have been a freedman of the Acili family, who were also connected to the Priscilla cemetery on Via Salaria, where the two initially were buried. Or he may have settled in Rome as a craftsman and trader, engaged the Acili as clients, and done well with his wife's connections. The "tents" that he and Prisca made very likely were not outdoor tents in the traditional sense but more like awnings that were used to cover the open areas of most Roman homes to shield them from the Mediterranean sun.

What finally persuaded me that the Aventine church must have been the site of Prisca and Aquila's home was the story about St. Peter's chair. According to the *Catholic Encyclopedia,* there were two early worship sites where St. Peter used a chair (*cathedra*) to sit in when he presided over meetings of the faithful and administered sacraments.[8] One chair, reportedly, was used at the Priscilla cemetery on the Via Salaria, which was lost in later centuries. A second chair was used by Peter at the house church where Santa Prisca is located. It is believed to have remained there and was celebrated on a *cathedra* feast day on February 22, which happens to be the same day honored as the dedication of Santa Prisca. Peter's chair at Santa Prisca became the place where successors to Peter, like Linus, presided and taught. That would make Santa Prisca a very holy site indeed—a true cradle of the church.

⁂

The early bishops and their deputies presided in a high-backed chair, cathedra, on a raised platform, just as the emperor had presided in basilica (royal) courts for policymaking or trials. The early bishops taught their congregations like a professor, hence early university professors also would preside over lecture rooms from tall chairs, which is why professors have "chairs" and why some churches are called cathedrals.[9]

⁂

But in the fourth century, Pope Damasus moved "St. Peter's chair" from Santa Prisca to the Vatican basilica that had been constructed over the tomb of St. Peter. Santa Prisca apparently had declined in influence after St. John Lateran became the residence of the popes in 314. Pope Damasus was intent on making sure Rome was the supreme center of the Christian church and that Peter was recognized as the cornerstone of the church. To reinforce that claim, he wanted Peter's historic chair for his new baptistery at the Vatican Basilica. For centuries after that, the chair was exhibited once a year to the faithful. In the seventeenth century, the chair was enclosed above the altar of St. Peter in a gigantic casing of bronze, supported by the four doctors of the church: Augustine, Ambrose, Athanasius, and Chrysostom.

So Peter's chair was lost to Santa Prisca, but it provided an important clue that the early house church near the site must have been large enough for meetings "chaired" by Peter. Custom was for Romans to combine their workplace with their home, with the commercial enterprise on the ground floor and living quarters above, which would result in a large abode. It makes more sense that such a large dwelling could have belonged to a couple of veteran believers with a successful business than to a teenaged believer who became a martyr—unless, of course, she was their daughter.

After the removal of Peter's chair, Santa Prisca's prominence continued to diminish. Even though the church was connected to the earliest preaching and baptizing in Rome, it was supplanted by bigger, grander basilicas in importance. Indeed, when the Vatican and the city of Rome inaugurated a new bus tour in 2005 to showcase the city's Christian heritage, "Roma Christiana," the buses made stops at seven major spiritual sites: St. Peter's Basilica, the Colosseum, Santa Maria Maggiore Basilica, St. John Lateran, St. Peter in Chains, San Clemente, and Santa Maria in Aracoeli. Not included on the stops was Santa Prisca, a humble structure with chronic leaks in the underground rooms.

Still, something about Santa Prisca drew me back yet a third time. It was a chilly fall Sunday when I hurried over to the Aventine to attend the morning Mass. When I opened the heavy wooden doors, there was no one inside. How sad, I thought. People don't even come to Mass here any more. It was cold outside, so I decided to sit in the pew and reflect for a while.

A tall dark-skinned priest walked over to me. "I bet you forgot about the change to daylight saving time. You are an hour early," he said gently, with a singsong English accent that told me he was not a native Italian. He said if I could wait an hour, there would be another Mass.

So I sat and waited and tried to assemble pieces of what I had learned looking for Junia. It had been quite a journey. I had gotten on the wrong train once and missed my train once, running as fast as I could through the Rome terminal with my bag and purse flapping. I had been robbed in my hotel room while I was fast asleep but luckily still had my passport.

Most important, I had learned that Junia was not a recent feminist fad but a historical woman of faith:

- She was recognized by church fathers and scholars as an apostle from the first century through the twelfth century.
- She has been honored as a saint by the Orthodox Church since the tenth century.
- Most Bible translations and leading scholars, male and female, now recognize her name.

So, no, Junia is not a new invention to fit a revisionist agenda. She is a historic figure, lost over time, now being rediscovered. Some scholars might caution against reading too much into the Romans text about Junia. But as one said, the greater danger would be to read too little into it.

Finding Junia is not a "silver bullet" to end once and for all the questions about whether women should be ordained. But her precedent offers yet another reason to widen the debate. And that is the challenge before us today: How can we use the information coming to light about women in the early church to make a stronger church? Can the divide in the debate be bridged? Can we really understand where we are in the journey if we don't look at the beginning with clear eyes? It pays to ask ourselves what really made us the way we are, what things have we carried from the past that determine why we believe what we do. The questions are tough:

- Why is it that some believers cling to scriptures that limit the role of women in faith and yet turn a blind eye to all those that include women in leadership roles?
- Why is it that when there is a "jump ball" between two countervailing scriptures regarding women, the negative one wins?
- Why is that some believers can put scriptures condoning slavery into perspective as being from a different era but insist that subordinate roles for women remain the same?

- Why is it that some believers will make exceptions to the restrictions on divorce for male leaders but not for restrictions on roles for women?

Is the point of the Bible to teach us about patriarchy—or salvation? And how can we have a civil conversation on this? I thought back on the comments of the most conservative ministers that I talked to. They worry that the "egalitarian" movement is dangerous because it might weaken gender differences and thus weaken the family as well as the church. I understand their concern at a time when families struggle with all manner of cultural pressures. But I suspect having female ministers won't weaken religion or the culture any more than having female news reporters weakens the content of the evening news or having a female secretary of state makes our country weaker. The calling and character count more than gender.

Yet many men and women cling to some patriarchal roles because they think it will make the church stronger to go back to the "way things used to be." The problem is they might not be looking at the right model. They are looking at the "Church fathers" model that emerged hundreds of years after Jesus' death, not at the way Jesus brought women into his ministry during his lifetime. Women have served as the outward and visible signs of an inward and spiritual grace.

❦

If you look for them, you will find women in addition to Junia playing important roles in the establishment of Christianity:

- *Philip's daughters.* The evangelist had four unmarried daughters who were prophets (Acts 21:8). Today we distinguish between apostles and prophets, but in the early church their roles were often similar. According to Karen King, Christian prophets not only prophesied and spoke in tongues, they offered prayer, provided guidance, interpreted scriptures, and taught. The *Teaching of the Twelve Apostles,* sometimes called the *Didache,* the earliest work on church order, also confirms that the prophets provided instruction, performed the Eucharist, and led prayer.

- *Tabitha.* Also known by her Greek name, Dorcas, Tabitha was a disciple of Jesus in Jaffa and was raised from the dead by St. Peter (Acts 9:36). She was well known for helping the needy and sewed clothes for the widows.

- *Lydia.* Lydia was a successful businesswoman in Philippi and became the first of Paul's converts in Europe (Acts 16:14–15, 25–34). The baptism of her household marked the beginning of the Philippian church.

- *Damaris.* Damaris was prominent in the congregation in Athens (Acts 17:34). Some ancient manuscripts ascribe to her "high standing"; others delete the reference, perhaps to discourage the recognition of women in public.

- *Chloe.* Chloe was apparently a well-to-do woman whose home was used for church gatherings in Corinth. She possessed sufficient clout to send a delegation to Paul to appeal for his intervention in factionalism in the Christian community there and got a favorable response from him (1 Cor. 1:11).

- *Claudia.* Claudia is named in 2 Timothy 4:21, along with two very prominent leaders of the church in Rome: Pudens, a senator whose home later became a *titulus* church, and Linus, who followed Peter as leader of the church and made allowances for women to be admitted to the holy places and attend functions with their heads covered.

- *Eudora and Syntiche.* Paul refers to these two women as co-workers in Philippi who were active evangelicals, spreading the Gospel (Phil. 4:2). He uses emphatic language to describe their labor, saying, "They fought at my side in spreading the Gospel."

- *House church leaders.* Virtually all the house churches mentioned in Acts are identified with a woman, implying she was the "head" of that household. There were congregations in Lydia's home (Acts 16:14–15, 40), Mark's mother's home (Acts 12:12), and Nympha's home (Col. 4:15). In Philemon 2, Paul greets Apphia, along with Philemon and Archippus, suggesting she shared leadership with them in the house church there.
- *Salome.* Salome was one of three women named as present at Jesus' crucifixion (Mark 15:40) and his tomb (Mark 16:1). Notably, she is not identified by her children or husband or town. She apparently was one of the women who had been followers of Jesus from Galilee and remained faithful until the end.
- *Lois and Eunice.* The apostle Paul commends Timothy's mother and grandmother for shaping his strong faith through their teaching and example. It is ironic that Paul's letter to Timothy is often used to prohibit women teaching men—"I do not allow a woman to teach" (1 Tim. 2:12)—when Paul also praises Lois and Eunice for instructing Timothy in the faith.[10]

The best argument for allowing women more leadership roles in churches is that requiring women to stay in the background tamps down half the strength of the church. Bringing more talent into leadership ranks will make the church stronger, not weaker. The church should be challenging women of faith, not to sit down and be quiet but to speak up more boldly about the social concerns in their communities—the homeless, the mentally ill in jails, the abductions of children by pedophiles, domestic violence, corruption in corporations, and more. It's going to take efforts of both men and women of faith to make a difference in these areas. Not all women are called to leadership roles, just as not all men are called to leadership roles. But some might have great gifts of teaching and administration that could make a powerful difference.

As I sat among the empty pews of Santa Prisca, I remembered the story of a friend who became the first woman elder at a large Presbyterian church. At the first dinner for the new elders, the man sitting on one side of her said in a loud voice where all could hear, "Well, I guess next they're going to have us doing the dishes!" But as the years passed, guess what? The women did not relegate the men to the kitchen. They did not take over the church and lord it over men. The church did not deteriorate. The work of the church continued just as it had before, only there were women standing next to the men at the front of the church.

The stories of Junia and Prisca and Phoebe and the many Marys teach us that there were role models of Christian women from the very beginning who worked hand in hand as respectful partners with men to do God's work. Two thousand years after they lived, the struggle to resolve the roles of men and women in the church still goes on. Today's women still must balance two systems—one public, one private. They stand with one foot in home and hearth and one in the public world. They are beginning to find their footing in some denominations. They are asking questions in theology schools. They are writing books about Mary Magdalene and now, Junia. Perhaps the time would come, I thought, when . . .

Then I noticed a little girl and a young boy had come into Santa Prisca. They were skipping through the pews, picking up programs from an earlier mass. After looking shyly at me several times, the little girl brought me one and then ran off to the church office, where her mother put an altar robe on her and one on her little brother. A whoosh of cold air came through the wooden doors. People were beginning to flow into the church. A father with two squirming young boys. An old married couple, bent over, wearing the same colors. Several young families with babies and toddlers. Some teenagers in low-cut jeans. The church was almost full. The people in the pews all looked like local folks, no tourists. As the service started, there were altar girls, as well as altar boys, lining up to help with the service. Two women stepped to the lectern to read the scriptures of the day. The priest invited everyone to the parish pizza dinner to raise money for the homeless. The old pipe organ wheezed somewhat into tune as everyone stood to sing. Prisca's church was full of life after all! How perfect, I thought. The church wasn't a museum. It was still renewing itself, generating faith. It was different, but the same. It was evolving, but still holy.

I had come to realize that the unity of the church is important. Change takes time and discernment. If we are discerning, the sheep will hear the sound of the Shepherd's voice. If we going toward holiness together, hearts have to be melted, not corralled.

Time to go home, I thought. Time to write what I had seen and learned about the women of the early church.

When I got back from Rome and walked in the door, my youngest son asked me, "Well, Mom, did you find Junia?" I just smiled and nodded. In the end, I realized that I did not find Junia. She found me.

The Lord says, "When you search for me, you will find me."
JEREMIAH 29:13

DISCUSSION QUESTIONS

Chapter One

- How would you go about looking for a missing apostle?
- Do you have a women's Bible commentary at home? Or a reference book about women in the Bible?
- Has it ever occurred to you to question *why* stories about women of the Bible are not given more prominence in church teaching?
- What surprises you about what you learned about women in the church in this chapter? How does it compare to your experiences?
- Why do you think some women feel invisible in our society?
- What do you think Paul meant for believers to do in their lives when he wrote his letter to the Galatians, in which he said, "There is neither Jew nor Greek, there is neither bond nor free, there is neither male nor female: for ye are all one in Christ Jesus"?

Chapter Two

- Can you name the twelve disciples by memory?
- Can you name the "other" apostles?
- What is the significance for women today of Junia's role as a preacher and teacher?

- How are women serving as leaders in *your* church?
- Who do you know around you who have been "messengers" for Christianity today?
- Would they say the same thing about you?

Chapter Three

- Learning without a goal to teach, says Kathryn Riss, can result in lesser achievement. She contends the best students are future teachers because the best way to learn something well is to take responsibility for teaching it to others. Can you take what you have learned about Christianity and put it into your own words?
- What kinds of messages do you communicate about *your* faith to your children, your friends, and your coworkers?
- Remember, you can deliver a message in hundreds of ways. One of the easiest and most effective ways is simply to respond to someone encountering difficulties that you will pray for them. You'll find it rare that anyone asks you not to do that.
- What does the story of Mary Magdalene make you curious about in the story of women in the early church?

Chapter Four

- If women like Thecla could be accepted as "equal-to-the-apostles" in the early centuries of the church, why not in this century? What reasons are given that women are not considered equal to those who preach and teach?
- What do you think it means to say God calls for his people to be a prophetic voice?
- How do you go in search of the God who is seeking us? Would you leave your comfort zone to do so? As Carolyn Osiek says in *Families in the New Testament World,* "hearing God's will demands interrupting normal activity and living differently." What does that say to you?
- Joan Anderson, author of *A Year by the Sea,* says, "The habit of deference can grow like a cancer on the soul of a woman until the pattern of her

future is out of her hands." What do you think she means? Do you think women are deferential by nature or by habit? Are church women more or less deferential than women in general?

- Why do we feel uncomfortable about people who ask nettlesome questions?
- Contrast and compare the words of Paul in 1 Timothy 5:14 and Titus 2:5. What did Paul mean when he encouraged women to "keep house" and become "workers at home?" How does this admonition to "stay at home" reconcile with the virtuous woman depicted in Proverbs 31:10–31?
- Thecla was much admired by women of the day. Do we show similar regard for women of faith in our culture today? Or do women who are notorious get more of the spotlight? What can be done about it?

Chapter Five

- Early Christians risked their jobs, their safety, their lives, to speak up about their faith. Do you think today's church women are as willing to speak up? Have you ever shied away from saying what you really think for fear of making waves?
- Do women of the church question the hierarchal status quo? If not, why not?
- Does Jesus explicitly say at any time that women are inferior to men or that the spiritual gifts and callings are conferred only upon men?
- Have you ever had a study group meet in your home? What gives you a sense of community and connectedness? The anchor was a popular symbol in the early church. What does that mean to you today?
- If the story of your life were examined years from now, what would readers say about the importance of your faith?

Chapter Six

- When was the last time you read through the book of Romans? Do you have a favorite verse? Are there passages you can recall by memory?
- Imagine how Paul's Epistle was received by the earliest members of the church in Rome, perhaps at night after a communal meal as testimony

was shared by the light of oil lamps. When you imagine the scene, what passages stand out for you? Why?

- The concept of receiving grace from God, which often comes before we even know we need it and comes whether we "deserve" it or not, was a life-changing concept for many early Christians. Have there been moments in your life in which you realized God's grace has been with you, whether you realized it at the time or not?
- Why do you think women of the early church were especially drawn to it?
- If you had to give an accounting of your life to God, as Paul says in Romans 14, what would the balance sheet say?

Chapter Seven

- Why do you think the roles of women like Mary of Magdala and Junia have been discounted by some church authorities?
- Do you think the medieval church's negative views about women have influenced cultural attitudes about women today?
- How can lingering biases against women be addressed in a constructive way?
- Some theologians believe that the roles of men and women in the church are "complementarian"—that they have different roles within the home and church but that those roles are of equal dignity and worth. Others say the church should be "egalitarian"—affirming for women all the same opportunities to serve God as men, including pastoral oversight. What do *you* think?
- Many churches today believe that women should not teach or serve in public ministry because women are more easily deceived by false teaching than men. What assumptions lie behind this? What are your observations?
- Some Christians have taught that Eve was more guilty than Adam when they sinned in the Garden of Eden. What do you think?
- List some of the effects that the curse of sin, mentioned in Genesis 3:16, has had on women. How did the coming of Christ reverse this curse?

Did Christ bring a "new covenant?" What did it mean to say Mary was the "the new Eve"?

- Is the ideal marriage based on a model of partnership or patriarchy? Why?
- Explain how you interpret the apostle Paul's words to Ephesians 5:22: "Wives submit to your husbands."
- The first disciples sought to live out the attitudes and character they had observed in Jesus' own life. What do you think that means to "disciples" today?

Chapter Eight

- How should Christians today consider the human errors that occurred in translations?
- Which translation of the Bible do you use? Why?
- Have you ever compared the wording of verses in two or three different Bibles?
- What does it mean to you to say the Bible is the "inspired word of God" as opposed to the "inerrant word of God"?
- What is your interpretation of 1 Timothy 2:15? Do you think it is contrary to the heart of the gospel to suggest that women must have children to be saved? What does Paul say in Romans about how we are saved?
- God described Eve as a helper for Adam. What do you think that means in light of the fact that the same Hebrew word for "helper" is used to describe God?
- Do you feel comfortable asking questions about the details of your faith?
- What role does asking questions play in faith? How are questions and doubt important to exercising free will?

Chapter Nine

- How do you think Christian women today should view the lives of the saints?
- Is there any artwork in your church that celebrates the role of early Christian women like Phoebe, Prisca, Mary, Mary Magdalene, Junia, Lydia?

- Are you in a church class that might sponsor such artwork? Who would you choose to spotlight? Why?
- Many of the early Christian women who were martyrs for their faith were praised for their bravery and constancy. Are there ways in which modern women can be brave in modeling their faith?
- In *Equal to Serve,* Gretchen Gaebelein Hull describes the "secular feminist" as someone who wants her rights and wants to be able to compete on an equal basis with men. She says the "Biblical feminist" is someone who wants to be free to be the person that God created her to be and to be able to follow Christ as he calls her. Which description applies to the "saints" of the church?

Chapter Ten

- What we think as mature adults is often an outgrowth of everything we have learned over the years. Have you been willing to reexamine the ideas that you held in the past?
- In the Greco-Roman world, authors based authority in patriarchal society on alleged intellectual and physical distinctions, so that slaves and women were considered weaker. If that distinction is no longer valid for slaves, should it be valid for women?
- What qualities could you exhibit that would be worthy of the early women of faith?
- Could you initiate a Bible study for or about women? What would you focus on?
- In Acts 18:24–28 we read that Prisca and Aquila took the skilled preacher Apollos aside to teach him more accurately the way of God. Was Apollos spiritually emasculated by submitting to Prisca's correction? Or was his ministry strengthened?
- Have your ever talked with your minister about the need to include more stories about women of faith in the curriculum for youngsters?
- How can you carry on Junia's work? In what ways can you be as brave as Junia?

- How can we find reconciliation for male-female roles in the church? Is it possible for women to assume more equal standing in the church without men feeling overthrown?
- What does it mean to say, "We are the Bibles the world is reading, we are the creeds the world is needing, we are the sermons the word is heeding?"

NOTES

Chapter One

1. Telling sidelights can be found in the footnotes at the bottom of the page. The *New Interpreter's Bible* archly states in its footnote on Romans 16:7, "The KVJ has 'Junia,' though until recently most other versions read 'Junias,' the masc. form. . . . See R. S. Cervin, 'A Note Regarding the Name "Junia(s)" in Romans 16:7,' . . . demonstrating that the name is certainly fem., despite the desperate attempts of many earlier lexicographers, some MSS, and some translations to this day, to suggest otherwise.

2. John Thorley, "Junia, a Woman Apostle," *Novum Testamentum,* 38.01, pp. 18–29.

3. According to Francesco Gioia, the pontifical administrator of the Patriarchal Basilica of St. Paul in Rome, Tarsus was an important cultural and trading center at the time of Jesus' emergence. Many Jews, including Paul's parents, had settled there. Paul was proud of his Tarsus roots and stated to Roman military authorities, "I am a Jew and a citizen of the well-known city of Tarsus in Cilicia" (Acts 21:39). He returned to his native city, having been forced to

leave Jerusalem because of a conspiracy against him by the Hellenistic Jews (Acts 9:30). He remained in Tarsus for almost four years, until Barnabas came in search of his help in evangelizing Antioch of Syria (Acts 11:25), after which there is no further mention of Paul's having returned to Tarsus. Since he greets Junia and Andronicus with familiarity in Romans 16, it is possible he knew them from years past in Tarsus or from the period when he returned to Tarsus before joining Barnabas. See Francesco Gioa, *Paul of Tarsus* (Vatican City: Liberia Editrice Vaticana, 2002), p. 7.

Tarsus was a city with much history. Alexander the Great resided in Tarsus for a time, and it was there that Antony met Cleopatra. It was a city renowned for its learning, in certain ways comparable to Athens and Alexandria. It was also a center of tentmaking, perhaps where Paul learned the vocation he later shared with Prisca and Aquila (http://www.mustardseed.net).

4. Leon Morris, *Romans* (Grand Rapids, Mich.: Eerdmans, 1988).
5. Here is a more complete list of early theologians who acknowledged a female apostle in Romans 16:7:

    • *Origen of Alexandria* (c. 185–253), who is considered one of the greatest of all Christian scholars. His learning and his works were encyclopedic. He is reputed to have written six thousand books. He accepted Junia as a female apostle.

    • *Jerome* (340–419) was the translator of the Vulgate—the Latin translation of the Bible that was the standard Bible for Western Christendom for many years. Jerome based his translation of the Old Testament on the oldest Hebrew texts available and the New Testament on the oldest Greek texts available. He identifies the apostle as "Julia," but it is a woman's name.

    • *Hatto of Vercelli* (924–961) was the Bishop of Vercelli and was well versed in Greek and legal history. He wrote *Capitulare,* a series of instructions for the clergy, as well as a lengthy commentary on the Pauline epistles and eighteen sermons. He was considered a foe of superstition and a voice for education. He is in agreement that Junia was a female apostle.

- *Theophylact* (c. 1050–1108) became a deacon at Constantinople, attained a high reputation as a scholar, and became the tutor of Constantine VII, for whom he wrote *The Education of Princes.* He later became Archbishop of Achrida in Bulgaria. His commentaries on the Pauline epistles are esteemed for "appositeness, sobriety, accuracy and judiciousness." He cites Junia as a female apostle.

- *Peter Abelard* (1079–1142) may be best known today for his ill-starred romance with his pupil Heloise, but during the twelfth century, he was renowned as a French philosopher and theologian. He is considered the founder of the University of Paris and wrote extensively on Paul's works, naming Junia as a female apostle.

- *John Chrysostom* (344 or 354–407), also known as John of Antioch, was a notable Christian bishop and preacher during the fourth century in Europe. He is famous for his eloquence and his denunciation of the abuse of authority by the church at the time. The Eastern Orthodox Church and the Roman Catholic Church both honor him as a saint. He generously praises a female Junia as an apostle.

  Other patristic exegetes (experts in critical interpretation of the Bible) who understood the second person mentioned in Romans 16:7 to be a woman included Ambrosiaster (c. 339–397), Theodoret of Cyrrhus (c. 393–458), Primasius (sixth century), John Damascene (c. 675–749), Haymo (d. 1244), Oecumenius (sixth century), Lanfranc of Bec (c. 1005–1089), Bruno the Carthusian (c. 1032–1101), and Peter Lombard (c. 1100–1160).

6. John Chrysostom, in J. P. Migne, *Patrologica Graeca,* Vol. 60 (Paris, 1862), cols. 669–670.

7. Thorley, "Junia," p. 28.

8. Migne, *Patrologica Graeca,* Vol. 51, cols. 668ff.

9. Daniel Wallace, *Junia Among the Apostles: The Double Identification Problem in Romans 16:7* (http://www.bible.org).

10. C.E.B. Cranfield, *The Epistle to the Romans,* Vol. 2, pp. 788–789; see also Helmut Koester, "St. Paul: His Mission to the Greek Cities and His Competitors," address delivered Sept. 13, 1997, at the Foundation for Biblical Research, Charlestown, N.H.

11. Karen Jo Torjesen, *When Women Were Priests: Women's Leadership in the Early Church and the Scandal of Their Subordination in the Rise of Christianity* (San Francisco: HarperSanFrancisco, 1995), p. 10.

12. Interviews with Michael White, Karen Jo Torjesen, and Carolyn Osiek.

13. Robert Banks, *Paul's Idea of Community* (Sydney: Anzea, 1979), p. 144; Susanne Heine, *Women and Early Christianity* (London: SCM Press, 1985), p. 88.

14. *Roman and Italian Catacombs, Domitilla* (Vatican City: Pontificia Commissione di Archeologica Sacra, 2002), p. 51.

15. Elisabeth Schussler Fiorenza, *In Memory of Her* (New York: Crossroad, 1992), p. 52.

16. Bernadette Brooten, "Junia: Outstanding Among the Apostles" (Romans 16:7), in Leonard Swidler and Arlene Swidler (eds.), *Women Priests: A Catholic Commentary on the Vatican Declaration* (Mahwah, N.J.: Paulist Press, 1977); database search by Nathan Wood, Perkins School of Theology, Southern Methodist University.

Chapter Two

1. The Twelve Disciples are named in Matthew (10:1–4), Mark (3:13–19), Luke (6:12–16), and Acts 1:13:

   Simon, a fisherman called Peter (Greek, *petros, petra*) by Jesus, also known as Simon bar Johan and Simon bar Jochanan; earlier called Cephas in Aramaic by Paul

James, a fisherman

John, a fisherman, sons of Zebedee, called Jesus Boanerges
in Aramaic

Andrew, a fisherman, brother of Peter and disciple of John the
Baptist

Philip, from Bethsaida of Galilee

Bartholomew, from Cana

Matthew, tax collector

Thomas, from Galilee

James, "the younger"

Thaddeus, also known as Jude or Judas

Simon, the Zealot

Judas Iscariot, the betrayer

However, there are discrepancies in the names. The names of the
Twelve are listed with some differences. The lists agree on eleven
names: Peter (Simon Peter), Andrew, James, John, Philip,
Bartholomew, Thomas, Matthew, James the son of Alphaeus,
Simon, and Judas Iscariot. But the gospels of Matthew and Mark
list "Thaddeus" as the other disciple, while Luke and Acts of the
Apostles list "Judas, the son of James." Some versions of scripture
name the twelfth disciple as "James, the brother of James," "Leb-
baeus," or "Judas the Zealot." While some point to the multiple
names as proof there were inconsistencies in the lists of the
Twelve Disciples, the answer may be that they are different ways
of referring to the same man.

2. James D. G. Dunn, *Word Biblical Commentary on Romans* (Waco,
    Tex.: Word Books, 1988), pp. 894–895.

3. *Romans* (New York: United Bible Societies, 1988).

4. Craig S. Keener, *Paul, Women, and Wives: Marriage and Women's
    Ministry in the Letters of Paul* (Peabody, Mass.: Hendrickson, 2004),
    pp. 241–242.

5. Bruce W. Winter, *Roman Wives, Roman Widows: The Appearance of New Women and the Pauline Communities* (Grand Rapids, Mich.: Eerdmans, 2003), p. 203. Winter also mentions that Richard Bauckham contends that Junia could have been the same person as Joanna, the wife of Chuza, Herod's steward, in *Gospel Women: Studies in the Named Women in the Gospels* (Grand Rapids, Mich.: Eerdmans, 2002), ch. 5 and pp. 182–186. However, this theory has been little adopted. Not only would it have required a variation in Junia's name, but it would also have required Andronicus, generally presumed to have been Junia's husband, to have had his name changed from Chuza.

6. Ben Witherington III, *Women in the Earliest Churches* (New York: Cambridge University Press, 1988), pp. 115–116.

7. N. T. Wright, *Paul for Everyone: Romans, Part Two* (Louisville, Ky.: Westminster/John Knox Press, 2004), p. 134.

8. Garry Wills, *What Jesus Meant* (New York: Viking, 2006), p. 50.

9. Charles Hodge, *Romans* (Wheaton, Ill.: Crossway Books, 1994), ch. 11; "Romans," *Catholic Encyclopedia* (http://newadvent.org).

10. Ray Schultz, "Romans 16:7: Junia or Junias?" *Expository Times,* Jan. 1987, p. 109.

11. Stanley J. Grenz and Denis Muir Kjesbo, *Women in the Church: A Biblical Theology of Women in Ministry* (Downers Grove, Ill.: Intervarsity Press, 1995), p. 79.

12. Evangelical minister Ken Bowles states on his Web site (http://SpiritualInsightsPage.org) that the case for Andronicus and Junias (male name) as *formal* apostles is not strong. Bowles asserts that the verse probably means that the two were well known to the Twelve Apostles, not that they were apostles themselves. The following versions are cited as examples supporting that view:

"Remember me to Andronicus and Junias, my tribal kinsmen and once my fellow prisoners. They are men held in high esteem

among the apostles, who also were in Christ before I was."
(Amplified Bible)

"They are respected among the apostles." (New Living Translation)

"They have been respected missionaries." (New Life Version)

"They are well known to the apostles." (English Standard Version)

"They are highly respected by the apostles." (Contemporary
English Version)

"The apostles think they are good men." (World Wide English)

Bowles's conclusion is that there were apostles that were like the missionaries of today but who did not have the position, authority, or abilities of the Twelve and of Paul.

13. Michael H. Burer and O. B. Wallace, "Was Junia Really an Apostle? A Reexamination of Rom 16.7," *New Testament Studies,* 2001, *47,* 76–91.

14. Ross Sheppard Kraemer and Mary Rose D'Angelo (eds.), *Women and Christian Origins* (New York: Oxford University Press, 1999), p. 210.

15. John Hunwicke, "Junia: A Woman Apostle?" *New Directions,* Mar. 2001 (http://ourworld.cs.com/francisgardom/MR01JUNI.htm).

16. Joseph Fitzmyer, *Anchor Bible Commentary* (New York: Doubleday, 1993), pp. 736–741.

17. Dennis J. Preato, "Romans 16:7: Resolving the Interpretive Issues" (http://www.cbeinternational.org/new/pdf_files/free_articles/Romans167.pdf).

18. F. F. Bruce, *Romans* (Grand Rapids, Mich.: Eerdmans, 2003), p. 258.

19. John A. Witmer, *The Bible Knowledge Commentary: An Exposition of the Scriptures* (Hiawatha, Iowa: Parsons Technology, 1997).

20. Douglas Moo, *The Epistle to the Romans* (Grand Rapids, Mich.: Eerdmans, 1996), pp. 916–927.

21. Wills, *What Jesus Meant,* p. 79.

22. N. T. Wright, "Women's Service in the Church: The Biblical Basis," paper presented at the symposium "Men, Women and the Church," St. John's College, Durham, England, Sept. 4, 2004.

Chapter Three

1. Marianne Dormann, "Women in the Apostolic Church" (http://mariannedorman.homestead.com/Women.html).

2. Ann Graham Brock, *Mary Magdalene: The First Apostle* (Cambridge, Mass.: Harvard Theological Studies, 2003), pp. 60, 171.

3. Bruce Chilton, *Mary Magdalene: A Biography* (New York: Doubleday, 2005), p. 114.

4. Darrell L. Bock, *Breaking the Da Vinci Code* (Nashville, Tenn.: Nelson, 2004), p. 143.

5. Karen L. King, *The Gospel of Mary of Magdala: Jesus and the First Woman Apostle* (Santa Rosa, Calif.: Polebridge Press, 2003), p. 144.

6. John Rivera, "Scholars Set the Record Straight on Mary Magdalene," *Baltimore Sun,* Apr. 19, 2003; see also "Mary Magdalene and the Da Vinci Code" (http://www.bibletruths.net).

7. The attitude of church leaders like Cyril, Bishop of Alexandria (376–444), toward Mary Magdalene shows how difficult it has been to gain acceptance for women in the ministry of Jesus. Although Cyril was a dedicated theologian, he was hostile to Jews, driving thousands from their synagogues and homes in Alexandria, and was hostile to women. Despite the fact that Alexandria had produced numerous literate women of note, Cyril contended that women were uneducated and not able to understand difficult matters easily. In explaining why Mary Magdalene did not initially recognize Jesus after his Resurrection, Cyril scoffed at women in general, saying that the woman Mary Magdalene, or rather the female sex as a whole, "is slow in comprehension." His attitude is ironic, considering that the most prominent woman of his time, the most celebrated mathematician

and philosopher in Alexandria, was a woman named Hypatia. Hypatia was known for her eloquence, modesty, and beauty. Her career was ended by Christian monks who dragged her from her chariot into a Christian church, stripped her naked, cut her throat, and burned her part by part. According to historian Leonard Swidler, Cyril was involved indirectly if not directly. See Swidler's *Biblical Affirmations of Woman* (Louisville, Ky.: Westminster/John Knox, 1979), pp. 344–345.

8. Michael Baigent, Richard Leigh, and Henry Lincoln, *Holy Blood, Holy Grail* (New York: Dell, 1983); Dan Brown, *The Da Vinci Code* (New York: Doubleday, 2003).

9. "Mary Magdalene," *Catholic Encyclopedia* (http://newadvent.org).

10. "Mary Magdalene in Provence" (http://www.about provence .com); "In Search of the Magdalene, the Black Madonna, and the Lost Goddess" (http://www.magdalenetours.com).

11. Orthodox Church of America (http://www.oca.org). The Orthodox Church came into being after the biggest rift within Christianity. Disputes over doctrine and church governance precipitated a split in 1054 that divided the church into the Western and Eastern branches. England, France, the Holy Roman Empire, Scandinavia, and Western Europe were in the Western camp, which became known as the Roman Catholic Church. Greece, Russia, Slavic lands such as Anatolia, and the Christians in Syria and Egypt made up the Eastern camp, which became known as the Eastern Orthodox Church. This split is often referred to as the Great Schism.

12. "Acta Pilati," *Catholic Encyclopedia* (http://newadvent.org); Johannes Quasten, *Patrology* (Allen, Tex.: Christian Classics, 1983), Vol. 1, pp. 115–116.

13. The Orthodox Church preserves an ancient Greek manuscript that supports the tradition of the Paschal eggs and Mary Magdalene's missionary role. The parchment is kept in the monastery library of St. Athanasius near Thessalonica. On it is a prayer, read on the day of Holy Pascha for the blessing of eggs and cheese:

"Thus have we received from the holy Fathers, who preserved this custom from the very time of the holy Apostles, therefore the holy Equal of the Apostles Mary Magdalene first showed believers the example of this joyful offering."

There is also a murkier tradition related to Mary Magdalene that bears mentioning: the remnants of Christ's heart are said to remain inside an egglike vessel, and this vessel is the basis for the Sacred Heart motif in Catholicism. In some church legends, the Sacred Heart exists as a guarded sacred object or a metaphysical essence that brings spiritual clarity. The "heart" supposedly was passed from hand to hand, and Mary Magdalene is listed among the noteworthy caretakers. I hesitated to include the legend because it veers into the fantastic territory that *The Da Vinci Code* would embrace. But it is typical of the symbolism and legends of those times. The fact that Mary Magdalene was included as a worthy caretaker shows, once again, that many early believers held her in high regard.

14. King, *Gospel of Mary of Magdala;* Brock, *Mary Magdalene;* Chilton, *Mary Magdalene.*
15. Ibid.

Chapter Four

1. Stephen J. Davis, *Cult of St. Thecla: A Tradition of Women's Piety in Late Antiquity* (New York: Oxford University Press, 2001), pp. 5–6.
2. Martha Ann Kirk, *Women of Bible Lands: A Pilgrimage to Compassion and Wisdom* (Collegeville, Minn.: Liturgical Press, 2004), pp. 318–323.
3. Nancy Carter, "The Acts of Thecla: A Pauline Tradition Linked to Women" (http://gmgm-umc.org).
4. "St. Thecla," *Catholic Encyclopedia* (http://newadvent.org); Davis, *Cult of St. Thecla.*
5. Tera Kirk, "Honor in the Ancient World" (http://www.geocities.com/HotSprings/Spa/7262/honor.html); Halvor Oxnes, *The*

Social Sciences and New Testament Interpretation (http://www .hendrickson.com); Margaret Y. MacDonald, *Early Christian Women and Pagan Opinion* (New York: Cambridge University Press, 1996), pp. 27–30.

6. "The Acts of Paul and Thecla" (http://gbgm-umc.org/umw); Bart D. Ehrman, *After the New Testament: A Reader in Early Christianity* (New York: Oxford University Press, 1999), pp. 278–284.

7. "Acts of Paul and Thecla: The Story of Thecla" (http://en .wikipedia.org).

8. Ibid.; Carter, "Acts of Thecla"; Antiochian Orthodox Christian Archdiocese of North America, "Thekla, Equal to the Apostles and First Martyr" (http://www.antiochian.org).

9. L. Michael White, *From Jesus to Christianity* (San Francisco: Harper-SanFrancisco, 2004), p. 401.

10. John Dominic Crossan and Jonathan L. Reed, *In Search of Paul: How Jesus' Apostle Opposed Rome's Empire with God's Kingdom* (San Francisco: HarperSanFrancisco, 2004), pp. xii–xiv.

11. Davis, *Cult of St. Thecla,* pp. 7–8.

12. Bart D. Ehrman, *Lost Christianities: The Battles for Scripture and the Faiths We Never Knew* (New York: Oxford University Press, 2003), p. 39.

13. Elizabeth Clark, *From Jesus to Christ,* 1998. PBS Home Video.

14. Sarah Barnett, "Death and the Maidens" (http://www .sydneyanglicans.net/culture/thinking/369a).

15. Anne Jensen, *God's Self-Confident Daughters: Early Christianity and the Liberation of Women* (Louisville, Ky.: Westminster/John Knox, 1996), pp. 87–89.

16. "Saint Irene" (http://en.wikipedia.org).

17. "Ammas and Abbas" (http://www.etss.edu); Eileen McGuckin, *Icon of Amma Syncletica* text; Kirk, *Women of Bible Lands,* pp. 219–222.

Chapter Five

1. Antonio d'Ambrosio, *Women and Beauty in Pompeii* (Los Angeles: Getty Trust Publications, 2001), p. 7.

2. Barbara F. McManus, "Roman Clothing: Women" (http://www.vtoma.org/bmcmanus/clothing2.html).

3. Winter, *Roman Wives, Roman Widows.*

4. Mark Simpson, "When Is a Kiss Holy?" *Christian Cambridge,* Jan. 18, 2005 (http://www.christiancambridge.uklinux.net).

5. Paul Veyne (ed.), *A History of Private Life from Pagan Rome to Byzantium* (Cambridge, Mass.: Belknap Press, 1987), pp. 39–40; Winter, *Roman Wives, Roman Widows,* p. 81.

6. Charles Sturt University, "Roman Society in the Time of Cicero" (http://hsc.csu.edu.au/ancient_history/societies/rome/2533/Cicero.html).

7. Marilyn Yalom, *A History of the Wife* (New York: HarperCollins, 2001), p. xvii.

8. Witherington, *Women in the Ministry of Jesus;* Yalom, *History of the Wife;* Yalom, *History of the Wife.*

9. Charles Sturt University, "Roman Society in the Time of Cicero."

10. Rodney Stark, *The Rise of Christianity* (New York: HarperCollins, 1997), pp. 118–121.

11. Ibid, pp. 119–121.

12. Veyne, *History of Private Life.*

13. Jerome Carcopino, *Daily Life in Ancient Rome* (New York: Penguin, 1941), pp. 110–111; Yalom, *History of the Wife.*

14. Winter, *Roman Wives, Roman Widows,* pp. 40–47.

15. Corpus of Latin Inscriptions, CIL 6.15346.

16. Winter, *Roman Wives, Roman Widows,* p. 161.

17. Witherington, *Women in the Earliest Churches,* p. 18; Carolyn Osiek, Margaret Y. MacDonald, and Janet H. Tuloch, *A Woman's Place* (Minneapolis, Minn.: Augsburg Fortress, 2006), pp. 82–90.

18. Cullen Murphy, "Is the Bible Bad News for Women?" *Wilson Quarterly,* Summer 1998, p. 22.

19. *Guide to the Mamertine Prison* (Rome: Futura Edizioni, 2004).

20. Lionel Casson, *The Ancient Mariners: Seafarers and Sea Fighters of the Mediterranean in Ancient Times* (Princeton, N.J.: Princeton University Press, 1991); Lionel Casson, *Travel in the Ancient World* (Baltimore: Johns Hopkins University Press, 1994).

21. *Complete Guide to the Bible* (Pleasantville, N.Y.: Reader's Digest, 1998), p. 397.

22. Loren Cunningham and David Joel Hamilton. *Why Not Women? A Fresh Look at Scripture on Women in Missions, Ministry, and Leadership* (Seattle, Wash.: YWAM Publishing, 2000), p. 91.

23. Gillian Clark, *Christianity and Roman Society* (New York: Cambridge University Press, 2004); Gillian Clark, *Women in Late Antiquity: Pagan and Christian Lifestyles* (New York: Oxford University Press, 1993); Gillian Clark, *Roman Women* (ser. 2), 1981; *28,* pp. 193–212.

24. Winter, *Roman Wives, Roman Widows,* p. 78; Keener, *Paul, Women and Wives,* pp. 22–30.

25. Wayne Meeks; *The First Urban Christians: The Social World of the Apostle Paul* (New Haven, Conn.: Yale University Press, 1983), p. 31.

26. Elizabeth Hamid, "Origins of Namelessness in Women," 2003 (http://www.slis.ualberta.ca/feminism/betsy/origens.htm).

27. Cunningham and Hamilton, *Why Not Women?* pp. 87–89.

28. MacDonald, *Early Christian Women,* p. 244.

29. Winter, *Roman Wives, Roman Widows*, p. 202; Richard Bauckham, "Joanna the Apostle," in *Gospel Women,* ch. 5 and pp. 182–186. Bauckham has argued that the Junia of Romans 16:7 is to be identified with Joanna, the wife of Chuza, Herod's steward mentioned in Luke 8:3. That would make her a woman of status. Part of Bauckham's basis for that contention is the practice in Jewish

circles of adopting Latin names that sounded similar to their Semitic names and the fact that Joanna was a witness to the Resurrection.

30. Rodney Stark, "From Jesus to Christ," *Newsweek,* March 28, 2005, p. 48.29.

31. See the following Web sites:

http://www.crystalinks.com/romegods.html

http://www.novaroma.org/religio_romana/deities.html

http://ancienthistory.about.com/library/bl/bl_gregory_gods.htm

http://www.geocities.com/Athens/Troy/1203

http://www.roman-empire.net/children/gods.html

http://www.factmonster.com/ipka/A0197622.html

http://www.loggia.com/myth/gods1.html

http://www.inamma.virtualslave.net/roman.html

http://www.famromo.wiccan.net/kidgods.htm

See also "Gods and Goddesses of Children and Childhood," *Encyclopedia Mythica* (http://www.pantheon.org).

Other pertinent goddesses worshiped by women of Rome:

- *Ceres* was the Roman goddess of agriculture, grain, and the love a mother bears for her child. Ceres was the only one of the gods who was involved on a day-to-day basis in the lives of the common folk. While others occasionally "dabbled" in human affairs when it suited their personal interests, or came to the aid of "special" mortals they favored, the goddess Ceres was considered a nurturer of humankind.

- *Liberta* was the Roman goddess of freedom. Originally a goddess of personal freedom, she later became the goddess of the Roman commonwealth. Liberta was depicted on many Roman coins as a female figure with a pileus, a felt cap, worn by slaves when they were set free; a wreath of laurels; and a spear.

- *Fortuna*, the Roman personification of good fortune, originally was a goddess of blessing and fertility and in that capacity, mothers especially worshiped her.
- *Diana* was later known as goddess of the hunt but originally as the Roman goddess of nature, fertility, and childbirth. Like Bona Dea, she was worshiped mainly by women as the giver of fertility and easy births. She was given a temple in the working-class area on the Aventine Hill where she was worshiped by the lower-class (plebeians) and the slaves, of whom she was the patroness. Slaves could also ask for asylum in her temple.
- *Juno* was queen of the gods. She was also honored as Juno Lucina, protectress of childbirth, in which the child is brought into light; and as Juno Sospita, who protects labor and delivery of children. Women who worshiped Juno Lucina had to untie knots and unbraid their hair lest these entanglements symbolically block delivery.
- *Venus* was the Roman goddess of love and beauty and was originally a vegetation goddess and patroness of gardens and vineyards. Both Julius Caesar and the Emperor Augustus named her the ancestor of their (Julian) family: the "gens Julia." Caesar also introduced the cult of Venus Genetrix, the goddess of motherhood and marriage, and built a temple for her in 46 B.C.E.
- *Vesta* was one of the most popular and mysterious goddesses—goddess of the hearth. She was at first worshiped only in Roman homes, then her adoration evolved to a state cult. The Vestal Virgins maintained the fire in her temple until 394, even after Christianity was made the official religion of the Roman Empire. The sanctum of the Vesta temple, which was kept closed the entire year, was opened on the first day of her festival for women who came to bring offerings barefooted. Vesta's sacred animal is the ass, whose braying supposedly kept the lascivious Priapus away. Vesta is portrayed as a stern woman, wearing a long dress and with her head covered.

- *Isis* was an imported Egyptian goddess highly favored by women. Isis was quoted as saying, "I am the one called the Deity by women." Isis, however, should not be considered a "women's libber." She was a patron of marriage and a defender of chastity.
- *Cybele* was originally a Phrygian goddess who became highly popular through the Roman Empire as Magna Mater, "Mother of the Gods." She was worshiped in wild, emotional, bloody, orgiastic ceremonies, and castrated priests tended to her shrine. As the goddess of nature and fertility, she had a special appeal for women who needed to produce an heir to keep their spouse.
- Women also made special sacrifices to fertility gods like *Matinus Matunus* and to goddesses of childbirth, such as *Carmentalia.* They honored minor gods like *Fabulinus,* who supposedly taught children to utter their first words, and goddesses like *Abeona,* who protected children when they left the house for the first time, and *Edusa,* who helped small children learn to eat. *Paventia* protected children from sudden fright. Parents who became childless invoked *Orbona,* begging her to grant them children again.

32. Meeks, *The First Urban Christians: The Social World of the Apostle Paul,* pp. 29–30; Peter Lampe, *From Paul to Valentinus* (Minneapolis, Minn.: Augsburg Fortress, 2003), pp. xiii–xv.

33. Peter Connolly, *Pompeii* (New York: Oxford University Press, 1990).

34. The ancient Romans ate a nutritious diet: fish from the Mediterranean was abundant, little beef because cattle were needed as laboring animals, fresh vegetables from nearby gardens, cheese, fruit, fresh lemons (which doubled as a moth repellant for woolen garments), olives, capers, honey, whole-grain bread, and of course, wine. Despite our cinematic image of Roman emperors devouring everything but the drapes at decadent banquets, the

staple meal for most Romans was cereal grains. The Romans woke early to take advantage of the daylight and ate a hearty breakfast of last night's leftovers or bread and cheese and fruit. They ate their breakfast with their hands while standing up. Lunch was a snack, sometimes taken during a break from work at hot-food stands called *thermopolia*. Examples have survived in Pompeii and Herculaneum of walk-up "snack bars" that had marble counter-tops with large circular holes to hold food pots.

Dinner was the main meal and might include grains, soups, vegetables, milk, cheese, olives, fruit, and, occasionally, lard.

35. Jerome Carcopino, *Daily Life in Ancient Rome* (New York: Penguin, 1991); Luciana Jacobelli Cantarella, *A Day in Pompeii* (Rome: Gruppo Mondadori Electa, 2003).

36. Connolly, *Pompeii.*

37. "Slave and the Law" (http://ccat.sas.upenn.edu/~thurley legal.html); "Roman Civilization" (http://abacus.batres.edu/ !mimber/Reiv/slavery.htm); John Madden, "Slavery in the Roman Empire: Numbers and Origins" (http://www.ucd/ie/ classics/classicsinfo/96/Madden96.html).

38. MacDonald, *Early Christian Women,* pp. 110–113.

39. Meeks, *First Urban Christians,* pp. 142–150; "Justin Martyr" (http://ChistianityToday.com).

40. Karen Armstrong, *A History of God* (New York: Knopf, 1993), p. 105.

41. Clark, *From Jesus to Christ.*

42. Ibid.

43. Swidler, *Biblical Affirmations of Woman,* p. 353.

44. Frank Daniels, "The Role of Women in the Church" (http://www.scs.unr.edu/-fdaniels/rel/women.htm); Marianne Dorman, "Women in the Apostolic Church (http://marianne dorman.homestead.com/women).

45. Clark, *From Jesus to Christ.*

Chapter Six

1. Garry Wills, *Augustine* (New York: Penguin, 1999); "Augustine,"
    Catholic Encyclopedia (http://newadvent.org); Peter Brown,
    Augustine of Hippo (Berkeley: University of California Press,
    1967). Scholars like Garry Wills contend that Augustine's sup-
    posed "sins" may have been less lascivious than some interpreters
    have suggested and more a matter of a sensitized conscience.

2. Maureen McKew, "Augustine on Women: Misogynist, Apologist,
    or Simply Mixed Bag?" (http://Villanova.edu); Edmund Hill, "St.
    Augustine: A Male Chauvinist?" (http://www.its.caltech.edu).

3. Clark, *From Jesus to Christ*.

4. "Now I am deeply joyful not only because you have been deliv-
    ered from sickness, but even more because you are bearing adver-
    sities with such fortitude, calling them trifles—a characteristic of
    a soul filled with power and abounding in the rich fruits of
    courage. You are not only enduring misfortune with fortitude, but
    are making light of it in a seemingly effortless way, rejoicing and
    triumphing over it—this is proof of the greatest wisdom." John
    Chrysostom, *Homilies and Letters* (http://www.chrysostom
    .org/writings.html); St. John Chrysostom, *On Modesty*
    (http://www.catholicmodesty.com).

5. J. Lee Grady, *10 Lies the Church Tells Women: How the Bible Has Been
    Misused to Keep Women in Spiritual Bondage* (Lake Mary, Fla.:
    Charisma House, 2000), p. 30.

6. "Martin Luther," *Catholic Encyclopedia* (http://newadvent.org).
    Helena, the mother of Emperor Constantine, brought the marble
    staircase to Rome in the fourth century in the belief it was the
    stairway from Pilate's palace, which Jesus ascended to be
    condemned to death. For centuries since then, penitents have
    climbed the steps on their knees, step after painful step, as a way
    of pledging their faith. Alister McGrath, *In the Beginning* (New
    York: Anchor/Doubleday, 2001), p. 41.

7. Andrew Thornton, preface to the *Letter of St. Paul to the Romans,* by Martin Luther (http://www.iclnet.org/pub/resources/text/ wittenberg/german.bible/rom-eng.ltxt).

8. "Katie Luther: Establishing a Pattern for a Christian Family," *Glimpses,* 2004, 76 (http://chi.gospelcom.net/GLIMPSEF/ Glimpses/glmps076.shtml); Ken Curtis and Dan Graves (eds.), *Great Women in Christian History: 37 Women Who Changed the World* (Camp Hill, Pa.: WingSpread, 2005); Irving Wallace, *The Intimate Sex Lives of Famous People* (New York: Simon & Schuster, 1965), p. 281.

9. John Munsey Turner, *John Wesley, the Evangelical Revival and the Rise of Methodism in England* (London: Epworth Press, 2002).

10. Glendora Goodwin, "Susanna Wesley: Mother of Methodism," *Herald Times,* May 11, 2001 (http://www.HeraldTimesOnline .com).

11. General Board of Global Ministries, United Methodist Church, "Women and Wesley's Times" (http://www.gbgm-umc.org).

12. "Grace Murray, Model Leader and John Wesley's True Love" (http://gbgm-umc.org/umw/Wesley/wesleywomen.stm).

13. "Karl Barth," *Boston Collaborative Encyclopedia of Western Theology* (http://www.bostoncollaborativeencyclopedia.com); Karl Barth, *The Epistle to the Romans* (New York: Oxford University Press, 1933).

14. Suzanne Selinger, *Charlotte von Kirschbaum and Karl Barth: A Study in Biography and the History of Theology* (University Park: Pennsylvania State University Press, 1998).

15. Hodge, *Romans,* p. xi.

16. Lareta Haltmann Finger, "Getting Along When We Don't Agree: Using Simulation and Controversy to Help Students and Lay Persons Interpret Romans," in Shiela E. McGinn (ed.), *Celebrating Romans: A Template for Pauline Theology* (Grand Rapids, Mich.: Eerdmans, 2004).

17. Who was with Junia in the early Christian community in Rome?
    Judging from the list in Romans 16, the group included the
    following people:

    • Epaenetus, who apparently was Paul's first convert in Athens
      and must have been close to Paul, since *beloved* is not a term he
      uses carelessly.

    • Several married couples, Prisca and Aquila, who had worked
      with Paul in Corinth and "risked their necks" for him; Junia and
      Andronicus, who had been in prison with Paul and were con-
      sidered noteworthy among the apostles.

    • Other women who had helped him—Persis, Mary, and the
      mother of Rufus. Some scholars speculate that the greeting to
      "Mary who labored much for us" could have referred to the
      mother of Jesus, Mary Magdalene, Mary of Bethany, Mary the
      mother of John Mark (in whose house the disciples met), or
      Mary the wife of Cleopas (who witnessed the crucifixion).

    • Philologus and Julia, who may have been brother and sister or
      husband and wife. Her name suggests she may have had some
      connection to the imperial Julian household, perhaps as a slave
      to the emperor.

    • Nereus and his sister, who may be the same Nereus named as
      the servant of a distinguished Roman who was executed in 95
      C.E. for being a Christian and his wife banned. It is possible that
      Nereus brought the gospel to the Roman couple. According to
      tradition, he later was beheaded at Tarracina.

    • Several slaves, including Amplias, Urbanus, and Stachys.

    • Two sisters, Tryphaena and Tryphosa, whose names mean
      "delicate" and "dainty," though they labored to the point of
      exhaustion.

    • Two households of slaves of formerly famous people—
      Narcissus was possibly the well-known freedman who was
      secretary to Emperor Claudius. After Claudius was murdered,

Narcissus was forced to commit suicide by Agrippina. Paul apparently was sending greetings to the household of Narcissus and that of Aristobulus, who was possibly the grandson of Herod the Great.

- One somewhat famous Christian, Rufus, who possibly was the son of Simon of Cyrene, mentioned in Mark 15:21. According to later legends, Rufus became Bishop of Thebes. Paul says Rufus' mother has been like a mother to him too.
- Two well-known Jews—Apelles and Herodion (who may have been related to Herod).
- Numerous Roman men, who may have been slaves: Asyncritus, Phlegon, Hermas, Patrobus, Hermes, Olympas. Pseudo-Hippolytus makes Phlegon one of the seventy disciples and Bishop of Marathon. According to tradition, Hermes also may have been one of the seventy disciples and afterward Bishop of Dalmatia. Irenaeus, Tertullian and Origen agree in attributing to Hermas the work called *The Shepherd,* but it may have been a later work. It was never received into the canon, although it was generally cited with respect. The name Patrobus was connected to at least one member of the emperor's household. By some scholarly counts, as many as twelve of the people saluted by Paul may have been members of the emperor's household staff.

At least twelve of the people named appear to have been personally acquainted with Paul during his previous mission trips and probably lived at some time in the East and traveled between the East and Rome. The list shows that Romans was a letter written to a mix of ordinary people. Many were slaves or former slaves, some were well connected, and some were tradespeople.

18. Sarah Barnett, "Death and the Maidens" (http://www.sydney anglicans.net/culture/thinking/369a).
19. Quoted in Peter Steinfels, "Beliefs," *New York Times,* June 4, 2005.

20. Anna Quindlen, "Separate, Not Equal at All," *Newsweek,* May 2, 2005.

21. "Salvation Army" (http://Spartacus.schoolnet.co.uk/ REsalvation.htm). General Booth was deeply influenced by his wife, Catherine Booth, who believed that women were equal to men and it was only inadequate education and social custom that made them considered as men's intellectual inferiors. She was an inspiring preacher and helped promote the idea of women preachers. The Salvation Army gave women equal responsibility for preaching and welfare work.

Chapter Seven

1. Brooten, "Junia," pp. 141–144.

2. Joseph McCabe, *A Rationalist Encyclopaedia* (1948), quoted in "First Commandment" (http://www.adishakti.org/his_human _adversary/the_first_commandment.htm).

3. John O'Malley, "Excommunicating Politicians," *America, the Catholic Weekly,* Sept. 27, 2004.

4. Dianne D. McDonnell, "Junia, a Woman Apostle" (http://www .churchpfgoddfw.com).

5. "Order of St. Augustine" sec. 5 (http://augnet.org).

6. Joan Chittister, *Heart of Flesh: A Feminist Spirituality for Women and Men* (Grand Rapids, Mich.: Eerdmans, 1998), audio version.

7. Elizabeth Hallan, *Saints* (New York: Simon & Schuster, 1994),p. 57.

8. Aquinas, *Summa Theologica* (New York: Benziger, 1947).

9. Cunningham and Hamilton, *Why Not Women?*

10. Gail Thomas, personal communication, 2005; "Pandora," *Classics Pages* (http://www.users.globalnet.co.uk); "Greek and Roman Mythology: Prometheus and Pandora" (http://www .online-mythlogy.com/prometheus_pandora).

11. Piers Paul Read, *The Templars* (New York: DaCapo Press, 1999); *Columbia Electronic Encyclopedia,* 6th ed. (New York: Columbia University Press, 2005).

12. Antonio Lopez, *The Popes: Boniface VIII* (Rome: Futura Edizioni, 1997); *Columbia Electronic Encyclopedia; Catholic Encylclopedia* (http://newadvent.org); Slaves of the Immaculate Heart of Mary, "Bonifice VIII" (http://catholicism.org).

13. Societas Christiana (http://societaschristiana.com); *Encyclopaedia Britannica* (http://britannica.com); Order of St. Augustine (http://augnet.org).

14. In his legal opinion paving the way for Celestine's historic abdication, *De Remuntiatione Papae,* Giles essentially contended that although papal power was of divine origin, the power is conferred on an individual by a human act, the election by the College of Cardinals. That doesn't mean the cardinals then could depose or remove the pope, because upon becoming pope, the pope is above earthly law and answerable only to God. However, the pope still could depose himself, or abdicate, as Celestine did. It was an artful argument in that it laid the groundwork for Celestine's abdication without establishing any grounds for the removal of a pope, which could have jeopardized Boniface and subsequent popes. See "Giles of Rome," *Stanford Encyclopedia of Philosophy* (http://www.scop.leeds.ac.uk/archives/win2001/entries/giles).

15. Antonio Lopez, *The Popes: Clement V* (Rome: Futura Edizioni, 1997), pp. 68–70.

16. Stephen Dafoe, "Who Were the Knights Templar?" (http://www/templarhistory.com/who.html).

17. "Giles of Rome" (http://augnet.org).

18. "Giles of Rome," *Stanford Encyclopedia of Philosophy* (http://www.scop.leeds.ac.uk/archives/win2001/entries/giles).

19. "Parshat Tazria," Torat Emet (http://www.aishdas.org/toratemet/en_tazria.html).

20. "Edgido Colonna," *Catholic Encyclopedia* (http://newadvent.org).

21. Karen Armstrong, *A History of God* (Knopf, 1999), p. 77.

22. Pliny the Elder, *Natural History,* bk. 28, ch. 23, 78–80.

23. Teva Regule, "An Interview with Kyriaki Karidoyanes Fitzgerald," *St. Nina Quarterly,* 1999, *3*(2) (http://www.stnina.org/journal/art/3.2.6).

24. Kirk, *Women of Bible Lands,* pp. 162–163.

25. Alison Weir, *Eleanor of Aquitaine: A Life* (New York: Ballantine, 2001); Lisa M. Bitel, *Women in Early Medieval Europe, 400–1100* (New York: Cambridge University Press, 2002); Emilie Amt, *Women's Lives in Medieval Europe: A Sourcebook* (New York: Routledge, 1993); Joseph Gies and Frances Gies, *Marriage and Family in the Middle Ages* (New York: HarperPerennial, 1987).

26. Marygrace Peters, "The Beguines: Feminine Piety Derailed" (http://www.spiritualitytoday.org); Elizabeth T. Knuth, "The Beguines" (http://www.users.csbsju.edu/~eknuth/xpxx/beguines./html); "The Beguines" (http://www2.Kenyon.edu/Projects/Margin/beguines.htm); Abby Stoner, "Sisters Between: Gender and the Medieval Beguines" (http://userwww.sfsu.edu/~epf/1995/beguine.html).

Chapter Eight

1. Alister McGrath, *In the Beginning* (New York: Anchor/Doubleday, 2001), pp. 56–58.

2. "Ad Fontes" (http://demo.lutherproductions.com/historytotor/basic.reformation.genknow.ad_fontes.htm).

3. McGrath, *In the Beginning,* p. 55.

4. "John Wycliffe," *Catholic Encyclopedia* (http://newadvent.org); "John Wycliffe," Island of Freedom (http://island-of-freedom.com); "John Wycliffe," *Encyclopaedia Britannica* (http://britannica.com).

5. Paul Choo, "History of Believing Christianity V: The Lollards, Wycliffe's Disciples" (http://www.apibs.org/topical/hist5.htm); Ex Libris, "English Dissenters: Lollards or Wycliffites" (http://www.exlibris.org/nonconform/engdis/lollards.html).

6. Johan Huizinga, *Erasmus and the Age of Reformation* (New York: Harper Torchbooks, 1957; originally published 1924); Keith Stump, "How We Got the Bible in English," Worldwide Church of God, 1994 (http://wcg.org/lit/bible/english.htm); "Desiderius Erasmus," *Catholic Encyclopedia* (http://newadvent.org).

7. *The Textus Receptus* (http://www.skypoint.com).

8. John Cereghin, *In Defense of Erasmus* (http://watch.pair.com/ · erasmus.html).

9. Eldon Epp, *Junia, the First Woman Apostle* (Minneapolis, Minn.: Augsburg Fortress, 2005), p. 28.

10. Adam Nicolson, *God's Secretaries: The Making of the King James Bible* (New York: HarperPerennial, 2003), p. 222.

11. British Library, *William Tyndale's New Testament* (http://www.bl.uk/onlinegallery).

12. McGrath, *In the Beginning,* p. 88.

13. Brooten, "Junia," p. 142.

14. Epp, *Junia,* p. 38.

15. Ken Collins, "What Is a Sacrament?" (http://www.kencollins.com).

16. Thorley, "Junia," pp. 18–29.

17. Epp, *Junia,* pp. 62, 63, 66; database research by Nathan Wood.

18. Epp, *Junia,* pp. 53–54; Bruce M. Metzger, *A Textual Commentary on the Greek New Testament,* 2nd ed. (Stuttgart, Germany: Deutsche Bibelgesellschaft and United Bible Societies, 1994), p. 475.

19. Paul N. Tobin, "New Testament Manuscripts and Text Types," 2000 (http://www.geocities.com/paulntobin/ntmanuscript.html).

20. Research by Nathan Wood.

21. Sarah Heaner Lancaster, *Women and the Authority of Scripture* (Philadelphia: Trinity Press, 2002).

22. Albert C. Outler, *John Wesley* (New York: Oxford University Press, 1964).

23. Jon Temple Bristow, *What Paul Really Said About Women* (New York: HarperCollins, 1991), p. 92.

24. Cunningham and Hamilton, *Why Not Women?* pp. 95–97.
25. Peachtree Editorial and Proofreading Service.

Chapter Nine

1. *Roma Sacra,* "The Vatican Necropolis," *Fabrica of St. Peter's,* pp. 2–6.
2. Ibid., p. 25.
3. Ibid., p. 61.
4. "St. Peter, Prince of the Apostles," *Catholic Encyclopedia* (http://newadvent.org).
5. *Roma Sacra,* p. 31.
6. Vincenzo Fiocci Nicolai, Fabrizio Bisconti, and Danilo Mazzoleni, *The Christian Catacombs of Rome* (Regensburg, Germany: Schnell & Steiner, 2006).
7. Umberto Fascola, "Living in Eternity," *Christian Catacombs of Rome* (http://www.catacombe.roma.it/enrcjercje/ricera7.html).
8. Ibid.
9. "Nero Persecutes the Christians, A.D. 64" (http://www.eyewitness tohistory.comp/christians.htm).
10. There is a minority view about the fate of the alleged male apostle "Junias." Scholars John Piper and Wayne Gruden state that Epiphanius (315–403) wrote an index of disciples, including "Iounias, of whom Paul makes mention, became bishop of Apameia of Syria." According to them, Epiphanius wrote "of whom" as a masculine relative pronoun, thereby indicating that he thought Iounias was a man. However, Douglas Moo calls into question the reliability of Epiphanius's evidence, because in the same passage, Epiphanius thought "Prisca" was a man. Epiphanius also wrote, "The female sex is easily seduced, weak and without much understanding. The Devil seeks to vomit out this disorder through women. . . . We wish to apply masculine reasoning and destroy the folly of these women." Epiphanius, "Adversus Collyridianos, Migne," *Patrologia, Graeca,* Vol. 42, col. 740 F.

11. "Tacitus' Account of Nero's Persecution of Christians" (http://drew.edu/doughty/christianorigins/persecutions/ tacitus.html).

12. "Persecution of Christians" (http://en.wikipedia.org).

13. Tacitus, *Annales* XV, p. 44.

14. Quoted in Adriano La Regina, *Archaelogical Guide to Rome* (Rome: Electa, 2005), pp. 206–207.

15. Robert Ellsberg, *All Saints* (New York: Crossroad, 2001), p. 36.

16. La Regina, *Archaeological Guide to Rome,* pp. 206–207.

17. Matthew W. Mahan (ed.), *Let's Go to Rome* (New York: St. Martin's Press, 2004), p. 86.

18. Tacitus, *Annales* XIII, p. 32.

19. Kathryn J. Riss, "Martyrs" (http://www.godswordtowomen.org/ myrt.htm).

20. Tacitus, *Annales* XV, p. 44.

21. Quoted in Riss, "Martyrs."

22. Marianne Dorman, "Feminine Martyrs" (http://mariannedorman .homestead.com/femalemartyrs~ns4.html).

23. G. A. Oshitelu, "Tertullian" (http://www.dacb.org/stories/ tunisia/tertullian_.html).

24. "Converting the Empire: How the Early Church Evangelized a Hostile Pagan World," *Christian History,* 1998, *57*(1).

25. Ibid.

26. Stark, *Rise of Christianity*.

27. Bob Buford, Jan. 2, 2006 (http://activeenergy.net).

28. Orthodox Church in America, "Saints: Andronicus" (http://oca .org); the tradition that Andronicus went on to become Bishop of Panonia may have come from Epiphanius's fourth-century *Index Discipulorum*. This document is considered dubious. Interestingly, it also is the sole Greek source to give Junia and Prisca a masculine name. In fact, both women, who are said to be men in this document, are also said to have become bishops (the male Junia

supposedly became Bishop of Apameia and the male Prisca of Colophon.

29. Fitzmyer, *Romans.*

30. Elizabeth Hallam, *Saints* (New York: Simon & Schuster, 1994), pp. 6–9.

31. John Cereghin, "In Defense of Erasmus" (http://watch.pair .com/erasmus.html).

32. Ottavio Traverso, *The Basilica of Santa Cecilia in Rome* (Rome: Marconi, 1992).

33. *San Clemente* (Rome: Collegio San Cemente, 1992).

34. Lodovico Ferretti, *Saint Catherine of Siena* (Rome: Edizioni Cantagalli, 1996).

35. Hallam, *Saints,* p. 31.

36. Philip Sheldrake, *Spirituality and History,* 2nd ed. (London: SPCK, 1995), p. 78.

37. Richard P. McBrien, *Lives of the Saints* (San Francisco: HarperSan-Francisco, 2001), pp. 14–15.

38. Barbara Reid, "Leading Ladies of the Church," *U.S. Catholic,* Feb. 2006.

Chapter Ten

1. Catherine Clark Kroeger and Mary J. Evans (eds.), *The IVP Women's Bible Commentary* (Downers Grove, Ill.: Intervarsity Press, 2002), p. 762; Mary Rose d'Angelo, "Hebrews," in Carol A. Newsom and Sharon H. Ringe (eds.), *Women's Bible Commentary* (Louisville, Ky.: Westminster/John Knox, 1992), pp. 455–459; Kenneth Barker (ed.), *NIV Study Bible* (Grand Rapids, Mich.: Zondervan, 1984, p. 1895; Joseph Gardner (ed.), *Complete Guide to the Bible* (Pleasantville, N.Y.: Reader's Digest, 1998), p. 411.

2. Andrea Lemma and Antonio Lombardi, *The Church of Saint Prisca and Its Mithraea* (Rome: Tipolitografia Trullo, 2000).

3. June Hager, "Dazzling Discoverings" (http://www.catholic

.net/RCC/periodicals.insider/05-97/churches.html); "Titulus," *Catholic Encyclopedia* (http://newadvent.org).

4. Lemma and Lombardi, *Church of Saint Prisca.*

5. "The Church in Rome in the First Century," note B, "Aquila and Prisca or Prsicilla" (http://www.ccel.org/ccel/edmundson/ church.xii.ii.html).

6. "St. Prisca," *Catholic Encyclopedia* (http://newadvent.org); "Churches of Rome: Santa Prisca" (http://roma.katolsk .no/prisca.htm).

7. Jouette M. Bassler, "Prisca," in Carol Meyers (ed.), *Women in Scripture* (Grand Rapids, Mich.: Eerdmans, 2000), p. 137; McBrien, *Lives of the Saints,* pp. 273–274.

8. "Chair of Peter," *Catholic Encyclopedia* (http://newadvent.org); see also "Chair of Peter, It's Clear" (http://www.network54 .com/forum).

9. Clark, *Christianity and Roman Society,* p. 7.

10. See Meyers, *Women in Scripture*; Kirk, *Women of Bible Lands*; Torjesen, *When Women Were Priests;* and Mary Ann Getty-Sullivan, *Women in the New Testament* (Collegeville, Minn.: Liturgical Press, 1942).

BIBLIOGRAPHY

Alexander, D., and Alexander, P. (eds.). *Eerdmans Handbook to the Bible.* Grand Rapids, Mich.: Eerdmans, 1974.

Amt, E. (ed.). *Women's Lives in Medieval Europe: A Sourcebook.* New York: Routledge, 1993.

Aries, P., and Duby, G. (eds.). *A History of Private Life: From Pagan Rome to Byzantium.* Cambridge, Mass.: Harvard University Press, 2003.

Armstrong, K. *A History of God.* New York: Knopf, 1993.

Armstrong, K. *Through a Narrow Gate,* New York: St. Martin's Press, 1981.

Balch, D. L., and Osiek, C. (eds.). *Early Christian Families in Context: An Interdisciplinary Dialogue.* Grand Rapids, Mich.: Eerdmans, 2003.

Beck, J. R., and Blomberg, C. L. (eds.). *Two Views on Women in Ministry.* Grand Rapids, Mich.: Zondervan, 2001.

Bisel, S. C., with J. Bisel and S. Tanaka. *The Secrets of Vesuvius.* New York: Scholastic, 1990.

Bitel, L. M. *Women in Early Medieval Europe, 400–1100.* Cambridge: Cambridge University Press, 2002.

Bock, D. L. *Breaking the Da Vinci Code.* Nashville, Tenn.: Nelson Books, 2004.

Bonfante-Warren, A. *Saints: Seventy Stories of Courage.* London: Courage Books, 2000.

Boyle, L.O.P. *A Short Guide to St. Clement's Rome.* Rome: Kina Italia/EuroGrafica, 1989.

Briffault, R. *The Mothers: The Matriarchal Theory of Social Origins.* New York: Grosset's Universal Library, 1963.

Bristow, J. T. *What Paul Really Said About Women.* New York: HarperCollins, 1991.

Brock, A. G. *Mary Magdalene: The First Apostle.* Cambridge, Mass.: Harvard Theological Studies, 2003.

Bruce, F. F. *The Epistle of Paul to the Romans: An Introduction and Commentary.* Downers Grove, Ill.: Intervarsity Press, 2003.

Burstein, D. (ed.). *Secrets of the Code: The Unauthorized Guide to the Mysteries Behind the Da Vinci Code.* New York: CDS Books, 2004.

Cantarella, E., and Jacobelli, L. *A Day in Pompeii: Daily Life, Culture, and Society.* Rome: Electa Napoli, 2003.

Capasso, G. *Journey to Pompeii: Virtual Tours Around the Lost Cities.* Naples: Capware, 2004.

Carcopino, J. *Daily Life in Ancient Rome: The People and the City at the Height of the Empire.* New York: Penguin, 1991.

Cary, M. *A History of Rome: Down to the Reign of Constantine.* (2nd ed.) Old Tappan, N.J.: Macmillan, 1967.

Casson, L. *The Ancient Mariners: Seafarers and Sea Fighters of the Mediterranean in Ancient Times.* Princeton, N.J.: Princeton University Press, 1991.

Chadwick, H. *The Early Church.* (Rev. ed.) New York: Penguin, 1993.

Chilton, B. *Mary Magdalene: A Biography.* New York: Doubleday, 2005.

Chittister, J. *Heart of Flesh: A Feminist Spirituality for Women and Men.* Grand Rapids, Mich.: Eerdmans, 1998.

Clark, E. A. *Women in the Early Church: Message of the Fathers of the Church.* Collegeville, Minn.: Liturgical Press, 1983.

Clark, G. *Women in Late Antiquity: Pagan and Christian Lifestyles.* New York: Oxford University Press, 1993.

Clark, G. *Christianity and Roman Society.* New York: Cambridge University Press, 2004.

Clouse, B., and Robert, G. *Women in Ministry: Four Views.* Downers Grove, Ill.: Intervarsity Press, 1989.

Connolly, P. *Pompeii.* New York: Oxford University Press, 1990.

Crossan, J. D., and Reed, J. L. *In Search of Paul: How Jesus' Apostle Opposed Rome's Empire with God's Kingdom.* San Francisco: HarperSanFrancisco, 2004.

Cunningham, L., and Hamilton, D. J., with J. Rogers. *Why Not Women? A Fresh Look at Scripture on Women in Missions, Ministry, and Leadership.* Seattle, Wash.: YWAM (Youth with a Mission) Publishing, 2000.

d'Ambrosio, A. *Women and Beauty in Pompeii.* Los Angeles: Getty Trust Publications, 2001.

Davis, S. H. *The Cult of St. Thecla: A Tradition of Women's Piety in Late Antiquity.* New York: Oxford University Press, 2001.

Ehrman, B. D. *After the New Testament: A Reader in Early Christianity.* New York: Oxford University Press, 1991.

Ehrman, B. D. *Lost Christianities: The Battles for Scripture and the Faiths We Never Knew.* New York: Oxford University Press, 2003.

Ehrman, B. D. *Lost Scripture: Books That Did Not Make It into the New Testament.* New York: Oxford University Press, 2003.

Ehrman, B. D. *The New Testament: A Historical Introduction to the Early Christian Writings.* New York: Oxford University Press, 2004.

Ehrman, B. D. *Truth and Fiction in the Da Vinci Code.* New York: Oxford University Press, 2004.

Ehrman, B. D. *Misquoting Jesus.* San Francisco: HarperSanFrancisco, 2005.

Eisler, R. *The Chalice and the Blade: Our History, Our Future.* New York: Harper-Collins, 1988.

Ellsberg, R. *All Saints: Daily Reflections on Saints, Prophets, and Witnesses for Our Time.* New York: Crossroad, 1997.

Epp, E. J. *Junia, the First Woman Apostle.* Minneapolis, Minn.: Augsburg Fortress, 2005.

Ferretti, L. *Saint Catherine of Siena.* Rome: Eisioni Cantagalli, 1996.

Fiorenza, E. S. (ed.). *Searching the Scriptures: A Feminist Introduction.* New York: Crossroad, 1997.

Fiorenza, E. S. *In Memory of Her: A Feminist Theological Reconstruction of Christian Origins.* New York: Crossroad, 2004.

Fitzgerald, K. K. *Women Deacons in the Orthodox Church—Called to Holiness and Ministry.* Brookline, Mass.: Holy Cross Orthodox Press, 1998.

Fitzgerald, K. K., (ed.). *Encountering Women of Faith, Saint Catherine's Vision Collection, Volume 1,* Berkeley, Calif.: InterOrthodox Press, 2005.

Fraschetti, A. *Roman Women.* Chicago: University of Chicago Press, 1994.

Gardner Associates (eds.). *Reader's Digest Complete Guide to the Bible: An Illustrated Book-by-Book Companion to the Scriptures.* Pleasantville, N.Y.: Reader's Digest, 1998.

George, M. *Mary, Called Magdalene.* New York: Penguin, 2003.

Getty-Sullivan, M. A. *Women in the New Testament.* Collegeville, Minn.: Liturgical Press, 2001.

Gies, F., and Gies, J. *Marriage and the Family in the Middle Ages.* New York: HarperCollins, 1987.

Gioia, F. *Paul of Tarsus: The Apostle for All to Know.* Rome: Libreria Editrice Vaticana, 2002.

Grady, J. L. *10 Lies the Church Tells Women: How the Bible Has Been Misused to Keep Women in Spiritual Bondage.* Lake Mary, Fla.: Charisma House, 2000.

Grady, J. L. *25 Tough Questions About Women and the Church.* Lake Mary, Fla.: Charisma House, 2003.

Grenz, S. J., and Kjesbo, D. M. *Women in the Church: A Biblical Theology of Women in Ministry.* Downers Grove, Ill.: Intervarsity Press, 1995.

Hallam, E. *Saints: Who They Are and How They Help You.* New York: Simon & Schuster, 1994.

Heine, S. *Women and Early Christianity, A Reappraisal.* Minneapolis, Minn.: Augsburg Fortress, 1988.

Hodge, C. *Romans.* Wheaton, Ill.: Crossway Books, 1994.

Huizinga, J. *Erasmus and the Age of Reformation.* New York: HarperTorchbooks, 1957. (Originally published 1924.)

Jensen, A. *God's Self-Confident Daughters: Early Christianity and the Liberation of Women*. Louisville, Ky.: Westminster/John Knox, 1991.

Keck, L. E. (ed.). *New Interpreters Bible*, Vol. 10 (Acts, Romans, 1 Corinthians). Nashville, Tenn.: Abingdon, 2002.

Keener, C.S.P. *Paul, Women, and Wives: Marriage and Women's Ministry in the Letters of Paul*. Peabody, Mass.: Hendrickson, 2004.

King, K. L. (ed.). *Images of the Feminine in Gnosticism*. Philadelphia: Trinity Press, 2000.

King, K. L. *The Gospel of Mary of Magdala: Jesus and the First Woman Apostle*. Santa Rosa, Calif.: Polebridge Press, 2003.

Kirk, M. A. *Women of Bible Lands: A Pilgrimage to Compassion and Wisdom*. Collegeville, Minn.: Liturgical Press, 2004.

Kling, D. W. *The Bible in History: How the Texts Have Shaped the Times*. New York: Oxford University Press, 2004.

Kraemer, R. S. *Her Share of the Blessings: Women's Religions Among Pagans, Jews, and Christians in the Greco-Roman World*. New York: Oxford University Press, 1992.

Kraemer, R. S., and D'Angelo, M. R. (ed.). *Women and Christian Origins*. New York: Oxford University Press, 1999.

Kroeger, C. C., and Evans, M. J. (eds.). *The IVP Women's Bible Commentary*. Downers Grove, Ill.: Intervarsity Press, 2002.

La Regina, A. *Archaeological Guide to Rome*. Rome: Electa, 2005.

Lampe, P. *From Paul to Valentinus: Christians at Rome in the First Two Centuries*. Minneapolis, Minn.: Augsburg Fortress, 2003.

Lancaster, S. H. *Women and the Authority of Scripture: A Narrative Approach*. Philadelphia: Trinity Press, 2002.

Lemma, A., and Lombardi, A. *The Church of Saint Prisca and Its Mithraea*. Rome: Tipolitografia Trullo, 2000.

Lopes, A. *The Popes: The Lives of the Pontiffs Through 2000 Years of History*. Rome: Futura Edizioni, 1997.

MacHaffie, B. J. *Women in Christian Tradition*. Minneapolis, Minn.: Augsburg Fortress, 1986.

Mahan, M. W. (ed.). *Let's Go to Rome*. New York: St. Martin's Press, 2004.

Mancinelli, F. *The Catacombs of Rome and the Origins of Christianity*. Rome: SCALA, 1981.

Manser, M. H. (ed.). *The Westminster Collection of Christian Quotations*. Louisville, Ky.: Westminster/John Knox, 2001.

Marshall, I. H. *Acts: The Tyndale New Testament Commentaries*. Grand Rapids, Mich.: Eerdmans, 1980.

Martimort, A. G. *Deaconesses, An Historical Study*. San Francisco: Ignatius Press, 1986.

McBrien, R. P. *Lives of the Saints from Mary and St. Francis of Assisi to John XXIII and Mother Theresa*. San Francisco: HarperSanFrancisco, 2001.

McGrath, A. *In the Beginning: The Story of the King James Bible and How It Changed a Nation, a Language, and a Culture.* New York: Anchor/Doubleday, 2002.

McKinion, S. A. (ed.). *Life and Practice in the Early Church: A Documentary Reader.* New York: New York University Press, 2001.

Meeks, W. A. *The First Urban Christians: The Social World of the Apostle Paul.* New Haven, Conn.: Yale University Press, 1983.

Meyers, C., Craven, T., and Kraemer, R. S. (ed.). *Women in Scripture: A Dictionary of Named and Unnamed Women in the Hebrew Bible, the Apocryphal/Deuterocanonical Books, and the New Testament.* Grand Rapids, Mich.: Eerdmans, 2001.

Mickelsen, A. *Women, Authority, and the Bible.* Downers Grove, Ill.: Intervarsity Press, 1986.

Moo, D. *The Epistle to the Romans.* Grand Rapids, Mich.: Eerdmans, 1996.

Newsom, C. A., and Ringe, S. H. (eds.). *Women's Bible Commentary.* Louisville, Ky.: Westminster/John Knox, 1998.

Nicolai, V. F., Bisconti, F., and Mazzoleni, D. *The Christian Catacombs of Rome: History, Decoration, Inscriptions.* Regensburg, Germany: Schnell & Steiner, 2006.

Nicolson, A. *God's Secretaries: The Making of the King James Bible.* New York: HarperPerennial, 2003.

Osiek, C., and Balch, D. L. *Families in the New Testament World: Households and House Churches.* Louisville, Ky.: Westminster/John Knox, 1997.

Osiek, C., and Macdonald, M. Y., with J. H. Tulloch. *A Woman's Place: House Churches in Earliest Christianity.* Minneapolis, Minn.: Augsburg Fortress, 2006.

Pagels, E. *The Gnostic Gospels.* New York: Vintage Books, 1989.

Pagels, E. *Beyond Belief: The Secret Gospel of Thomas.* New York: Random House, 2003.

Panati, C. *Sacred Origins of Profound Things.* New York: Penguin, 1996.

Pelikan, J. *Whose Bible Is It? A History of the Scriptures Through the Ages.* New York: Viking Penguin, 2005.

Pergola, P. *Early Christian Rome, Past and Present: Catacombs and Basilicas.* Los Angeles: Getty Trust Publications, 2000.

Piper, J., and Grudem, W. (eds.). *Recovering Biblical Manhood and Womanhood: A Response to Evangelical Feminism.* Wheaton, Ill.: Crossway Books, 1991.

Pomeroy, S. B. *Goddesses, Whores, Wives, and Slaves: Women in Classical Antiquity.* New York: Schocken Books, 1995.

Pontificia Commissione di Archeologica Sacra. *Roman and Italian Catacombs, Domitilla.* Vatican City: Pontificia Commissione di Archeologica Sacra, 2002.

Read, P. P. *The Templars.* New York: Da Capo Press, 2001.

Richards, S. P., and Lawrence, O. *Women of the Bible: The Life and Times of Every Woman in the Bible.* Nashville, Tenn.: Nelson, 2003.

261

Schneiders, S. M. *Women and the Word: The Gender of God in the New Testament and the Spirituality of Women.* Mahwah, N.J.: Paulist Press, 1986.

Sproul, R. C. *The Gospel of God: Expositions of Paul's Letter to the Romans.* Fearn by Tain, Scotland: Christian Focus Publications, 2002.

Stark, R. *The Rise of Christianity.* New York: HarperCollins, 1997.

Swidler, L. *Biblical Affirmations of Woman.* Louisville, Ky.: Westminster/John Knox, 1979.

Swidler, L., and Swidler, A. *Women Priests: A Catholic Commentary on the Vatican Declaration.* Mahwah, N.J.: Paulist Press, 1977.

Torjesen, K. J. *When Women Were Priests: Women's Leadership in the Early Church and the Scandal of Their Subordination in the Rise of Christianity.* San Francisco: HarperSanFrancisco, 1995.

Trible, P. *God and the Rhetoric of Sexuality.* Minneapolis, Minn.: Augsburg Fortress, 1978.

Turner, J. M. *John Wesley, the Evangelical Revival and the Rise of Methodism in England.* London: Epworth Press, 2002.

Unger, M. F. *The New Unger's Bible Dictionary.* Shelton, Wash.: Moody Press, 1988.

Veyne, P. (ed.). *A History of Private Life: From Pagan Rome to Byzantium.* Cambridge, Mass.: Belknap Press, 1987.

Weir, A. *Eleanor of Aquitaine: A Life.* New York: Ballantine, 1999.

White, L. M. *From Jesus to Christianity: How Four Generations of Visionaries and Storytellers Created the New Testament and Christian Faith.* San Francisco: HarperSanFrancisco, 2004.

Wilken, R. L. *The Christians as the Romans Saw Them.* New Haven, Conn.: Yale University Press, 2003.

Winter, B. W. *Roman Wives, Roman Widows: The Appearance of New Women and the Pauline Communities.* Grand Rapids, Mich.: Eerdmans, 2003.

Witherington, B., III. *Women and the Genesis of Christianity.* New York: Cambridge University Press, 1990.

Witherington, B., III. *Women in the Earliest Churches.* New York: Cambridge University Press, 1988.

Witherington, B., III. *Women in the Ministry of Jesus: A Study of Jesus' Attitudes to Women and Their Roles as Reflected in His Early Ministry.* New York: Cambridge University Press, 1998.

Wright, N. T. *What Saint Paul Really Said: Was Paul of Tarsus the Real Founder of Christianity?* Grand Rapids, Mich.: Eerdmans, 1997.

Wright, N. T. *Paul for Everyone: Romans, Part One and Part Two.* Louisville, Ky.: Westminster/John Knox, 2004.

Yalom, M. *A History of the Wife.* New York: HarperCollins, 2001.

THE AUTHOR

Rena Pederson's distinguished career in journalism includes serving for sixteen years as editorial page editor of the *Dallas Morning News*. She is a former finalist for the Pulitzer Prize and was a member of the Pulitzer Prize board for nine years. A winner of multiple writing awards, Pederson is the author of two books—*What's Next? Women Redefining Their Dreams in the Prime of Life* (Perigee/Penguin Putnam, 2001) and *What's Missing? Inspiration for Women Seeking Faith and Joy in Their Lives* (Perigee/Penguin Putnam, 2003). She has appeared on PBS, CNN, *The Oprah Winfrey Show,* Fox News, MSNBC, and ABC-TV.

Pederson earned a bachelor's degree, with honors, from the University of Texas at Austin and a master's in journalism from Columbia University in New York. She is an active member of Highland Park United Methodist Church in Dallas and has two sons, Greg Gish and Grant Gish.

If you would like to schedule Rena Pederson to speak to your group, you may contact The Barnabas Agency at (800) 927-0517 ext. 110, or visit www.barnabasagency.com.

INDEX

This page is a continuation of the copyright page.